APOCALYPTICISM IN THE DEAD SEA SCROLLS

Since the photographs of the Dead Sea scrolls were released in 1992 there has been an explosion of interest in them. This volume explores the issue of apocalypticism in the scrolls; how the notions of the "end," Messianic expectation and eternal life affected the Dead Sea sect, influenced Judaism and filtered into Christianity. Collins' volume provides a valuable and accessible introduction to the interpretation of the scrolls, which is an informative addition to the series examining the major themes of the scroll texts.

John Collins is currently the Professor of Hebrew Bible and Post-Biblical Judaism at the University of Chicago. His books include *Between Athens and Jerusalem* (1983); *The Apocalyptic Imagination* (1984); *Daniel* (Hermeneia Commentary, 1993); and *The Scepter and the Star* (1995). He has served as editor of the Journal of Biblical literature and President of the Catholic Biblical Association.

This new series, *The Literature of the Dead Sea Scrolls*, provides in six volumes an overall introduction to the principal kinds of literature amongst the Dead Sea scrolls. Since all the unpublished texts came into the public domain in 1991, there has been much scholarly activity in editing the materials. However, little has been published to provide the interested student with a concise guide to the complete extant literary corpus. This new series aims to fill that gap through its popular presentation of the main ideas and concerns of the literature from Qumran and elsewhere in the Judaean wilderness.

The series is intended for all interested in the Dead Sea scrolls, especially undergraduate and graduate students working in Biblical Studies or the study of Jewish history and religion in the late Second Temple period. Written by the foremost experts in their particular fields, the series serves to advance general knowledge of the scrolls and to inform the discussion of the background to the self-definition of early Judaism and nascent Christianity.

APOCALYPTICISM IN THE DEAD SEA SCROLLS

John J. Collins

London and New York

First published 1997
by Routledge
11 New Fetter Lane, London EC4P 4EE

Simultaneously published in the USA and Canada
by Routledge
29 West 35th Street, New York, NY 10001

© 1997 John J. Collins

Typeset in Garamond by
RefineCatch Limited, Bungay, Suffolk

Printed and bound in Great Britain by
Creative Print and Design (Wales), Ebbw Vale

British Library Cataloguing in Publication Data
A catalogue record for this book is available from the British Library

Library of Congress Cataloguing in Publication Data
A catalogue record for this book has been requested

ISBN 0-415-146364 (hbk)
ISBN 0-415-146372 (pbk)

CONTENTS

SERIES EDITOR'S PREFACE

The Literature of the Dead Sea Scrolls is a six-volume series designed to provide introductions to the principle literary genres found among these very important texts. From the outset the intention behind the series has been to focus on the texts themselves, before trying to assert what their historical or theological significance might be. The series treats principally the finds from the eleven caves at Qumran, but some other contemporary texts found in the Judaean wilderness in the last fifty years are also considered.

In 1991 all the unpublished manuscripts from Caves 4 and 11 at Qumran became available to the scholarly world at large and to the general public. Much has been done to incorporate all the new information into scholarly debates about Jewish religion and history in the late Second Temple period, but little of the overall significance of the whole literary corpus has been put in the public domain. A major aim of this series is to step back from the debates about the history and identification of the community or movement responsible for writing or preserving these manuscripts. In so doing, entirely fresh consideration can be given to the literary corpus as a whole within the context of Jewish literature of the three centuries before the fall of the temple in 70 CE. On such fresh and newly constructed foundations firmer opinions can be offered about the importance of the scrolls for emerging forms of Judaism and for nascent Christianity.

It is important for those interested in Jewish history and religion of this period to have access to the primary resources, the texts, for themselves, so that anybody can make up their own minds about them. However, some of the textual evidence is very fragmentary and difficult to assess, some of it is entirely new evidence in the discussions. Students of all kinds need straightforward guides to the literature to enable them to trace a secure path through the mass of material. It is not the purpose of this series to provide detailed translations and commentaries on individual texts, though in some chapters of some of the volumes in the series this is the case. Though small extracts and quotations are often given, to make the most of what is written in each volume readers will need to have access to one of the standard translations of the Dead Sea scrolls in English. Nor is the purpose of the series to cover every single text. But the general reader will find here a valuable and up-to-date companion to the principal literary genres found in the scrolls.

Such companions as these may be especially useful to those studying similiar genres in related fields such as the Hebrew Bible, the New Testament, or Jewish halakhah, so that those too are not studied in isolation from this extensive literary corpus which provides so much insight into the development of genres in the period.

I am grateful to my colleagues in the field of Dead Sea scrolls research who have taken the time to contribute to this worthwhile venture and to the editors at Routledge, especially Richard Stoneman, for the enthusiastic welcome given to this series and its individual volumes.

George Brooke

BIBLIOGRAPHIC NOTE

Apart from the biblical book of Daniel, the apocalyptic literature cited in this book can be found in H. F. D. Sparks (ed.) *The Apocryphal Old Testament* (Oxford: Clarendon, 1984) and in J. H. Charlesworth (ed.) *The Old Testament Pseudepigrapha* (2 vols. New York: Doubleday, 1983, 1985).

The most complete translation of the Dead Sea scrolls is that of F. García Martínez, *The Dead Sea Scrolls Translated* (Leiden: Brill, 1994). Most of the material to which reference is made here can also be found in G. Vermes, *The Dead Sea Scrolls in English* (London: Penguin, 1995). A new translation by M. Abegg, E. Cook and M. Wise, to be published by Harper (San Francisco) was not yet available when the manuscript of this book was completed.

Use of square and round brackets: square brackets indicate that there is a lacuna in the text, and the letters in brackets are restored. Round brackets are added for the sake of sense in English but have no counterparts in the original.

LIST OF ABBREVIATIONS

DEAD SEA SCROLLS AND RABBINIC SOURCES

Ar Levi Apoc
The Aramaic Levi Apocryphon, or Apocryphal Levi. An Aramaic text that partially corresponds to the Greek Testament of Levi (which is a section of the Testaments of the Twelve Patriarchs).

b.
Babylonian Talmud (e.g. b. Sanhedrin = tractate Sanhedrin of the Babylonian Talmud).

Berēšît Rabbah
Midrash on Genesis.

CD
The Damascus Document, of which two copies were found in the Cairo Geniza, and fragments of several other copies were found in Qumran Cave 4.

Eighteen Benedictions
Early Jewish liturgical text.

j.
Jerusalem Talmud (e.g. j. Ketubot = tractate Ketubot of the Jerusalem Talmud).

m.
Mishnah tractate (e.g. m. Soṭah = Mishnah tractate Ṣotah).

messianic apocalypse
= 4Q521, a Hebrew text that speaks of "the messiah of heaven and earth."

New Jerusalem text
Aramaic text from Caves 4 and 11 describing eschatological Jerusalem.

p.
pesher; a distinctive type of commentary on biblical (primarily prophetic) texts found at Qumran.

Pesikta de R. Kahana
Homiletic midrash of uncertain origin.

pseudo-Daniel
Fragmentary Aramaic texts from Cave 4 (4Q243–244, 245) that mention

	Daniel but are distinct from the biblical book).
pseudo-Ezekiel	Fragmentary Hebrew text based on Ezekiel from Cave 4 (= 4Q385, 386, 387, 388).
pseudo-Moses	Fragmentary Hebrew text, found in parts of 4Q387, 388, 389, 390.
Q	Qumran (e.g. 4Q = a document from Qumran Cave 4).
1QH/4QH	The Hodayot, or Hymns Scroll.
1QM/4QM	*Serek-ha-milḥamah,* The War Rule.
1QS/4QS	*Serek-ha-yaḥad,* the Community Rule.
1QSa	The Messianic Rule; a rule for the community at the end of days.
1QSb	The Scroll of Blessings.
4QAmram	= Testament of Amram, an Aramaic apocalyptic text from Cave 4.
4QCatena	An exegetical text from Cave 4 (4Q177) sometimes regarded as part of a larger text, the "Eschatological Midrash" which also included 4QFlorilegium.
4QDibHam	A prayer called "The Words of the Heavenly Luminaries" (*Dibrê ha-Meôrôt*).
4QFlorilegium	An exegetical text from Cave 4 (4Q174), sometimes regarded as part of a longer "Eschatological Midrash" which also included 4QCatena.
4QMMT	*Miqṣat Maʿaśê ha-Tôrāh* (literally: some of the works of the Torah) = the Halakhic Letter. A letter outlining legal interpretations in which the Qumran sect differed from the Jerusalem authorities.
4Qmess ar	An Aramaic text from Cave 4 which mentions a figure called "the Elect of God," who is variously identified as Noah or as a future messianic figure (= 4Q534).
4QpIsa	The commentary (pesher) on Isaiah.
4QpMic	The commentary on Micah.
4QpNah	The commentary on Nahum.

4QPrNab	The Prayer of Nabonidus. An Aramaic narrative from Cave 4 that is related to chapter 4 of the book of Daniel.
4QpPss	The commentary on Psalms.
4QSapiential Work A	A fragmentary wisdom text from Cave 4 (= 4Q415, 416, 417, 418 and 423).
4QTest	The Testimonia (4Q175); a collection of passages with eschatological import.
11QMelchizedek	A midrash text from Cave 11 which ascribes an eschatological role to an angelic figure named Melchizedek.
11QShirShabb	*Shirôt ha-Shabbat*. The Songs of Sabbath Sacrifice, also known as The Angelic Liturgy.
11QTemple	The Temple Scroll.
Sifre Deut	A rabbinic midrash on Deuteronomy.
Son of God text	= 4Q246, Aramaic text that mentions a figure who will be called "Son of God." Also known as "Aramaic Apocalypse."
S	Serek = Rule (as in Community Rule; War Rule).

APOCRYPHA AND PSEUDEPIGRAPHA

Animal Apocalypse	= 1 Enoch 85–90. Dates from Maccabean era. Attested in Aramaic at Qumran.
Apocalypse of Abraham	Apocalypse from about 100 CE, preserved in Slavonic.
Apocalypse of Weeks	= 1 Enoch 93:1–10; 91:11–17. Maccabean era. Attested in Aramaic at Qumran.
Astronomical Book of Enoch	= 1 Enoch 73–82. Pre-Maccabean. Attested at Qumran.
2 Baruch	Apocalypse from about 100 CE. Preserved in Syriac.
3 Baruch	Greek apocalypse from late first century CE.

Dreams, Book of	1 Enoch 83–90, including Animal Apocalypse.
1 Enoch	Composite work, fully preserved in Ethiopic. Aramaic fragments found at Qumran. Constituent parts include Book of Watchers, Astronomical Book, Animal Apocalypse, Apocalypse of Weeks, Epistle of Enoch (all found at Qumran) and Similitudes (not found at Qumran).
2 Enoch	Apocalypse preserved in Slavonic. Origin uncertain. Usually thought to derive from Hellenistic Judaism.
3 Enoch	= Sefer Hekaloth. Mystical Hebrew text. Dates from third to sixth centuries CE.
Epistle of Enoch	1 Enoch 91–104.
4 Ezra	= 2 Esdras 3–14. Jewish apocalypse from late first century CE. Fully preserved in Latin.
Giants, Books of	Fragmentary Aramaic work found in Cave 4. Related to the Enoch corpus.
Hermas, Shepherd of	Early Christian apocalypse, early second century CE.
Isaiah, Ascension of	Christian apocalypse from second century CE.
Jubilees	A re-writing of Genesis with distinct halakhic and apocalyptic interests. Fully preserved in Ethiopic. Hebrew fragments found at Qumran. Dates from second century BCE.
1 Maccabees	History of Maccabean rebellion and Hasmonean dynasty.
2 Maccabees	History of Maccabean rebellion, characterized by interest in martyr stories.
Mani Codex	A text from the fifth century CE relating to the life of Mani, the third century CE Gnostic teacher, which contains references to several apocalypses.
Noah, Book of	Fragmentary work, partially preserved in 1 Enoch, and possibly also in some Qumran documents.

NRSV	New Revised Standard Version.
Pss Sol	Psalms of Solomon. Jewish psalms from first century BCE.
Sibylline Oracles	Jewish and Christian oracles in the name of the pagan sibyl. The earliest Jewish oracles date from the second century BCE.
Sir	The apocryphal wisdom book of Ben Sira (= Sirach, = Ecclesiasticus). Early second century BCE.
T. Levi	Greek Testament of Levi. Part of the Testaments of the Twelve Patriarchs.
Tob	The apocryphal book of Tobit. Fully preserved in Greek and Latin. Hebrew and Aramaic fragments found at Qumran.
Paul, Apocalypse of	Early Christian apocalypse. Third century CE.
Peter, Apocalypse of	Early Christian apocalypse. Second century CE.
Similitudes of Enoch	1 Enoch 37–72. Not preserved at Qumran. Probably dates from first century CE.
Watchers, Book of	1 Enoch 1–36. Pre-Maccabean apocalypse, attested at Qumran.
Wis	The apocryphal Wisdom of Solomon, composed in Greek in Alexandria around the turn of the era.

OTHER SOURCES

Ant	The Antiquities of Josephus, late first century CE.
Aristokritos	Christian apologist, fifth century CE.
Atrahasis	Old Babylonian myth about creation and the flood.
Gathas	The hymns of the Persian prophet Zarathustra.
Hippolytus	Roman bishop, about 200 CE. Author of treatise refuting heresies.
Isis and Osiris	Treatise by Plutarch (about 100 CE) on various Hellenistic myths.

JW	The Jewish War, by Josephus.
Lactantius	Christian apologist. Third century CE.
Syncellus	Byzantine historian, about 800 CE.
Theopompus	Hellenistic historian about 300 BCE.

GLOSSARY

apocalypse	A revelation pertaining to the heavenly world and the eschatological judgment.
eschatology	Matters pertaining to the end of history or to the afterlife of the individual.
halakhic	Pertaining to Jewish law.
hekalot	Literally, palaces. Used in Jewish mysticism to refer to the various heavens.
J source	The oldest narrative source in the Pentateuch, which refers to God as Yahweh (German spelling, Jahweh).
Kittim	A code name for Greeks and especially Romans in Jewish texts. Derived from Citium in Cyprus.
Manichean	The Gnostic religion founded by Mani.
merkavah	Chariot. Used in Jewish mysticism with reference to the throne chariot of God, as described in Ezekiel 1.
Ptolemies	Greek rulers of Egypt after Alexander the Great.
Seleucids	Greek rulers of Syria after Alexander the Great.
yaḥad	Community (Hebrew).
Yasna	Individual songs in the Gathas.

1

WHAT IS APOCALYPTICISM?

In modern English, the noun "apocalypse" and the related adjective "apocalyptic" have come to connote a catastrophe of cosmic proportions. So one speaks of the possibility of a nuclear apocalypse, or of the apocalyptic landscape of some futuristic films. It may come as something of a surprise, then, to learn that the underlying Greek word, *apokalypsis*, means simply "revelation" or "uncovering." The catastrophic connotations of the word come from its use in the last book of the New Testament, the Apocalypse, or Revelation of St John. The Apocalypse is indeed a revelation. It reports the visions of St John, when he was in the spirit on the island called Patmos. But his revelation has a particular character. Much of it concerns visions of cosmic destruction. It culminates in a grisly banquet in which the birds of heaven are called "to eat the flesh of kings, the flesh of captains . . . the flesh of all both free and slave, both small and great" (Rev 19:18). This is followed by the resurrection and judgment of the dead, and then the revelation of "a new heaven and a new earth, for the first heaven and the first earth had passed away, and the sea was no more" (21:1). Because of the content of this particular revelation, the word "apocalypse" came to refer broadly to the end of this world, or to any catastrophe of such a scale that it seems to put this world in jeopardy.

THE LITERARY GENRE APOCALYPSE IN ANTIQUITY

The Revelation of John, however, was not an isolated literary phenomenon in the ancient world. We have a spate of Christian

1

apocalypses from the second and third centuries CE, in the names of Peter and Paul, Mary and John (Yarbro Collins 1979). According to the Mani Codex, which dates from around 400 CE, each of the forefathers, from Adam to Enoch, showed his own *apokalypsis* to the elect (Cameron and Dewey 1979). The use of the term *apokalypsis* as a genre label in the Christian era derives from its use in the canonical Apocalypse of John. But the Apocalypse also stood in a tradition of older Jewish literature, typified especially by the book of Daniel. The Jewish works were not generally labeled as "apocalypses" in antiquity, and have only been gradually identified as such in modern times because of their similarity to the Christian apocalypses. Most of the Jewish works in question were not handed down in Jewish tradition or preserved in their original languages. Instead they were preserved in Christian churches, in Ethiopic, Slavonic, Latin and Syriac translations. Only a few, such as 4 Ezra or 2 Esdras which was preserved in Latin, were known continuously in the West. The others, preserved in the Eastern Churches, only became known in the West in the nineteenth century.

The catalyst for the modern rediscovery of the Jewish apocalypses was the publication of the Ethiopic text of 1 Enoch in 1821 by Richard Laurence. This text had been brought back from Ethiopia to England by a traveler in the late eighteenth century. As early as 1832 the German scholar Friedrich Lücke recognized the importance of 1 Enoch and the related Jewish tradition for understanding the book of Revelation (Lücke 1832). The corpus available to Lücke included only the books of Daniel, Enoch, 4 Ezra and the Sibylline Oracles, but it was increased by subsequent discoveries. Laurence also published the Ascension of Isaiah in Ethiopic. Several other apocalypses came to light before the end of the nineteenth century: 2 Baruch in Syriac, 3 Baruch in Greek, 2 Enoch, and the Apocalypse of Abraham in Slavonic (see Koch 1972: 19). With the exception of the book of Daniel, however, none of this literature was extant in the Semitic language in which it had originally been composed, and so the suspicion lingered in some quarters that it was not really representative of Judaism in the centuries before and after the turn of the era. This suspicion has been definitively dispelled by the discovery of the Dead Sea scrolls.

Before we turn to discuss the impact of the scrolls on the study of Jewish apocalyptic literature, it is necessary to get a better impression of the character of this literature. We have noted that the apocalyptic genre was identified by modern (nineteenth-century) scholars primarily by analogy with the Apocalypse of John, and that great importance was attached to the motif of the end of this world and related concepts. These features, however, do not begin to exhaust the character of the apocalyptic literature. In brief, this literature may be divided into two types, one of which is distinguished by its interest in the unfolding of history over several epochs while the other has its primary focus on the mysteries of the heavenly world (Collins 1979, 1984). Both types, however, share some basic features. They are presented as supernatural revelations, mediated by an angel or some heavenly being, and they invariably focus on the final end of life and history. This final end usually entails the transformation of this world (the new creation of the book of Revelation) but it also involves the judgment of the individual dead and their assignment to eternal bliss or damnation.

As the name "apocalypse" suggests, the notion of revelation is fundamental to this literary genre. Sometimes the revelation is visual. Daniel has a dream in which he sees four beasts rising out of the sea (Daniel 7). John sees a woman sitting on a scarlet beast that has seven heads (Rev 17). Often these visions are allegories: Daniel's four beasts represent four kingdoms. The woman in Revelation 17 is Rome. At other times, however, the revelation takes the form of a discourse. In Daniel 10–12, an angel tells Daniel "what is written in the book of truth," which turns out to be a prediction of Hellenistic history, culminating in the resurrection of the dead. Enoch imparts to his children what he has read in the heavenly tablets: an overview of the periods of history from antediluvian times to the new creation (1 Enoch 93). Other revelations record the experiences of visionaries who were escorted through the heavens by angelic tour guides (2 Enoch, 3 Baruch). In all cases, the supernatural character of the revelation is emphasized. The information imparted is not such that anyone could have figured it out by human knowledge.

All of these revelations are presented in the name of visionaries who lived many centuries before the books were actually written. Enoch supposedly lived before the Flood, but the books attributed to him are not attested before the second century BCE. Daniel's career is set in the Babylonian exile, although his revelations are primarily concerned with the Hellenistic period, and were to a great degree written after the fact. The revelations, in short, are pseudonymous. Even if the real authors saw visions or had revelatory experiences, they present their revelations in the name of others, who were presumed to speak with greater authority. The Revelation

3

of John in the New Testament is exceptional in this regard, since John is apparently the actual name of the visionary. (Another Christian exception is found in the *Shepherd of Hermas*.) But all the Jewish apocalypses are pseudonymous, and this convention was also taken up in Christianity (in the Apocalypses of Peter, Paul, etc.). Moreover, we have several examples of pseudonymous prophecy from the surrounding pagan cultures, notably a string of Akkadian prophecies from Babylon which are sometimes thought to have influenced the Jewish apocalypses (Grayson 1975; Lambert 1978). Clearly, pseudepigraphy was a well-established convention. We can only guess at the underlying mentality. Attribution to a figure of great antiquity, such as Enoch, lent status and authority to the work. The common people presumably accepted the attribution at face value, but the literary fiction must have been transparent to the inner circle of those who produced these writings. Nonetheless, it may be too simple to regard the device of pseudonymity as a calculated act of deception. A person who reported a revelation in the name of Enoch may have felt that the attribution was appropriate, that this was the kind of thing that Enoch would have written, or may have identified with Enoch in his imagination. We have no authoritative explanation of the phenomenon from an ancient source. Interestingly enough, the main sectarian writings from Qumran do not rely on the device of pseudonymity, and the earliest Christian apocalypse also dispensed with it. While pseudonymity is a common feature of the genre it cannot be regarded as an indispensable element.

APOCALYPSE AND PROPHECY

Apocalyptic revelation obviously stands in some continuity with the prophetic revelations found in the Hebrew Bible. The account of the revelation in Daniel chapter 10, for example, draws heavily on Ezekiel 8–10. In the apocalyptic revelations, however, more emphasis is placed on the supernatural character of the revelation. The prophets sometimes receive their revelations from angels, especially in the later prophetic books, such as Ezekiel and Zechariah. In the apocalyptic writings, this feature is consistent. Apocalyptic symbolism is initially more bewildering than is usual in the prophets. Daniel's vision of the four beasts rising out of the sea is a case in point. The prophets are said to stand in the council of the Lord (Jer 23:18) but we do not find tours of heaven or hell in the prophetic books. When Ezekiel is taken on a guided tour by an angel in Ezekiel

40–8, he is shown the new Jerusalem, on earth, rather than some otherworldly regions. So while there is continuity between prophetic and apocalyptic revelation, there is also a clear shift in emphasis. The apocalyptic writers shroud their message in mystery to a far greater degree than was the case with the biblical prophets. The attribution of an apocalypse to an ancient figure such as Enoch adds to this sense of mystery.

Hand in hand with this emphasis on the supernatural goes the increased interest of the apocalyptic writers in angels and demons (Rowland 1982; Mach 1992). Ancient Israel was familiar with the notion of a divine council, which represented the survival of ancient polytheism in a religion where only one God was worshiped (cf. Psalm 82:1: "God has taken his place in the divine council; in the midst of the gods he holds judgment". Not until the books of Daniel and Enoch, however, are members of the heavenly host given individual names. Henceforth Michael and Gabriel, Raphael and Uriel play roles of increasing importance in human affairs. Correspondingly, there are also supernatural forces opposed to the God of Israel. The book of Isaiah drew on ancient mythology to conjure up battles between the Lord and Leviathan and "the dragon that is in the sea" (Isa 27:1; cf. Isa 51:9). In the apocalyptic literature the forces of evil become more organized, under the leadership of a figure variously known as Belial or Satan. There is considerable variation in the apocalyptic writings in the roles (and names) allotted to angels and demons, but the angelic world is undeniably more prominent in these writings than in the books of the prophets.

There are also differences in the ways in which prophetic and apocalyptic texts deal with history. The apocalyptic writers inherited from the prophets the belief that God would intervene in history at a decisive point to judge the world. (Amos gave classical expression to this belief when he spoke of a "day of the Lord" that would be darkness and not light, in Amos 5:18.) This divine intervention is sometimes envisaged as an "end" – Amos proclaimed that "the end has come upon my people Israel" (Amos 8:2). The "end" envisaged in the prophets is normally the "end" of Israel, or Judah, or Assyria, or Babylon. It is not the end of the world as such, although it is sometimes described poetically with cosmic imagery. (Cf. the description of "the day of the Lord" in Isaiah 13: "the stars of the heavens and their constellations will not give their light; the sun will be dark at its rising, and the moon will not shed its light.") Normally, too, the prophets address specific historical crises. They do not attempt to survey the course of history as a whole or measure out the time from beginning to end. The divine judgment that they envisage takes the form of the destruction of some earthly power, whether Israel or the nations, and the salvation they hope for is the restoration of Israel in its land.

The apocalyptic writers go beyond their prophetic predecessors in several respects. In the historically oriented apocalypses, we often find that history is divided into a set number of periods or epochs. In Daniel 9, Jeremiah's prophecy that Jerusalem would be desolate for seventy years is interpreted as referring to seventy weeks of years, or 490 years. This calculation was enormously influential in later writings, including the Dead Sea scrolls. Enoch divided the course of history into ten "weeks" (1 Enoch 93; 91) but predicted a decisive new departure in the seventh week, with the emergence of an elect group that eventually rises to power. In these texts there is a sense that history has a fixed duration and that it can be calculated in advance, so that the end of history, as we know it, can be predicted. The book of Daniel is the only Jewish apocalypse that actually attempts to calculate the number of days until the "end" would come. We shall consider this prediction in some detail later. But the notion that the "end" could be calculated has had enormous influence on apocalyptic movements down to modern times.

Perhaps the most momentous difference between apocalyptic and prophetic eschatology concerns the final goal of history. The apocalypses usually, though not always, envisage the restoration of Israel on earth in some form. (3 Baruch is an exception in this regard.) But the eschatology of the prophets is radically altered by the new belief in the judgment of the dead, and the possibility of the reward and punishment of individuals beyond the grave. Physical resurrection is only one of the forms that life after death can take. In some apocalyptic writings, the goal of life is transformation to an angelic state. (Such a hope is expressed clearly in 1 Enoch 104. See Himmelfarb 1991.) In this case, the hope of the apocalyptic writers conforms to their general fascination with the heavenly angelic world. The apocalypses give glimpses of that world in the present, and those that describe heavenly ascents give more extended glimpses of it. After death, the righteous can hope to participate forever in the heavenly world.

Other literary trajectories, besides that of prophecy, can also be traced in the apocalyptic literature. The German scholar Gerhard von Rad argued at length that the apocalypses were more closely related to wisdom literature than to prophecy (von Rad 1965), While this thesis has been generally rejected, it is true that apocalyptic revelation can be viewed as a kind of wisdom, and we shall find important lines of continuity with wisdom literature in the Dead Sea scrolls (Collins 1996a; see Chapter 3 below). The apocalyptic interest in the heavenly world, and especially in the heavenly temple, reflects the influence of priestly circles (Himmelfarb 1993). This priestly influence is especially important in the scrolls (see Chapter 8 below). Apocalypticism is not simply late prophecy, but is rather a new phenomenon of the Hellenistic age, which drew on many streams of tradition. Accordingly, we should expect to find varying emphases in different apocalyptic works.

THE APOCALYPTIC WORLDVIEW

The preceding sketch, brief as it is, should suffice to indicate the range of interests that we find in the apocalyptic writings. An apocalypse is not only a literary form. It also implies a particular view of the world (Collins 1991). Life on earth is shaped by supernatural forces, which are both good and bad. The course of history is determined in advance, although individuals still have some choice as to where they stand. There will be a divine judgment to reward the good and punish the wicked, and this judgment will have its effect not only on the last generation but also on the individual dead. This view of the world stands in fairly sharp contrast to that of the strand of biblical religion represented by the book of Deuteronomy. According to Deuteronomy, the word of God is "not in heaven, that you should say, 'who will go up to heaven to get it for us so that we may hear it and observe it?'" (Deut 30:13). The goal of life is to live long in the land, and to see one's children's children to the third and fourth generations. For the apocalyptic writers, however, the knowledge that gives life must be obtained from heaven by special revelations, and the goal of life is eternal fellowship with the angels rather than long life on earth. It is true that some aspects of the apocalyptic worldview, such as the belief in demonic powers, were widely shared in the Hellenistic age, and that others, such as judgment after death, eventually came to be widely shared in Judaism. In the last two centuries of the common era, however, apocalypticism constituted a distinctive worldview within Judaism, as can be seen by contrasting the Book of Enoch with Ben Sira, or Daniel with 1 Maccabees. It is impossible to say how widely this worldview was shared. Key elements of it were rejected by some Jews (e.g. the Sadducees rejected the judgment of the dead). But neither was it peculiar to a particular sect or the product of a single movement.

A worldview is not necessarily tied to any one literary form, and the apocalyptic worldview could find expression in other genres besides apocalypses. An apocalypse, as we have seen, is a formal report of a revelation mediated by a heavenly being. Essentially the same view of the world can be found in other compositions that are either revelations of another kind (such as the Sibylline oracles) or in compositions that presuppose divine revelation but do not describe it directly (such as the Pauline epistles). The distinction between apocalypticism as a worldview and apocalypse as a literary form is essential to appreciating the role of apocalypticism in the Dead Sea scrolls. Formal apocalypses are extremely rare in the Qumran corpus, but the influence of the apocalyptic worldview in other genres of writing is pervasive.

THE DIVERSITY OF THE SCROLLS

Also essential to our subject is an appreciation of the diversity of material in the Dead Sea scrolls. The corpus of the scrolls can be divided roughly into three categories: those that are clearly sectarian, those that show no signs of sectarian authorship, and those which may or may not be sectarian. In the first category are texts that clearly pertain to a sectarian community. The clearest examples are provided by the Community Rule and the Damascus Document, which legislate for forms of community life that are distinct from the communal organization of Israel. There are differences and discrepancies between these rule books, but they are also closely related. We group them together here as sectarian, on the assumption that they pertain to the same movement, although that movement may have allowed for some diversity. This movement is widely, and plausibly, identified with the Essenes, a sect which had two orders, according to Josephus, one of which married and one which did not (see Collins 1992; VanderKam 1995a: 71–98). Several other compositions from Qumran are closely related to the sectarian rule books, by various considerations. These include the biblical commentaries or pesharim, the thanksgiving hymns or Hodayot, and the Rule of the War of the Sons of Light against the Sons of Darkness.

At the other end of the spectrum are several books that were known before ever the scrolls were discovered, and that cannot be attributed to the sectarian group described in the Community Rule. These include the biblical texts (including Daniel) and apocryphal books such as Tobit and Ben Sira, but also, significantly for our purpose, fragments of 1 Enoch and Jubilees. Also in this category are several compositions that show no trace of sectarianism and that are almost certainly part of the common heritage of Judaism. These include the non-canonical psalms in the Psalms Scroll, and such writings as the Prayer of Nabonidus, which preserves an older form of the tradition contained in Daniel 4.

The third category constitutes a gray area between the other two. Several compositions have no distinctively sectarian vocabulary or motifs, and yet are quite compatible with the sectarian worldview. So, for example, the Aramaic work known as the Testament of Amram has all the rudiments of the dualism of the two spirits that finds its classical expression in the Community Rule. Yet the editor dated it, on the basis of palaeography, to the early or mid-second century BCE, and suggested that it was composed before the Dead Sea sect separated itself from the rest of Judaism (Milik 1972a). The so-called "Son of God" text (4Q246) likewise lacks specifically sectarian terminology, but we shall argue that it is fully compatible with the messianic expectations of the Dead Sea sect. In many of these cases it may be impossible to draw a clear line between compositions that are sectarian and those that are not. We must content ourselves with pointing out the affinities of these texts with both the Qumran scrolls and the wider literary context of Second Temple Judaism.

APOCALYPTICISM AND THE SCROLLS

On any reckoning, the corpus of actual apocalypses in the Dead Sea scrolls is quite scanty (Stegemann 1983). The chief exemplars of the genre among the scrolls are the books of Enoch and Daniel, which were already well known before the scrolls were discovered. The other works that come into consideration are found mainly in highly fragmentary remains of Cave 4, and most of them are in Aramaic (Dimant 1994a). The aforementioned "Son of God" text has been dubbed "the Aramaic Apocalypse" by its editor (Puech 1992a). It certainly shares many features of the apocalyptic genre, and is apparently the interpretation of a vision. We cannot, however, define its literary form with any confidence, since both the beginning and the end of the work are lost. The same problem besets the

Pseudo-Daniel fragments in 4Q243–5. These fragments include an overview of history, but it is not clear whether this is presented as a revelation, or is derived from common historical knowledge. In the case of the Testament of Amram we are fortunate to have the beginning of the work, which might warrant the categorization of the work as either an apocalypse or a testament. Only fragments of the body of the work survive, however, and so any comment on its genre must be very tentative. The Qumran corpus contains several pseudo-prophetic texts (4Q385–90) that have much in common with apocalyptic reviews of history, but again their fragmentary condition makes recognition of their genre hazardous.

It is a remarkable fact that none of the major sectarian compositions from Qumran is in the form of an apocalypse. Several of them are in the distinctive form of the Serek, or rule book. The genre of pesher is also distinctive and original in the scrolls. The sectarian writings often presuppose a claim of revelation, but they are not formally revelation reports. The Dead Sea scrolls do not enlarge our corpus of apocalypses, with the possible exceptions of some of the fragmentary texts from Cave 4.

Nonetheless, many scholars have taken the Dead Sea sect to be an "apocalyptic community" (Cross 1995: 76–8; Collins 1990) and not without reason. The most systematic presentation of a worldview in the scrolls is found in the Instruction on the Two Spirits in the Community Rule. This discourse is in the form of a sapiential instruction; it is not presented as a revelation. Nonetheless the content is strongly reminiscent of the apocalypses. Human behavior is shaped by supernatural forces; the era of conflict has a set limit; eventually there will be a divine judgment followed by eternal reward and punishment. Whether this dualistic understanding of the world is presupposed in all the sectarian scrolls is a matter of dispute, but the other scrolls have their own apocalyptic features. The Damascus Document has an overview of history reminiscent of the Enochic writings, and implies a calculation of the date of the "end" or decisive divine intervention. The Rule of the War is perhaps the most obviously "apocalyptic" book in the corpus, although its literary form is that of a rule book and not of a revelation. The subject of this book, the final conflict between the forces of light and darkness, presupposes the typical apocalyptic view of history moving towards a crisis, which will be the occasion of divine intervention. Other motifs in the sectarian scrolls that figure prominently in apocalyptic literature include messianic expectation, the hope for eternal life (which only rarely takes the form of resurrection), and the interest in the angelic world and the desire to participate in it.

The role of all these apocalyptic motifs in the scrolls will be examined in the following chapters. At the outset, it will be well to isolate the apocalyptic traditions that are clearly older than the Qumran sect. These are represented primarily in the books of Enoch and Daniel. Both of these books are found in multiple copies at Qumran, and there can be no doubt that they exercised a profound influence on the Dead Sea sect. Their worldview, however, is not simply adopted and reproduced in the sectarian documents. They represent a source for the ideology of the sect, not an expression of it. We can better appreciate the originality of the worldview of the Dead Sea sect if we are aware of the traditions it inherited and proceeded to modify.

2

DANIEL, ENOCH AND RELATED LITERATURE

DANIEL

The book of Daniel is the only example of an apocalypse in the Hebrew Bible, although various features of the genre are anticipated in the prophetic books. The apocalyptic features of Daniel are all found in the second half of the book, chapters 7–12, which were composed around the time of the Maccabean revolt (167–164 BCE). The first half, chapters 1–6, consists of older stories which establish the identity of Daniel and provide a fictional setting for the revelations in the Babylonian exile, some 400 years before the actual time of composition (see Collins 1993: 24–38). Fragments of eight manuscripts of Daniel were found at Qumran (two in Cave 1, five in Cave 4 and one, on papyrus, in Cave 6; for an index of the passages see Ulrich 1995: 106). Moreover, Daniel is cited in 4QFlorilegium and in 11QMelchizedek in ways that suggest that it was already regarded as authoritative scripture at Qumran.

The apocalyptic character of Daniel lies in large part in the manner of revelation. In chapters 7 and 8 Daniel sees bizarre visions that are interpreted for him by an angel. In chapter 9, an angel explains to him the true meaning of Jeremiah's prophecy that Jerusalem would lie desolate for seventy years. In chapter 10, he has an overpowering vision of an angel, who then predicts the history of the Hellenistic age as it is written in "the book of truth." The notion that truth is a mystery, and that revelation entails a process of interpretative decoding, is found already in the stories in Daniel 1–6, where Daniel interprets the dreams of King Nebuchadnezzar and deciphers the mysterious writing on the wall at Belshazzar's feast. The Aramaic terms for mystery (*rāzā'*) and interpretation (*pišrā'*) are cognate to the corresponding Hebrew words (*raz, pešer*) that appear frequently in the scrolls (see Mertens 1971: 124–30). Angelic revelations, however, are in short supply in the corpus of the scrolls. The primary importance of Daniel for the Qumran texts lies in the content of the revelations. We shall begin by highlighting several features of Daniel's visions that are influential in subsequent tradition.

DANIEL'S VISIONS

The first point that is likely to catch the eye of the reader of Daniel 7 is the prominence of vivid mythological imagery. Daniel sees four beasts coming up out of the sea. The sea (*yamm*) was personified in Canaanite mythology, and its mythical overtones are often in evidence in the poetic books of the Bible. (The Canaanite mythology is known to us from texts from the late second millenium BCE, which were found at Ugarit in northern Syria. The tradition continued long after these texts were composed.) It is often associated with a sea-monster, variously known as Rahab or Leviathan. In the process of creation God stilled or dried up the sea, smote Rahab and pierced the fleeing serpent (Job 26:12–13; cf. Ps 89:9–11; Isa 51:9–11). Isa 27:1 predicts a day when the Lord will "punish Leviathan the fleeing serpent, Leviathan the twisting serpent, and he will kill the dragon that is in the sea." In Daniel 7, the four beasts are identified as kings or kingdoms that arise on the earth, but they are invested with mythic cosmic significance by the imagery with which they are described. The vision suggests that there are superhuman, primordial powers at work in the history of earthly kingdoms. The figure of "one like a human being" who comes with the clouds of heaven is likewise reminiscent of the god Baal in Canaanite mythology, who is often described as "the rider of the clouds," a characterization usually reserved for Yahweh in the Hebrew Bible. At the center of Daniel's vision is the divine throne, where God appears as an "ancient of days," surrounded by myriads of heavenly attendants. While the vision is concerned with a specific period of history on earth, culminating in the persecution of the Jewish people by Antiochus Epiphanes, it sets this history against the backdrop of a heavenly court. The outcome of history is not determined by human endeavor but by divine decree. The interpreting angel explains that the kingdom that is given to the "one like a son of man" is given to "the holy ones of the Most High" or to "the people of the holy ones." In human terms, this is a prediction of the victory of the

13

Jewish people. Both in the Bible and in the Dead Sea scrolls, however, the term "holy ones" most often refers to heavenly beings, or angels. The use of the term in Daniel 7 suggests that the triumph of the Jewish people comes about because of the triumph of their angelic patrons in heaven. (For detailed argument see Collins 1993: 286–317).

The heavenly backdrop of history in Daniel is most clearly spelled out in Daniel 10–12. An angel appears to Daniel in a vision and tells him of a struggle in heaven with "the prince of Persia" in which he was helped by "Michael, one of the chief princes." After the "prince of Persia," the "prince of Greece" will come. The "princes" are the patron angels of the various peoples, corresponding to the national gods of older Near Eastern mythology (cf. Deut 32:8). At the end of the sequence predicted by the angel, "Michael, the great prince, the protector of your people shall arise" (12:1). This is the only time in the Hebrew Bible that the archangel Michael is named. We shall encounter him again in the scrolls. His role in Daniel 10–12 corresponds to that of the "one like a son of man" in chapter 7, with whom he should probably be identified: he is the heavenly representative of the Jewish people. As depicted in Daniel, the struggle between the Jews and the Seleucids in the Maccabean period is only the earthly reflection of the heavenly struggle between the patron angels, or of the primordial struggle between the rider of the clouds and the beasts from the sea. This mythical view of warfare is essential background for the expectation of an eschatological war in the scrolls, although it is adapted with significant alteration.

Three other aspects of Daniel's visions require comment.

First, there is the division of history into a set number of periods. Chapter 7 speaks of four kingdoms. This schema was used widely for political propaganda in the Hellenistic world (Flusser 1972). Other examples are found in Daniel 2 and the Fourth Sibylline Oracle. In chapter 9, Jeremiah's prophecy that Jerusalem would be desolate for seventy years is reinterpreted as referring to seventy weeks of years, or 490 years. We shall see that this schema figures prominently in the calculations of the Dead Sea sect.

The second feature is related to this. Daniel attempts to calculate the date at which the "end" will come. The end in question is not only the end of the persecution, but the end of the predetermined course of history, or of the 490 years. What is most remarkable is that the book of Daniel preserves different calculations of this "end," and even juxtaposes two of them in Daniel 12:11–12 ("From the time that the regular burnt offering is taken away and the abomination that makes desolate is set up, there shall be one thousand two hundred and ninety days. Happy are those who persevere and attain the thousand three hundred and thirty five days".) However these numbers are to be understood, there is no doubt that Daniel gave a powerful impetus to the attempt to calculate the date of divine intervention in human history. We shall consider this aspect of apocalypticism further in Chapter four.

Finally, the triumph of Michael in Daniel 12:1 is followed by the resurrection of the dead. It is not clear that bodily resurrection is involved. The "land of dust" from which people are raised is probably Sheol. The wise are said to shine with the brightness of the firmament and to be like the stars forever. The stars are the host of heaven, and to become like the stars is to become like the angels (cf. 1 Enoch 104:2–6). There are only a few clear references to resurrection in the Dead Sea scrolls, but there is plenty of evidence that the members of the sectarian community believed that they were destined for fellowship with the host of heaven.

PSEUDO-DANIELIC WRITINGS

In addition to the book of Daniel, other Danielic writings have been found at Qumran which may be described as apocalyptic, at least in a broad sense of the term. The name Daniel occurs in three manuscripts found at Qumran, 4Q243 (Pseudo-Daniel[a]), 4Q244 (Pseudo-Daniel[b]), and 4Q245 (Pseudo-Daniel[c]), (Milik 1956). 4Q243 and 244 overlap, and clearly belong to the same composition. Milik tentatively proposed that 4Q245 belonged to the same work, but this now seems doubtful. 4Q243–4 present a speech by Daniel in a royal court. His speech is an overview of history, beginning with Noah and the Flood, and continuing down to the Hellenistic period. (The document contained several personal names. Only one, Balakros, is preserved. This name was borne by several figures in the early Hellenistic period.) 4Q245 contains a long list of names. In part, this list gives the names of high priests from the patriarchal period (Qohath) down to the Hellenistic age (Onias, Simon). It then continues with a list of kings, including David, Solomon, and Ahaziah. It is difficult to see how these lists could be integrated into the document preserved in 4Q243 and 244. The latter document views Israel in the context of universal history, and is concerned with the problem of foreign domination. 4Q245 is focused on the internal history of Israel. The two documents may come from the same or related circles, but their relationship seems to be one of complementarity rather than identity.

We have forty fragments of 4Q243 and fourteen fragments of 4Q244. Both manuscripts are written in Herodian script (late first century BCE). Milik found affinities between this text and the book of Daniel in allusions to seventy years and a four-kingdom schema, while he found a reference to resurrection in 4Q245. Neither the seventy years nor the four-kingdom schema is actually found in the fragments. The reconstruction of "seventy years" seems more plausible than any alternative in 4Q243 fragment 16. (The passage is very fragmentary, but appears to say that someone is/will be oppressed for seventy years.) The reference, however, is not necessarily to the Exile, as it is in Daniel 9. 4Q390, the Pseudo-Moses text, has two references to seventy years, neither of them in an exilic context. The four-kingdom schema is inferred from the fourth line of the same fragment which reads *hî' malkûtā' qd[* ("this is the . . . kingdom"). Milik restored *qdmyt'*, "first." This reconstruction is problematic on two counts. First, two lines earlier in the same fragment we read that "he will save them." It seems unlikely that an act of salvation would be followed immediately by the inauguration of the first of a series of Gentile kingdoms. Second, if Milik's interpretation were correct this would be the only case where the four-kingdom sequence (familiar from the book of Daniel and the Fourth Sibylline Oracle) is inaugurated after deliverance from the Exile. The first kingdom is always either Babylon or Assyria. Alternative reconstructions are possible. The phrase can be read as *malkûtā' qadîštā'*, "holy kingdom," and the passage may be located in the eschatological phase of the prophecy.

4Q245 survives in four fragments, one of which contains the list of names already noted. The second fragment contains a passage reminiscent of CD 1, where some people are said to wander in blindness. There follows a statement that "these then will rise" (*yqwmwn*). Milik saw here a reference to resurrection and a parallel to Daniel 12, but the verb *qwm* is not used in Daniel 12, and does not necessarily refer to resurrection at all. The following line says that some people "will return" (*ytwbwn*). It seems then that these fragments may be largely independent of the book of Daniel.

We can only guess at the provenance of these compositions. Even without 4Q245, 4Q243–4 probably had an eschatological conclusion. 4Q243 fragment 24 speaks of the gathering of the elect, and fragment 25 seems to imply an eschatological battle ("the land will be filled ... with decayed carcasses"). Pseudo-Daniel a–b shares several motifs with other quasi-prophetic pseudepigrapha of the time. Israel at large lives in error, due to the influence of demonic spirits. Eschatological restoration is the destiny of an elect group, which walks in the way of truth, set in contrast to the "error" of others. The eventual emergence of this elect group is surely one of the major themes of this work. In this respect it resembles such works as the Animal Apocalypse (1 Enoch 83–90), the Apocalypse of Weeks (1 Enoch 93:1–10; 91:11–17), the Damascus Document, and the Pseudo-Moses text (4Q390). There are distinct parallels to the Damascus Document in the account of the exile as giving Israel into the hand of Nebuchadnezzar, for the desolation of the land (cf. CD 1:12; 5:20). Yet there is no mention of a community (*yaḥad*), and no unambiguously sectarian language, and so this text is not necessarily a product of the Dead Sea sect. Its relation to the sect may be analogous to that of Jubilees or the Enoch literature.

4Q245 also envisages a group that wanders in blindness, and another group that "returns." The key to the provenance of the document, however, lies in the list of names. The priestly names include Ḥôniah (Onias) and, in the following line, Shimeon. The name preceding Shimeon ends in -n, and the trace of the preceding letter seems more like *taw* than *nun*. The possibility arises that the text refers to Jonathan and Simon Maccabee (especially since Onias is represented as Ḥôniah, rather than Yôḥanan). If this is so, Jonathan and Simon may be presented simply as the culmination of a series of high priests, or the fragmentary text may have regarded them as usurpers of the priesthood. Since the following fragment speaks of people wandering in blindness and envisages some eschatological reversal, the latter possibility seems more likely. Nothing is certain, however, in view of the fragmentary state of the text.

While the name Daniel does not occur in 4Q246, the so-called "Son of God" text, it, too, shows a clear relationship to the book of Daniel (Collins 1995: 154–72). There is a general similarity in setting in the two compositions. 4Q246 is the interpretation of a vision, apparently the vision of a king, by someone who falls before the throne in the opening verse. There are verbal parallels to Daniel at column 2, line 5, "his kingdom is an everlasting kingdom" (cf. Dan

4:3; 7:27) and at 2:9, "his sovereignty is an everlasting sovereignty" (cf. Dan 4:31; 7:14). Another possible allusion to Daniel is the use of the word "to trample" (*dûš*) in 2:3 (cf. Dan 7:7). These parallels give rise to the suspicion that 4Q246 may be an adaptation of Daniel 7, although it is certainly not a systematic interpretation. Some scholars, however, prefer to regard the text as a roughly contemporaneous parallel to Daniel that shares some language with the biblical book (Puech, 1992a). We shall return to the Son of God text in a later chapter when we consider the subject of messianism.

THE ENOCH TRADITION

The book of Enoch is a composite book, containing five major works: the Book of the Watchers (chapters 1–36), the Similitudes (37–72), the Astronomical Book (73–82), the Book of Dreams, including the Animal Apocalypse (83–90), and the Epistle, including the Apocalypse of Weeks (91–105). Appended at the end are a brief Book of Noah (106–7) and a discourse on the last judgment, addressed to Methuselah. 1 Enoch is fully preserved only in Ethiopic, with some fragments in Greek. Aramaic fragments of all sections except the Similitudes and the concluding discourse (108) have been found at Qumran (Milik 1976). The Astronomical Book was copied separately, and is found in four copies (4Q208–11). Seven manuscripts contain fragments of the other sections. 4QEn^a and 4QEn^b (4Q201, 202) contain only fragments of the Book of the Watchers. 4QEn^d and 4QEn^e (4Q205, 206) combine fragments of the Book of the Watchers and the Book of Dreams. 4QEn^c (4Q204) has fragments of the Book of the Watchers, the Book of Dreams, the end of the Epistle and the Book of Noah (104–7), 4QEn^f (4Q207) has a fragment of the Book of Dreams and 4QEn^g (4Q212) has fragments of the Epistle. Moreover, there are allusions to the Enoch literature in sectarian compositions (e.g. CD 2:18 refers to the story of the Watchers. The motif of planting in the Apocalypse of Weeks, 1 Enoch 93:10 is echoed in CD 1:7 and other passages).

The books that make up the Enochic corpus may be viewed as a tradition that developed in the late third and early second centuries BCE (Stone 1978; VanderKam 1984). The oldest of the Enoch manuscripts from Qumran pertains to the Astronomical Book (1 Enoch 73–82), and dates to the late third or early second century BCE. This book is introduced in the Ethiopic translation as

The book of the revolutions of the lights of heaven, each as it is, according to their classes, according to their (period of) rule and their times, according to their names, and their places of origin and according to their months, which Uriel, the holy angel who was with me and is their leader showed to me; and he showed me all their regulations, exactly as they are, for each year of the world and forever, until the new creation shall be made which will last for ever.

(72:1)

There is no account of the actual revelation, but a heavenly tour seems to be implied (cf. 76:1; 81:5). Mention of the new creation gives the work an eschatological horizon, and chapter 81 (which may be a secondary addition) seems to imply some form of afterlife (81:4: "Blessed is the man who dies righteous and good, against whom no book of iniquity has been written"). But eschatology is marginal in this work. The primary emphasis is on the order of the heavens, and the movements of the sun, moon, and stars. Specifically, the work supports the contention that "the year amounts to exactly 364 days" (72:32). The 364-day calendar is also defended in the Book of Jubilees, and is of fundamental importance for the Dead Sea sect. Disagreement over the liturgical calendar appears to have been one of the reasons for the secession of the sect in the first place (cf. CD 2:14–15; 4QMMT, the so-called Halakhic Letter). The importance of the 364-day calendar at Qumran constitutes a point of continuity between the tradents of the Enoch literature and the Dead Sea sect.

The Book of the Watchers (1 Enoch 1–36) also dates from the time before the Maccabean revolt. It takes its name from the story of the Watchers, or fallen angels, which is elaborated in 1 Enoch 6–11 at much greater length than in Genesis 6. According to 1 Enoch, 200 Watchers came down to take wives from among human beings, led by Shemihaza and Asael. (Two variants of the story appear to be woven together; see Nickelsburg 1977.) They not only had illegitimate sexual intercourse, but also divulged forbidden information and caused the spread of sin and violence on earth. Eventually, the earth cried out against them and the angels appealed on its behalf to the Most High. The Watchers were confined under the earth to await a final judgment, and the earth was cleansed. Enoch carries a petition to heaven on behalf of the Watchers, but the appeal for mercy is rejected. The giants who were born from the Watchers and human women, however, become evil spirits on earth (1 Enoch 15:8) and evil spirits come out from their flesh and rise against humanity. It is possible that the story of the Watchers was composed as an allegory either of the impact of Hellenistic culture in Palestine or of the corruption of the priesthood. It is written, however, as an account of the origin of sin and evil in the world, and it is as such that it became an influential apocalyptic myth (Sacchi 1990). The origin of evil was the subject of much speculation and debate in Judaism in the second century BCE. The Enochic account, which emphasized the role of supernatural, demonic forces, was attractive to the Qumran sect, but the sect produced its own distinct account in the Instruction on the Two Spirits in the Community Rule.

In the Book of the Watchers, the judgment on the fallen angels provides the occasion for Enoch's ascent to heaven. This is the oldest Jewish account that we have of a "round-trip" journey to heaven, where the visionary ascends to heaven to receive a revelation and returns to impart it on earth. (It may be that such ascents were implied in prophets' claim to have stood in the council of the Lord, e.g. Jer 23:18, 22, but the ascent is never described in a prophetic text.) The climax of Enoch's ascent in 1 Enoch 14 is a vision of the divine throne, which has much in common with the vision of the "ancient of days" in Daniel 7. In both of these visions we have important witnesses to early Jewish mysticism (Gruenwald 1980: 29–42), and this tradition is also continued in the scrolls. Enoch's angelic tour guide also takes him to the ends of the earth, where he sees all sorts of cosmological mysteries, notably the place of judgment of the fallen angels (1 Enoch 18–19), the abodes of the dead, where they await a final judgment (chapter 22), and the tree of life (chapters 24–5).

The oldest Enochic writings, then, have a distinct cosmological emphasis. In some of the later writings of the corpus the emphasis falls rather on history. The Apocalypse of Weeks is a distinct composition embedded in the Epistle of Enoch (1 Enoch 91–105). In the Ethiopic translation the order of the text is disturbed. The first part of the apocalypse is found in 93:1–10, while the continuation is in 91:11–17. The correct transition between 93:10 and 91:11 is preserved in one of the Aramaic manuscripts from Qumran (4Q En^g). In the Apocalypse of Weeks, Enoch narrates "that which appeared to me in the heavenly vision, and which I know from the words of the holy angels and understand from the tablets of heaven" (93:2). He presents a highly schematized overview of history, divided into weeks (presumably weeks of years). Ultimately, ten periods are specified (followed by "many weeks without end"), but the crucial transition occurs in the seventh week with the election of a group called "the chosen righteous." Division of history into both ten and seven periods is well attested in Jewish apocalyptic literature (Yarbro Collins 1984). The tenfold division is probably derived ultimately from the Persian idea of the millennium. Multiples of seven are suggested by the system of sabbatical and jubilee years in the Israelite priestly tradition (Leviticus 25). The Apocalypse of Weeks is probably older than Daniel 9, and so cannot be influenced by Daniel's prophecy of seventy weeks of years. The two apocalypses draw on some common ideas and traditions.

The Apocalypse of Weeks also claims to find a pattern in history, whereby certain people or groups are chosen for salvation in times when wickedness prevails. In the second week, "great wickedness will arise . . . but in it a man will be saved." The reference is to Noah. The third week is marked by the election of Abraham: "a man will be chosen as the plant of righteousness forever." In the sixth week all are blinded, but "in it a man will ascend" (presumably Elijah). The seventh week is dominated by an apostate generation, but "at its end the chosen righteous from the eternal plant of righteousness" will be chosen. The eighth, ninth, and tenth weeks describe the eschatological finale. A sword will be given to the righteous that judgment may be executed. The righteous will acquire houses, and a new temple will be built. Finally, the world will be written down for destruction, eternal judgment will be executed on the Watchers and a new heaven will replace the old.

For purposes of comparison with the Dead Sea scrolls, the most intriguing aspect of this composition is the emergence of an elect group just before the dawn of the eschatological era. The Damascus Document describes the emergence of the Dead Sea sect in rather similar terms. A similar, or most probably the same, group plays a pivotal role in the other "historical" apocalypse in 1 Enoch, the Animal Apocalypse in 1 Enoch 85–90.

The Animal Apocalypse can be dated on internal grounds to the Maccabean revolt. It is a complex allegory (see Tiller 1993). The figures of biblical history are represented by animals. Adam is a white bull. Cain and Abel are black and red bullocks. The descent of the Watchers is described in chapter 86 as the descent or fall of stars from heaven. The giants begotten by them are elephants, camels, and asses. Then, "there came from heaven beings who were like white men." These are the angels who bind the Watchers and imprison them. Noah is initially a white bull, but he becomes a man, which is to say that he is transformed into an angel. Abraham and Isaac are bulls, but Jacob is a sheep. Moses is a sheep at first, but he, like Noah, becomes a man (89:36, 38).

The account of the kingdoms of Israel and Judah is similar to the sixth week of the Apocalypse of Weeks. The sheep (Israel) are blinded and go astray. The ascension of Elijah is noted. God delivers the sheep into the hands of the wild animals. Then seventy shepherds are appointed to watch over the sheep and destroy some of them while another is appointed to record what the shepherds do. The seventy shepherds are the patron angels of the nations. They are later grouped with the fallen angels at the judgment. Their reign is divided into four periods, which are allotted 12, 23, 23, and 12 shepherds respectively. The first period culminates with the rebuilding of the temple, but we are told that the offerings in this temple were unclean. This verdict on the Jewish restoration is quite compatible with the Apocalypse of Weeks, which simply refers to an "apostate generation."

At the end of the third period (90:6) "small lambs were born from these white sheep, and they began to open their eyes." This development corresponds to the emergence of "the chosen righteous" in the Apocalypse of Weeks. In 90:9 "horns came up on those lambs, but the ravens cast their horns down, and I looked until a big horn grew on one of those sheep and their eyes were opened." The big horn is a transparent reference to Judas Maccabee. The recording angel is said to come down to help Judas (a reference to the tradition that an angel appeared at the battle of Beth-Zur. 2 Macc 11:6–12). From this point onward the apocalypse is no longer describing historical events, but the anticipated eschatological finale. God comes down and sets up his throne for judgment. A sword is given to the "sheep" as it was given to the righteous in the Apocalypse of Weeks. The Watchers and seventy shepherds are destroyed, as also are the "blind sheep" or apostate Jews. All the righteous who had been destroyed are brought back, presumably by resurrection, and all are transformed into "white bulls" – the condition of Adam and the early patriarchs. All are gathered in the house of the Lord, which should probably be understood as the new Jerusalem, since the temple is represented in this apocalypse as a tower.

Here again, the emergence of a distinct (sectarian?) group, shortly before the outbreak of the Maccabean revolt, is intriguing in light of the Dead Sea scrolls. Devorah Dimant has even suggested that the "lambs" to which the apocalypse refers are in fact the community of the Teacher of Righteousness (Dimant 1984: 544–5). Most scholars demur at such a specific identification, but it is not unreasonable to suppose that there was some relationship between the movement described in the Animal Apocalypse and the Apocalypse of Weeks and the Dead Sea sect. We shall return to this question when we have completed our overview of Enochic traditions at Qumran.

The last major section of the book of Enoch, the Epistle (chapters 91–105) is an exhortation rather than an account of revelation, although it presupposes what Enoch has learned from the tablets of heaven and the writing of the holy ones (103:1–2). The bulk of the document is taken up with woes against the sinners and exhortations for the righteous. Some of the accusations against the sinners concern idolatry and blasphemy, but the bulk of them are social in character: "Woe to those who build their houses with sin, for from their whole foundation they will be thrown down" (94:8). Two other features of the Epistle are significant for our study of the scrolls.

First, the author takes issue with the account of the origin of sin that was presented in the Book of the Watchers and presupposed in the Animal Apocalypse. According to 1 Enoch 98:4: "as a mountain has not, and will not, become a slave, nor a hill a woman's maid, so sin was not sent on the earth, but man of himself created it." The Epistle evidently knows the tradition of the Watchers, but disputes it. If we view the various components of 1 Enoch as a tradition, it is evident that this tradition allowed for dispute and argumentation.

Second, the Epistle contains one of the clearest formulations of the hope for afterlife in the company of the angelic host. The righteous are promised in 1 Enoch 104: "you will shine like the lights of heaven and will be seen, and the gate of heaven will be opened to you . . . you will have great joy like the angels of heaven . . . for you shall be associates of the host of heaven" (104: 2,4,6). The Epistle also speaks of resurrection, as rising from sleep (92:3), but the book concludes with a strong emphasis on transformation to an angelic state. It is this mode of immortality that is most significant for the apocalyptic heritage of the Dead Sea scrolls.

A few other writings that are related to the Enoch tradition may be noted here briefly.

Milik claimed to have identified "ten, if not some twelve" copies of the Book of Giants, which was previously known as a Manichean work of the third century CE (Milik 1976: 4; cf. 2Q26; 4Q203; 4Q530–3; 6Q8). One of these manuscripts was copied by the same scribe as 4QEnᵃ and Milik has argued that it was originally part of an Enochic pentateuch, following on the Book of the Watchers. We do not, however, have any fragments that actually show that the Book of the Giants was copied in the same manuscript as any of the Enochic writings.

The Book of Noah was known only indirectly before the discovery of the scrolls. There is mention of such a book in Jubilees (10:13; 21:10), the Mount Athos manuscript that contains the apocryphal Levi material and in the Chronography of Syncellus. Fragments have been identified in 1 Enoch, notably in chapters 106–7, but there is no agreement as to how much material in 1 Enoch can be ascribed to the Book of Noah. In the scrolls, too, fragments of the Book of Noah can only be identified tentatively because of their content; no composition clearly identified as a book of Noah has been found. The most likely candidate is the text known as the "Elect of God" text or 4Qmess ar (4Q534). This text was initially thought to give the horoscope of the messiah, but it has been more plausibly explained as referring to the birth of Noah. It is also possible that the section of the Genesis Apocryphon dealing with Noah is a summary of the lost Book of Noah (García Martínez 1992: 40). Fragments of the book may also be found in 1Q19 and 6Q8, although Milik regards the latter as a copy of the Book of Giants.

JUBILEES

The Book of Jubilees also has notable affinities with the Enoch tradition. Jubilees is even more prominent in the scrolls than 1 Enoch. It is fully preserved in Ethiopic, but fragments of the Hebrew original have now been found in fourteen (possibly fifteen) manuscripts from Qumran: two (1Q17, 18) from Cave 1, two (2Q19, 20) from Cave 2, one (3Q5), from Cave 3, eight, possibly nine (4Q216–24) from Cave 4, and one (11Q12) from Cave 11: VanderKam 1992; VanderKam and Milik 1994). There are also three fragments that have been dubbed "pseudo-Jubilees" (4Q225, 226, and 227). All three mention Moses and have parallels to material dealt with in Jubilees, but do not correspond to the Ethiopic text of Jubilees. There appears to be an explicit reference to Jubilees in CD 16:3–4, where it is called "the book of the divisions of the periods according to their jubilees and their weeks." Another fragment 4Q228 may also refer to Jubilees as an authority or source of information. The sheer number of manuscripts is significant for the importance of Jubilees at Qumran. Only Genesis, Exodus, Deuteronomy, Isaiah, and Psalms are represented by more manuscripts than the pseudepigraphs of Enoch and Jubilees.

Jubilees is an expansionistic paraphrase of Genesis and, more briefly, of Exodus down to the revelation on Mount Sinai. Its focus is on halakhic matters. The account of creation highlights the sabbath in chapter 2, and the book concludes with instructions for the sabbath in chapter 59. Great attention is paid to the festivals and to rituals such as circumcision. Notably, Jubilees defends the 364-day calendar and warns against "the feasts of the Gentiles" and the aberration of the moon (6:32–8).

Jubilees has been shown to depend on 1 Enoch at several points (VanderKam 1978). Apart from the 364-day calendar, the most significant point of continuity concerns the story of the Watchers and the origin of sin on earth. Jubilees retells the story with some variations in chapter 5. Then in chapter 10 the unclean spirits descended from the Watchers begin to lead the children of Noah astray. When Noah asks the Lord to imprison them, their leader Mastema asks that some of them be allowed to remain on earth, since some of humanity is destined for corruption and to be led astray (10:8). His wish is granted, and one-tenth of the demons are allowed to remain at large.

While the Book of Jubilees does not devote much space to eschatology, the prospect of a final judgment is of crucial importance throughout: "the judgment of all is ordained and written on the heavenly tablets in righteousness" (5:13). Eschatological concerns are developed at greater length in two passages. Jubilees 1:23–9 anticipates a time when the Jews will turn to God and He will live among them for all eternity. There will be a new creation, "and all the luminaries (will) be renewed for healing and for peace and for blessing for all the elect of Israel." Jubilees 23 is more explicit. Here we get a rapid overview of all generations from the time of Abraham. There is an extended account of the decline of humanity and the abuses of "an evil generation" (23:14) of the Hellenistic age. One of the charges against this generation is that it has forgotten "feasts and months and sabbaths and jubilees" – a possible reference to a change of calendar. But then (23:26) "the children will begin to study the laws" and the transformation will begin. This development parallels the emergence of the "chosen righteous" in the Apocalypse of Weeks and "lambs" in the Animal Apocalypse. The "children" in Jubilees will drive out their adversaries and live in peace. Finally, "their bones shall rest in the earth and their spirits shall have much joy" – an apparent reference to afterlife without resurrection. This latter point is an interesting parallel to the mode of afterlife that we will find to be typical of the scrolls, and to the eschatology of the Essenes as described by Josephus. (See further Chapter 7, below).

THE APOCALYPSES AND THE ORIGIN OF THE DEAD SEA SECT

The books of Enoch and Daniel and related writings figure prominently in the corpus of the Dead Sea scrolls. There can be no doubt that these writings influenced the ideology of the Dead Sea sect, and were among the sources on which the sectarians drew. Many scholars, however, have believed that the relationship is closer than this, and that the apocalypses were actually produced by an early stage of the sectarian movement. This view has played an important part in two of the most widely held theories of the origin of the Dead Sea sect.

The view that the Dead Sea sect should be identified as the Essenes, and was an offshoot of the Hasidim of the Maccabean era, for a long time represented the consensus of scholarship (Cross 1961, 1995; Stegemann 1971) and is probably still the most widely held theory of the orgins of the Qumran community. The relation of the sect to the Hasidim bears directly on our present discussion. The Hasidim, as an organized party, are known from three passages in the books of Maccabees. They were "mighty warriors in Israel" (1 Macc 2:42) who supported Judas Maccabee (2 Macc 14:6). When a priest from the line of Aaron named Alcimus was appointed high priest by the Seleucid king Demetrius in 161 BCE, the Hasidim were the first to seek peace, and they were probably identical with the group of scribes who approached Alcimus to ask for terms. Their trust was ill-founded, and sixty of them were killed (1 Macc 7:12–16). Apart from these passages we have no direct information about the Hasidim. We know nothing of their beliefs and hopes, except that they supported Judas Maccabee and were more eager to make peace than the other militants. (For a full discussion of the Hasidim see Kampen 1988.)

Some scholars however have painted an enlarged portrait of the Hasidim, attributing to them the apocalyptic writings of Enoch and Daniel. (See especially Hengel 1974, 1:175–80. Scholars who relate the Essenes to the Hasidim do not necessarily agree with this attribution.) In brief, the Hasidim are assumed to be identical with the "chosen righteous" and the "lambs" of the Enochic apocalypses, with the "children" of Jubilees, and with the *maskilim* of Daniel. It is unlikely, however, that all these writings were produced by a single movement. The book of Daniel is notoriously lacking in enthusiasm for the Maccabean revolt, which it regards as, at most, "a little help" (Dan 11:34), and can hardly be a product of the militant Hasidim. The Enochic books are compatible with the Hasidim insofar as they do support the Maccabees. But there is nothing in the references to the Hasidim in the Maccabean books to suggest that they shared the Enochic fascination with the heavenly world. So while it is possible that the "chosen righteous" of the Apocalypse of Weeks are the Hasidim, it is by no means certain that this is so. Neither is there any hard evidence that the Essenes or the Dead Sea sect were related to the Hasidim, although a relationship is certainly possible. In short, the relation of the Hasidim to the apocalypses, on the one hand, and to the Dead Sea sect, on the other, is a matter of inference and speculation.

It is possible, however, to relate the apocalypses to the Dead Sea sect without recourse to the Hasidim. The so-called "Groningen Hypothesis" put forward by F. García Martínez and A. S. van der Woude (1990) argues that "the Essene movement" had its origin in apocalyptic circles before the Maccabean revolt. Here again the references to an emerging group in the Hellenistic period (the "chosen righteous," or the "lambs") are crucial. The classic account of the origin of the Dead Sea sect is provided by the Damascus Document as follows:

> He (God) left a remnant to Israel and did not deliver it up to be destroyed. And in the age of wrath, three hundred and ninety years after He had given them into the hand of King Nebuchadnezzar of Babylon, He visited them and He caused a plant root to spring from Israel and Aaron to inherit His Land and to prosper on the good things of His earth. And they perceived their iniquity and recognized that they were guilty men, yet for twenty years they were like blind men groping the way.
>
> (CD 1)

The blindness was eventually dispelled by the arrival of the Teacher of Righteousness.

If the reference to 390 years is taken literally, it should point to a date early in the second century BCE, even allowing for the fact that the author's chronology may have differed from ours. This is also the time that seems to be implied for the emergence of the "chosen righteous from the chosen plant of righteousness" in the Enochic apocalypses. It is tempting, then, to assume that the groups in question are one and the same. We should, however, bear in mind that the 390 years is a symbolic number derived from Ezekiel 4:5, and that it is by no means certain that it can be treated as reliable chronological information. It is also possible, of course, that more than one sectarian group emerged in the early second century CE. The crucial question is whether the Enochic apocalypses and the sectarian scrolls are so close ideologically that we should ascribe them to a single movement. García Martínez and van der Woude hold that we should: "the most important proof . . . lies in the demonstration that characteristic and fundamental ideas of Essenism and of the Qumran sect can already be found in one form or another within the Palestinian apocalyptic tradition" (García Martínez 1988: 119).

Whether we regard this claim as justified will depend on our judgment as to the degree of continuity that is required and the degree of alteration that may be tolerated. Continuity there certainly is. The 364-day calendar, which figures prominently in Enoch and Jubilees, was one of the major reasons for the secession of the Dead Sea sect. All this literature displays an intense interest in the heavenly world, attributes the origin of sin to demonic forces, and expects everlasting reward of the righteous and punishment of the wicked. The specific understanding of demonic forces and of eternal life, however, is somewhat different in the scrolls from what we find in the apocalypses. We must allow that other traditions besides that of the apocalypses played a part in the formation of the sectarian ideology. The apocalypses show no knowledge of the kind of community organization that is characteristic of the Dead Sea sect. Neither do they exhibit the distinctive pesher-style exegesis. The books of Enoch show little interest in halakhic issues, although these issues become very prominent in Jubilees.

It is possible to argue that the apocalypses, specifically the Enoch tradition, represent an early stage of the movement that became the Dead Sea sect, before the Teacher of Righteousness came on the scene and the most distinctive ideas of the sect crystalized. I should prefer, however, to envisage a looser relationship. The books of Enoch and Jubilees were composed over a considerable length of time, surely more than the twenty years allowed by the Damascus Document for the period of blindness before the coming of the Teacher. Enoch is not invoked as a revelatory authority in the literature of the Dead Sea sect. This would be surprising if the books of Enoch that we have were produced by an earlier stage of the same movement. Moreover, other lines of continuity can be traced in the scrolls – e.g. with the book of Daniel, and with Sadducean halakhic traditions (Schiffman 1994). It is likely that the Dead Sea sect was fed by more than one tributary stream.

Nonetheless, the continuity of the sectarian texts with the apocalyptic tradition of the books of Enoch and Jubilees is real and important. We know from the Damascus Document and from the so-called Halakhic Letter (4QMMT) that the primary issues that led to the separation of the sect from the rest of Judaism were calendaric and halakhic. These issues, however, were viewed in the light of an apocalyptic worldview, which was shaped to a great degree by the tradition embodied in the books of Enoch and Daniel. The tradition was not static. Other traditions also came into play and the sect adapted all of them to its needs. We shall examine key elements of the resulting sectarian worldview in the following chapters.

3

CREATION AND THE ORIGIN OF EVIL

THE MYTH OF THE WATCHERS

At the root of the apocalyptic tradition embodied in the books of Enoch is a mythic account of the origin of evil on earth through the agency of the Watchers or fallen angels (see Sacchi 1990). The fullest articulation of this myth is found in one of the oldest books of Enoch, the Book of the Watchers (1 Enoch 1–36). The fundamental myth utilized by the Book of the Watchers has been aptly characterized by Paul Hanson as "Rebellion in Heaven" (Hanson 1977: 195–223). The creation itself is good, just as it is in Genesis 1. The Watchers, led by angelic figures named Asael and Semiḥazah, revolt; they are not evil from the beginning. (Asael came to be identified with Azazel, the demon in the wilderness in Leviticus 16, as the tradition unfolded. The identification is attested at Qumran in 4Q180, a text variously known as "The Pesher on the Periods" or "The Ages of Creation" (Dimant 1979.)

The origin of this myth is unclear. Genesis 6 provides the starting point for the story with its enigmatic reference to "the sons of God" (or simply the divine beings, *bnê hā' elôhîm*), who have intercourse with human women, but Genesis does not posit rebellion in heaven. The "sons of God" are not accused of any sin in Genesis; their action is reported in a neutral way. The Nephilim or "mighty men of old," who were on the earth in those days and are usually taken to be the offspring of these unions, are described as "men of renown," surely a positive reference. The Flood is brought on by the wickedness of humankind, and the inclination of the thoughts of their hearts. Milik argued that the brief and elliptic Genesis narrative presupposed the fuller story of the Watchers, which we find in 1 Enoch (Milik 1976: 31), but this is unlikely. Genesis probably presupposes an older story of the cause of the Flood. The older myth, however, is more likely to conform to the Atrahasis epic, where the Flood is brought about by the increase of humanity rather than by sin (Batto 1992: 64–6). The Enochic Book of the Watchers clearly has its own sources, which variously ascribe leadership of the revolt to Semiḥazah or Asael. These sources can have originated no later than the third century BCE (Stone 1978).

In the Book of the Watchers, the union with human women is assumed to be sinful, probably because it involves the transgression of divinely appointed boundaries. The sin is compounded by the illicit revelation which the Watchers impart, and by the violence of the giants whom they beget. It is reasonable to infer that this sin is paradigmatic. Various allegorical applications have been suggested, to the spread of Hellenism (Nickelsburg 1977) or to the corruption of the priesthood (Suter 1979). In 1 Enoch 12–16, a secondary expansion of the story of the Watchers, the spirits of the giants become evil spirits on earth (1 Enoch 15: 8–10: "Evil spirits came out from their flesh, because from above they were created; from the holy Watchers was their origin and first foundation"). In this way the revolt of the Watchers becomes the ultimate cause of the existence of evil spirits and, by implication, of human sin.

The author of the Book of Jubilees knew and used the Book of the Watchers, but adapted it in several respects (VanderKam 1978). Jubilees is basically a retelling of Genesis, and unlike the Book of the Watchers it highlights the story of Adam and Eve (chapter 3). Sin does not originate in heaven, but on earth. The angels initially come down "to teach men to do what is just and right on earth" (4:15), and are subsequently attracted to human women. As in Enoch, the spirits of the giants become evil spirits on earth, and after the Flood, "the unclean demons began to lead the children of Noah's sons astray and to mislead them and destroy them" (Jub 10:1). They were created for the purpose of destroying (Jub 10:5–6), although they were not part of the original creation. These spirits now have a leader, Mastema, who is described as a prince, and who bears a strong resemblance to the Satan of Hebrew Scriptures. He first appears in Jubilees 10, and is presumably one of the spirits of the giants. Only one-tenth of the spirits are allowed to remain with him, for the purpose of destroying and misleading mankind. These spirits operate by divine permission, but they are not ultimately responsible for human sin, since Adam fell long before they came on the scene. In later tradition, Satan was identified with the serpent of the Garden of Eden, but that identification is not made in Jubilees.

THE SAPIENTIAL TRADITION

The apocalyptic tradition of Enoch and Jubilees was not the only account of the origin of evil on offer in Judea in the second century BCE. The subject was also pondered by wisdom teachers, and their legacy too was important for the Dead Sea sect. From the time of Ben Sira (Sirach), in the early second century BCE, the Torah of Moses was an object of study and discussion in wisdom schools. The central importance of the Torah at Qumran scarcely needs to be stressed. It was the "well" which the converts of Israel dug (CD 6:4) and the Community Rule stipulated that wherever ten members assembled there should not be lacking a man to interpret the Torah day and night (1QS 6:6). In view of all this intensive study of the Torah, it was inevitable that there should develop an explanation of the origin of evil based on the accounts of creation in Genesis 1–3.

In view of the importance attached to the sin of Adam in later Jewish and especially Christian tradition, it is surprising that no attention is paid to Genesis 2–3 in the Hebrew Bible. With the possible exception of some texts of uncertain date from Qumran, Ben Sira is the first to grapple with the implications of the story. Even the Book of Jubilees, which contains the oldest intact narrative paraphrase of these chapters, has surprisingly little to say about the sin of Adam (Vermes 1992b). It is not until the first century CE that the sin of Adam acquires central importance, in the letters of St Paul and in the apocalypses of 4 Ezra and 2 Baruch.

Ben Sira is also silent on the sin of Adam. He makes one notorious reference to the sin of Eve: "From a woman sin had its beginning and because of her we all die" (Sirach 25:24). There is an interesting parallel to this statement in a fragmentary wisdom text from Qumran (4Q184, the so-called Wiles of the Wicked Woman): "She is the beginning (*r'ēšît*) of all the ways of wickedness ... for her paths are paths of death." The Qumran text, however, implies no reference to Eve, and does not address the ultimate origin of sin and death. Ben Sira's statement remains anomalous in pre-Christian Judaism. It is also anomalous in the context of Sirach's own teaching, and it seems to be an *ad hoc* comment, made in the context of a tirade against the "wicked woman" rather than an integral part of a coherent theological system.

Sirach addresses the origin of sin directly in Sirach 15:11–20. The passage has the character of a disputation: "Do not say, 'It was the Lord's doing that I fell away,' for he does not do what he hates." The implied opponents apparently attribute the origin of evil to God, although those who attribute it to "the sons of God" in the manner of Enoch may also be in view. Some of Sirach's own pronouncements on creation could be understood to impute ultimate responsibility to God:

> Every man is a vessel of clay, and Adam was created out of the dust. In the fullness of his knowledge the Lord distinguished them and appointed their different ways. Some he blessed and exalted, and some he made holy and brought near to himself; but some he cursed and brought low, and turned them out of their place. Like clay in the hand of the potter, to be molded as he pleases, so all are in the hand of their Maker, to be given whatever he decides.
>
> (33:10–13)

The problem is how to balance a monistic belief in a good, omnipotent creator with the evident presence of evil in the world.

Sirach addresses this problem in Sirach 15:14: "God created the human being (*adam*) in the beginning and placed him in the power of his inclination (*bʾyad yiṣrô*)." The word *yēṣer*, inclination, is related to the word for "potter" in Sirach 33 (*yôṣēr*) and to the verb used in Genesis 2:7 ("the Lord God formed man out of the dust of the ground"). One might infer that the "inclination" is the form given to human beings by the creator. While there is no mention of an inclination in Genesis 1–3, the term appears twice in the Flood story (J source): Genesis 6:5, "every inclination of the thoughts of their hearts is evil continually" and Genesis 8:21: "the inclination of the human heart is evil from youth." The association of the *yēṣer* with evil is typical of biblical usage. Later, in rabbinic literature, the *yēṣer* acquires a technical sense, and is conceived as a force that determines behavior. Urbach summarizes the situation as follows:

> In Sirach, as in the Bible, the *yēṣer* is the natural inclination of man, and also in the teaching of the Tannaim and Amoraim it sometimes denotes the power of thought, or serves as a

synonym for the heart as the source of human desires. However, rabbinic teaching did to some extent personify "the Evil Inclination," to whom were ascribed attributes, aims and forms of activity that direct man, even before he was explicitly identified, as by the Amora Resh Laqish, with Satan and the angel of death.

(Urbach 1975: 1.472)

The potency of the evil inclination (or "evil heart," *cor malignum*) plays a prominent part in the apocalypse of 4 Ezra, written at the end of the first century CE: "For the first Adam, burdened with an evil heart, transgressed and was overcome, as were also all who were descended from him. Thus the disease became permanent; the Torah was in the people's heart along with the evil root, but what was good departed, and the evil remained" (4 Ezra 3:21–2; 4:20; Stone 1990: 63–7). Ezra stops short of saying that God created the evil heart, but the sages are explicit on this point. So Sifre Deuteronomy §45: "My children I have created for you the Evil Inclination, (but I have at the same time) created for you the Torah as an antidote."

Recent scholarship has been consistent in emphasizing the neutrality of the inclination in Sirach, and its conformity to the biblical view. It is clear from the following verses that Sirach envisages free choice. The formulation is Deuteronomic: "If you choose, you can keep the commandments . . . . Before each person are life and death, and whichever one chooses will be given" (Sirach 15:15,17; cf. Deut 30:15). The inclination is not an external, supernatural force. Yet if Sirach is credited with any coherence at all, this passage must be read in the light of chapter 33, which insists that people are clay in the hand of the potter ($y\bar{o}\d{s}\bar{e}r$), to be given whatever God decides. The exercise of human choice is conditioned by the inclination with which a person is fitted at creation, and so the word $y\bar{e}\d{s}er$ in Sirach 15:14 cannot be simply equated with free will (as it is in the New Revised Standard Version translation). The emphasis in Sirach's argumentation is influenced by the immediate context of a passage. In chapter 15, he is concerned to defend God from implication in human sin, and so he puts the emphasis on free will, but in chapter 33 his focus is on the omnipotence of God and the symmetrical order of creation. There is an unresolved tension in his thought between divine determination and human free will.

Sirach fills out his understanding of creation of humanity in

17:1–24. The clearest references are to Genesis 1 rather than Genesis 2–3, although the notice that God created the human being (*anthrōpon*, Adam) out of the ground shows that Genesis 2 is also in view. Sirach notes that humanity is made in the divine image and enjoys authority over the rest of creation, but he ignores the story of the "Fall." Death does not result from the sin of Adam (or Eve!) but is part of creation from the beginning (17:1–2; cf. 41:4). God filled humanity with knowledge and understanding and showed them good and evil (Sirach 17:7, cf. Gen 2:9). There is no suggestion, however, that they were forbidden to eat from the tree of the knowledge of good and evil. Instead, God "allotted to them the law of life. He established with them an eternal covenant and revealed to them His decrees. Their eyes saw His glorious majesty and their ears heard the glory of His voice" (11–13). The reference here is to the revelation at Sinai (cf. Exod 19:16–19). The designation "law of life" is derived from Deuteronomy 30:11–20. But Sirach allows no interval between the creation and the giving of the Torah. Rather, he implies that the law of life was given to humanity from the beginning. The sin of Adam (which Sirach does not even acknowledge) is no more significant than the sin of anyone else who breaks the Law.

Despite this vigorous endorsement of Deuteronomic theology and human responsibility, however, Sirach's overall position remains ambiguous. A Hebrew redactor of chapter 15 complemented the statement that God left humanity in the power of its inclination with the phrase "He set him in the power of his spoiler" (*ḥōtpô*). The phrase is not supported by the versions. The original Sirach had no place for a demonic "spoiler," and in this he differed both from the Enochic tradition and from the Qumran Community Rule. Consequently, the human "inclination" ultimately comes from God. There was, then, in Sirach's own theology a basis for the view that sin also comes from God, even though this inference was unacceptable to the sage.

THE ENOCH TRADITION IN THE SCROLLS

When we turn now to the Dead Sea scrolls, we find influences from both the apocalyptic and the sapiential traditions, but we also find, in the Instruction on the Two Spirits, a new synthesis that goes beyond any of its Jewish precedents. In view of the strong manuscript evidence for interest in the books of Enoch at Qumran, there is remarkably little appeal to the Enoch tradition in the major sectarian documents of Qumran. The Damascus Document cites the story of the Watchers in the course of an admonition to "walk perfectly on all his paths and not follow after thoughts of the guilty inclination and lascivious eyes" (CD 2: 15–16). The Watchers provide the first negative example in a review of human conduct: "because they walked in the stubbornness of their heart, the Heavenly watchers fell; they were caught because they did not keep the commandments of God." The fall of the Watchers is paradigmatic for human sinfulness, insofar as it illustrates a pattern that is repeated throughout history. It is not causative, however, and it is not understood as the origin or source of human sinfulness. That source lies rather in the inclination (*yēṣer*) of the human heart, as Ben Sira already taught. Azazel and the angels are given a more causative role in misleading Israel in 4Q180, but the text is very fragmentary. That text also resembles Enoch insofar as God is said to have established the sequence of the ages before creation, and engraved them on the heavenly tablets.

THE SAPIENTIAL TRADITION IN THE SCROLLS

The importance of the *yēṣer* or human inclination is also underlined in the sapiential writings found at Qumran. A lengthy wisdom text known as 4QSapiential Work A is found in several fragmentary manuscripts (1Q26, 4Q415–18, 423. See Harrington 1996). Unlike Ben Sira and the older biblical wisdom tradition, this work appeals to the authority of heavenly books and special revelation, in a manner hitherto associated with apocalypses rather than with wisdom:

> Engraved is the ordinance, and ordained is all the punishment. For engraved is that which is ordained by God against all the iniquities of the children of Seth. And written in His presence is a book of memorial of those who keep His word. This is the vision of the Hagu (Meditation), the book of memorial. And He gave it as an inheritance to Man (*'enoš*), together with a spiritual people. For according to the model of the holy ones is his inclination [or: He fashioned him; the unpointed Hebrew, *yṣrw*, is ambiguous]. But no more has Hagu been given to fleshly spirit, for it knew not the difference between good and evil according to the judgment of its spirit.

> (4Q417 2:14–18)

The "book of memorial" is an allusion to Malachi 3:16: "a book of memorial was written before Him of those who revered the Lord and thought on His name." In the Qumran context, this book has strong apocalyptic overtones. Heavenly tablets and books figure prominently in the books of Enoch, Daniel and Jubilees (1 Enoch 47:3; 93:1–2; 108:3; Dan 7:10; 10:21; 12:1; Jub 30:20–2. Lange 1995: 69–79). The reference to engraving also recalls 1QH 9:24 (formerly 1:24): "All things are graven before Thee with the stylus of remembrance for everlasting ages." In some of these cases the emphasis is on the record of rewards and punishments (e.g. Dan 12:1; cf. also 4QDibHam 6:14) but in others the whole divine plan is implied (e.g. 1 Enoch 93:1–2).

The knowledge contained in the Book of Hagu is angelic. (Compare 1 Enoch 93:1–2: "Enoch began to speak from the books ... according to that which appeared to me in the heavenly vision, and which I know from the words of the holy angels and understand from the tablets of heaven.") It is given to *'ĕnôš* (Man) because his inclination is (or: he was fashioned) after the model (*tabnît*) of the holy ones (Lange 1995: 88). The reference to *'ĕnôš* here has puzzled commentators. The Hebrew word *'ĕnôš* may be either the proper name of the son of Seth (Gen 4:26; 5:6–7; 9–11) or a general designation for a human being. Harrington takes it in the latter sense. *'ĕnôš* in the sense of human being occurs repeatedly in the Hodayot, Community Rule and other scrolls. Here we are told that his *yēṣer* (inclination, nature) is after the likeness of the holy ones. The interpretation is disputed, but Lange is on the right track when he takes the point to be the affinity of *'ĕnôš* with the holy ones, or angels. The "spiritual people" linked with *'ĕnôš* is contrasted with "the spirit of flesh" which failed to distinguish between good and evil.

This latter phrase holds the key to the correct interpretation of the passage. The context is supplied not by Genesis 4–5 (Enosh) but by the creation of humanity in Genesis 1–3. Like Sirach, the author holds that the knowledge of good and evil is set before humanity from the beginning. (This is also clear in 4Q423. See Elgvin 1994: 188). The story of Adam in Genesis 3, which is understood as a "Fall" in later tradition, is taken here as a failure to distinguish between good and evil. But this is not the only depiction of Adam in Genesis 1–3. According to Genesis 1:27 he was created "in the image of God" (*bᵉṣelem 'ĕlōhîm*). I suggest that the *'ĕnôš* of the Sapiential Text is none other than the Adam of Genesis 1:27. In fact the word *'ĕnôš* is used in precisely this context in 1QS 3:17 in the

Instruction on the Two Spirits: "he created *'ᵉnôš* to rule the world." The likeness of the holy ones, in which his *yēṣer* is fashioned, represents an interpretation of the image of God. (The word *'elōhîm* is often used in the sense of angels, holy ones, in the scrolls.) It is well known that Philo of Alexandria understood Genesis to refer to a double creation of Man, and that he derived this understanding from an exegetical tradition. In the words of T. H. Tobin: "The double creation of man is an interpretation which tries to explain why the description of the creation of man occurs twice in Genesis. In such an interpretation this is taken to mean that two different 'men' were created, the one heavenly and part of the intelligible world, the other earthly and part of the sensible world" (Tobin 1983: 108). Philo understands the two Adams in his own philosophical framework. The Qumran Sapiential Text understands them as two types of humanity, a spiritual people in the likeness of the holy ones and a "spirit of flesh." The duality of human existence is formulated differently in the Instruction on the Two Spirits in the Community Rule: God created *'ᵉnôš* to rule the world and appointed for him two spirits. The two formulations, however, are attempting to express the same conviction: that humanity is divided dualistically right from creation.

THE INSTRUCTION ON THE TWO SPIRITS

A much more elaborate explanation of the origin of evil is found in the Instruction on the Two Spirits, in the Community Rule (1QS 3:13–4:26; for text and translation see Charlesworth 1994). The literary genre of instruction falls within the scope of wisdom literature. A mythological account of creation is presupposed, but it is not recounted in an extended narrative as it is in the Book of the Watchers. Rather it is subordinated to the exposition of the two ways in which human beings walk. The literary context in which the teaching is presented is shaped by the tradition inherited from Ben Sira and the Sapiential Text. Nonetheless, the worldview presented in this text is thoroughly apocalyptic, and bears considerable similarity to that of Enoch and Jubilees.

The key passage in the Instruction reads as follows:

> From the God of knowledge comes all that is and is to be. Before ever they existed He established their whole design, and when, as ordained for them, they come into being, it is in

accord with His glorious design that they accomplish their task
without change . . . . He has created man to govern the world,
and has appointed for him two spirits in which to walk until the
time of His visitation: the spirits of truth and wickedness.

(1QS 3:15–19)

The passage goes on to describe the origin, characteristics and destiny of those who walk in each of the two spirits (Licht 1958). They
spring respectively from a fountain of light and a source of darkness.
The righteous are ruled by "the Prince of Light" and are assisted by
the God of Israel and his Angel of Truth. The wicked are ruled
by "the Angel of Darkness" and all their unlawful deeds are caused
by his dominion. The passage describes the attributes of each spirit:
on the one hand, humility, goodness, and wisdom; on the other,
greed, wickedness, and falsehood. Those who are ruled by the spirit
of light are destined for "healing, plentiful peace in a long life,
fruitful offspring with all everlasting blessings, eternal enjoyment
with endless life, and a crown of glory with majestic raiment in
eternal light" (IQS 4:6–8). They shall inherit all the glory of Adam.
Those who are ruled by the spirit of darkness, in contrast, are destined for "punishments at the hands of all the angels of destruction
in the fire of the dark regions." God has established the spirits in
equal measure until the final age, and has set everlasting hatred
between their divisions. But God in the mysteries of His understanding "has ordained an end for injustice and in the time of the
visitation he will destroy it forever." God has allotted these spirits to
humankind so that they may know good and evil, and that their
destiny may be according to their spirit. There is some tension within the Instruction as to the degree to which people are ruled by the
relevant spirit and the degree to which they have free choice. The
beginning of the discourse gives the impression that people are
entirely in the one camp or the other. Later, however, we read that all
people have a portion of both spirits, and their retribution is "according to whether each one's portion in their two divisions is great or
small" (1QS 4:15–16). The two spirits fight their battle "in the heart
of man" (1QS 4:23). This has given rise to speculation that the
Instruction has undergone some revision, and that a myth of cosmic
conflict has been psychologized, by locating the conflict in the
human heart. Von der Osten-Sacken (1969: 11–27) distinguishes
three strata: 3:13–4:14; 4:15–23a; 23b-6. This is possible, but the
tension remains in the text as we have it.

The Instruction on the Two Spirits is indebted to both apocalyptic and sapiential traditions. There are numerous terminological parallels between this instruction and 4QSapiential Work A (Lange 1995: 128–9). These include the title "God of knowledge," and the phrase "to know good and evil." The Sapiential Text refers repeatedly to "the mystery that is to be" (*raz nihyeh*), an unusual expression, involving the *niphal* of the verb "to be." (The phrase seems to refer to all the mysteries of creation, including the eschatological resolution of history, Lange 1995: 60.) The Instruction on the Two Spirits says that God established "all that is and is to be (*nihyeh*) using the same *niphal* form of the verb to be. (The phrase *raz nihyeh* also occurs later in the Community Rule, in 1QS 11:3.) Moreover, the two documents share certain presuppositions about the nature of creation and history. Humanity is divided between two spirits. The Sapiential Text distinguishes between "people of spirit" or "spiritual people" and the "spirit of flesh"; the Instruction between the spirits of light and darkness. History is divided into periods (*qēṣ*) in both documents, and both envisage an eschatological conclusion with appropriate retribution.

Some scholars have exaggerated the affinity of the Instruction on the Two Spirits with the sapiential tradition by arguing that the two spirits should be understood in terms of the good and evil inclinations. P. Wernberg-Møller has written:

> It is significant that our author regards the two "spirits" as created by God, and that according to IV, 23 and our passage both "spirits" dwell in man as created by God. We are therefore not dealing here with a kind of metaphysical, cosmic dualism represented by the two "spirits," but with the idea that man was created by God with two "spirits" – the Old Testament term for "mood" or "disposition." That RWHWT is used here as a psychological term seems clear; and the implication is that the failure of man to "rule the world" is due to man himself because he allows his "spirit of perversion," that is to say his perverse and sinful propensities, to determine his behaviour. We have thus arrived at the rabbinic distinction between the evil and the good YEṢER.
>
> (Wernberg-Møller 1961: 422)

It is certainly true that the two spirits have a psychological dimension. They struggle in the heart of human beings (1QS 4:23). It is also true that the entire passage is based, however loosely, on

Genesis 2–3. The Instruction begins by saying that God created man (*'ʿnôš*) to rule the world (cf. Gen 1:28) and concludes with a statement that God "has given a legacy to the sons of men for knowledge of good [and evil]," a statement that suggests that this document, like Sirach and 4QSapiential Work A, may not have regarded the tree of knowledge as off limits. Significantly, the Community Rule, like CD, promises the elect that "the glory of Adam" will be theirs (1QS 4:23). But Wernberg-Møller's inference that "we are therefore not dealing here with a kind of metaphysical, cosmic dualism" is a *non sequitur*. The Instruction clearly identifies the two spirits with the Prince of Light and the Angel of Darkness (3:20–1). The dualism is simultaneously psychological, moral, and cosmic. There is a synergism between the psychological realm and the agency of the supernatural angels or demons.

There are then significant differences between the Instruction on the Two Spirits and the sapiential tradition. The Sapiential Text does not describe the dualistic character of creation in such explicit terms as the Instruction. It lacks the terminology of light and darkness, and it does not embody the opposing spirits in angelic powers, such as the Prince of Light and Angel of Darkness in the Instruction. In short, the Instruction has a developed mythological dimension that is not paralleled in the Sapiential Text, or in any older Hebrew wisdom literature.

ZOROASTRIAN INFLUENCE

The mythological aspect of the Instruction bears at least a phenomenological similarity to the worldview of the Enoch literature. Heavenly or demonic beings influence the behavior of human beings, and lead them towards a final retribution beyond this world. Yet there are surprisingly few parallels in detail. There is no allusion to the myth of the Watchers in the Instruction. The origin of evil is located in God's act of creation, not in some subsequent rebellion. There is, however, an echo of Jubilees at 1QS 3:23–4, which refers to the dominion of the Spirit of Darkness as "the dominion of his enmity" (*memšelet maśtēmātô*) and refers to the spirits of his lot who cause the sons of light to stumble. (Similarly in the War Rule, 1QM 13:10–12, Belial is called "the angel of Mastema".) There is a general similarity to the apocalyptic tradition, insofar as angelic and demonic beings play a role in shaping human destiny. But the specific explanation of the origin of evil is quite different, and entails a different understanding of creation (cf. Davidson 1992: 297). The Instruction on the Two Spirits is fully as mythical in its conception as the story of the Watchers, but the underlying myth is different. This myth was recognized almost as soon as the scroll was published. It is the myth of Persian dualism (Dupont-Sommer 1950: 107, 113, 119; 1953: 157–72; Kuhn 1952: 296–316. For the debate on the issue see Kobelski 1981: 84–98. For the most recent exposition see Philonenko 1995).

In the Gathas, the oldest part of the Avesta, which are generally considered to be the work of Zoroaster himself, humanity and even the supreme God has to choose between two spirits, one of whom is holy and the other a destroyer. The two spirits are the twin children of Ahura Mazdah, the Wise Lord (Zaehner 1961: 50–1) although later the holy spirit is identified with Ahura Mazdah, and the spirit of destruction is primordial (Kobelski 1981: 92. This development is attested as early as the fourth century BCE by Eudemus of Rhodes, a pupil of Aristotle). These spirits were associated with light and darkness from an early time, as evidenced by Plutarch (*Isis and Osiris,* 46–7), who cites Theopompus (about 300 BCE) as his source (Gwyn Griffiths 1970: 471). The two spirits are described as follows in the Gathas:

> In the beginning those two Spirits who are the well-endowed (?) twins were known as the one good and the other evil, in thought, word, and deed. Between them the wise chose rightly, not so the fools. And when these Spirits met they established in the beginning life and death that in the end the followers of the Lie should meet with the worst existence, but the followers of Truth with the Best Mind. Of these two Spirits he who was of the Lie chose to do the worst things; but the Most Holy Spirit, clothed in rugged heaven, [chose] Truth as did [all] who sought with zeal to do the pleasure of the Wise Lord by [doing] good works.
>
> (Yasna 30; trans. Zaehner 1961: 42)

The same Yasna speaks of a time when Evil shall cease to flourish and those who have acquired good fame shall reap the promised reward. (Cf. also Yasna 45, 47; Duchesne-Guillemin 1952.)

There is, of course, considerable adaptation of the Persian myth in the Jewish context. God creates rather than begets the two spirits. As creator, God is clearly transcendent, above both light and darkness. This doctrine was already affirmed by Second Isaiah, who claimed for his God the sovereignty Zoroaster attributed to Ahura Mazda: "I form light and create darkness, I make weal and create woe; I the Lord do all these things" (Isa 45:7). This affirmation of the creator, however, has the consequence of making responsibility for evil rest with God. In the Persian myth, the evil spirit still becomes evil by choice. In the Jewish treatise, it is created evil by God. There are several precedents in biblical tradition for the notion that evil comes from the Lord (cf. 2 Sam. 19:9, Amos 3:6, Sirach 33:14–15). Such a monistic view is typical of the Deuteronomic tradition, with its negative attitude towards mythology. There is a sharp difference, however, between Deuteronomic monism and the dualism under God that we find in the scroll. There is an equally sharp difference between the scroll and earlier apocalyptic tradition on this point. The myth of opposing forces of light and darkness, evenly balanced until the end of history, has no precedent in Jewish tradition. The similarity to the Zoroastrian myth cannot be coincidental. The possibility of such influence is not especially problematic in the Hellenistic period, when there had already been contact between Jews and Persians for several hundred years, even though we can not at present trace the channels through which Zoroastrian dualism was actually transmitted.

DUALISM IN A JEWISH CONTEXT

The Instruction on the Two Spirits is arguably the most strikingly distinctive text in the entire corpus of the scrolls. For this reason it is often assumed to be the quintessence of the theology of the Dead Sea sect, and thought to represent the teaching of the Teacher of Righteousness (Charlesworth 1994: 15). There is no agreement among scholars, however, as to where it should be located in the development of the ideology of the sect. Hartmut Stegemann regards it as "certainly pre-Essene, and influenced by Babylonian Judaism" (Stegemann 1993: 154; cf. Lange 1995: 126–8). Others have argued that the dualism is a late development, and that a progression towards a more pronounced dualism can be seen in the redactional history of several texts (Davies 1985; Duhaime 1987).

It may be well at this point to pause in order to clarify what we mean by the words "dualism" and "dualistic." The historian of religion Ugo Bianchi has defined dualism as "the doctrine of the two principles . . . dualistic are all those religions, systems, conceptions of life which admit dichotomy of the principles which, coeternal or not, cause the existence of that which does or seems to exist in the world" (Bianchi 1980: 15). He goes on to distinguish various kinds of dualism. The distinction between "radical" and "softened" dualism is most immediately relevant here. The early form of Zoroastrian dualism, where the two spirits are the twin children of Ahura Mazda, is "softened" dualism; the later form, where the spirit of evil is primordial, is radical. In the Instruction on the Two Spirits, the dualism is "softened," since the dichotomous spirits are subordinate to a transcendent God.

Some scholars restrict the use of the terms dualism and dualistic to situations where we have "two equal and opposing influences, conceived cosmologically and/or ethically, and, in a Jewish context, subordinated to the sovereignty of one God" (Davies 1985: 50). On such a definition, the role of Mastema in Jubilees, or of Satan in Christian tradition, is not dualistic, since the Prince of Evil is not paired with a corresponding equal spirit. Such a definition is unduly restrictive, however. The alternative usage speaks of dualism wherever human affairs are subjected to the influence of a supernatural agent who is hostile to God. It should be emphasized that the Hebrew Bible knows of no such agent in the ethical sphere: Satan only acquires his diabolical character in the post-biblical period. In this usage, dualism does not require that the prince of darkness be paired with an equal adversary, as he is in the Instruction on the Two Spirits. The Angel of Light is only the agent of God and has no independent agenda. We may also speak of dualism when God's agent is not mentioned and a Satanic figure is opposed directly to the deity. Passages in the Dead Sea scrolls that speak of the dominion of Belial are inherently dualistic, even if no mention is made of Belial's angelic adversary (*contra* Davies 1985: 50).

Dualism is obviously highly compatible with a sectarian ideology. It provides a way of explaining why the truth, as the sect sees it, is utterly rejected by others, even those who profess to worship the same God, especially if the Spirit of Darkness holds dominion for a period. The belief that this division is fore-ordained by God is comforting to the believer, as it entails an assurance that God is in control, despite current appearances to the contrary. It is reasonable to suppose that the sharp separation between light and darkness posited in the Instruction on the Two Spirits reflects the alienation of the Dead Sea sect from the world around it and its decision to separate itself from the majority of the people (4QMMT C 7; cf. 1QS 8:13–14). The claim that the opponents are under demonic influence is especially typical of sectarian division, between parties that both claim to have the true expression of the same religion (Pagels 1991, 1995).

A CORPUS OF DUALISTIC WRITINGS

It is possible to identify a small corpus of writings among the scrolls, in several different genres, which attest to an explicit dualism of two spirits, although they may differ from the Instruction in 1QS in terminology and in emphasis. The most obvious and important text is the War Rule, which will be the subject of an extended discussion in Chapter 6. The focus of the War Rule is different from that of the Instruction; the one describes and gives directions for the final battle between the forces of light and darkness, while the other is a discourse on creation and human nature. Yet the two share a dualistic worldview in which the opposing factions are associated with light and darkness. The opposing angels are identified in the War Rule as Michael and Belial. While these names are not mentioned in the Instruction on the Two Spirits, there is an obvious correspondence between the two documents in this respect. Belial is also linked with the dualism of light and darkness in other texts, such as the "Eschatological Midrash" (4Q177. 2.8: "the lot of light that was mourning during the dominion of Belial") and 4Q286 (see pp. 46–7, below).

The different names of the opposing angels are explicitly addressed in a fragmentary composition known as 4QAmram, or the Testament of Amram, an Aramaic writing preserved in five copies (Milik 1972a,1972b; Kobelski 1981). This composition might be classified either as a testament or as an apocalypse, since it is simultaneously the deathbed speech of a patriarch and the report of a vision. Amram, son of Qohath, son of Levi, tells his sons about a vision in which two angelic figures were quarreling over him. When he asks who they are he is told: "we rule over all humanity," and they ask him by which of them he chooses to be ruled. One of them is identified as a "watcher" (like the fallen angels in 1 Enoch) and he is said to rule over all darkness. He is named Melchiresha ("king of wickedness"). Since the other, who rules over all light, is said to have three names, it is likely that Melchiresha has other names too. Melchiresha is the only name preserved, but it is possible to make a plausible conjecture about the others. The negative figure appears elsewhere in the scrolls as Belial and the Angel (or Prince) of Darkness. (Other possibilities, less frequently attested, are Mastema and Satan). The positive figure appears most often as Michael or the Prince of Light. His third name is almost certainly Melchizedek ("king of righteousness"), the counterpart of Melchiresha. Melchizedek is the central figure in the eschatological midrash known as 11QMelchizedek, in which he plays the role of God's agent in the eschatological judgment. It seems then that the principal angels of light and darkness could also be called by other names at Qumran. Each of the pairs in question, Michael/Belial, Melchizedek/Melchiresha, angel of light/angel of darkness, implies a dualistic structure. It is possible, of course, that 4QAmram is effecting a synthesis of traditions that were originally diverse, but in fact none of these pairs is attested in any Jewish writing that is demonstrably older than the Dead Sea scrolls. This fact would lead us to suppose that dualism in this form first arose in Judaism in the context of the Dead Sea sect. The Testament of Amram, however, is an early manuscript. In the judgment of the editor, J. T. Milik, one of the manuscripts (4QAmram[b]) is "certainly from the second century BCE, possibly even from its first half" on palaeographic grounds (Milik 1972a: 78). If this judgment is accepted (and it has not been challenged) the form of dualism preserved in the Testament must have developed at a very early stage of the sect's formation, even before the establishment of the settlement at Qumran.

The various names for the angel of darkness are also rehearsed in a number of liturgical texts (Kobelski 1981: 37–48). In 1QS 2, in the context of the renewal of the covenant, we read that "the Levites will curse all the men of the lot of Belial. They will speak up, saying: "Cursed be you in all your guilty wickedness. May God set you trembling at the hand of all the avengers. . . . May God not be compassionate to you when you call. . . . May there be no peace for you in the mouth of all who make intercession." Much of the same language is used in 4Q280 fragment 2, in a curse on Melchiresha: "Cursed be you Melchiresha. . . . May God set you trembling at the hand of the avengers. . . . May God not be compassionate to you [when] you call. . . . And may there be no peace for you in the mouth of all who make intercess[ion]."

In 4Q286 10 ii 1–13 we find the curse directed against Belial: "Cursed be [B]elial in his hostile [sc]heme, and damned be he in his guilty domination. Cursed be all the spiri[ts] of his [lo]t in their wicked scheme. . . . Indeed [they are the lo]t of darkness; their punishment is in the eternal Pit." The text continues with curses against the sons of Belial, the Angel of the Pit, and Spirit of Abaddon. The latter two are simply variant names for Belial.

One of the most fascinating dualistic texts from Qumran is in the form of a horoscope. 4Q186 uses physical characteristics to determine the share of an individual in the lot of light and darkness: "his thighs are long and lean, and his toes are thin and long. He is of the second Column. His spirit consists of six (parts) in the House of Light and three in the Pit of Darkness." Another figure has "teeth of uneven length. His fingers are thick and his thighs are thick and very hairy, each one. His toes are thick and short. His spirit consists of eight (parts) in the House of Darkness and one from the House of Light." This text makes clear that the psychological understanding of the two spirits was not an idiosyncrasy of 1QS but was the subject of a diagnostic practice in the community. We have no way of knowing how widely it was practiced, or over how long a time.

It is apparent then that the dualism of the two spirits played a central role in a cluster of texts from Qumran. The question remains whether it was central to the ideology of the sect as a whole, or a view of the world that was held by some members of the sect and rejected by others.

DUALISM AND THE IDEOLOGY OF THE SECT

The first point to consider is the inclusion of the Instruction on the Two Spirits in two copies of the Community Rule. Since at least one manuscript (4QS^d; probably also 4QS^e) apparently did not include the first four columns of 1QS, there is reason to believe that the Instruction was added as a secondary or tertiary expansion. (In the case of 4QS^b, fragments of columns 1, 2, 5, 9, 10, and 11 are preserved, but not 3 and 4, where the Instruction on the Two Spirits is found in 1QS. It should be noted, however, that some of the manuscripts that lack the Instruction were copied later than manuscripts in which it is found.) It has been suggested that 1QS is a collection of independent compositions (Stegemann 1993: 153). But even if the different components of this manuscript were composed independently, they are brought together by purposeful redaction. 1QS 1:1–3:12 describes a ceremony of covenant renewal for the members of the community. The Instruction on the Two Spirits provides an understanding of the order of creation. These two compositions taken together establish the theological context within which the rules of the community must be understood. The juxta-position was not peculiar to 1QS. It is also attested in 4QS^c. The importance attached to this edition of the Community Rule is shown by the care with which it was stored in a manuscript jar in Cave 1.

Moreover, the covenant renewal ceremony in 1QS 1:1–3:12 pre-supposes a dualistic view of the world. The ceremony is prescribed for "all the days of Belial's dominion." The curses of the covenant are directed against "all the men of the lot of Belial." There is no reference to light and darkness, and no reference to creation, but the reference to "the lot of Belial" implies a division of humanity simi-lar to that expounded in the Instruction on the Two Spirits. It is not clear, however, whether the covenant ceremony presupposes the Instruction or whether the Instruction is a more advanced formula-tion of the dualism that is implied but not fully articulated in the ceremony.

A similar problem is presented by the other major sectarian rule book, the Damascus Document (CD). This document lacks the deterministic language of the Instruction on the Two Spirits, and seems to give a much greater role to human free will, in accordance with the Deuteronomic tradition. Here again the community rules are preceded by introductory material, which may well have been added in several stages. One of the introductory exhortations begins in CD 2:14: "And now, my sons, listen to me and I shall open your eyes so that you can see and understand the deeds of God, so that you can choose what He is pleased with and repudiate what He hates, so that you can walk perfectly on all His paths and not follow after the thoughts of a guilty inclination and lascivious eyes." Not only is the guilty inclination the cause of human error; it was also the downfall of the Watchers: "for having walked in the stubbornness of their hearts the Watchers of heaven fell; on account of it they were caught, for they did not follow the precepts of God." In this passage, the Damascus Document seems to rely on a theology of the human inclination (*yēṣer*) that is similar to what we have found in the sapiential tradition. (The elect are also promised "the glory of Adam" in CD 3:20.) Other passages in the document, however, have strongly apocalyptic overtones.

The most explicitly dualistic statement in the Damascus Docu-ment is made as a parenthetic example in CD 5:18–19: "For in ancient times there arose Moses and Aaron, by the hand of the

Prince of Lights and Belial, with his cunning, raised up Jannes and his brother during the first deliverance of Israel." Belial is evidently identical with the "angel of darkness" of the Instruction on the Two Spirits. Because of the parenthetical nature of the statement, and the lack of any other reference to the "Prince of Lights" in CD, it has been argued that this verse is a secondary insertion (Duhaime 1987: 51–5). Belial, however, has an integral role in CD. In CD 4:13 we read: "And during these years Belial will be sent against Israel." The notion that a period of history is subject to the dominion of Belial has been called "the very heart of the sectarian thought" (Dimant 1984: 493). We have seen it in the covenant renewal ceremony at the beginning of 1QS. It is also found in the Hodayot (1QH 11:28, formerly 3:28). It is probably identical with·"the period of wrath" in CD 1:6. The errors of Israel are ascribed to "the three nets of Belial" (CD 4:15). Sinners are those over whom "the spirit of Belial dominates" (12:2). Those who abandon the covenant will be delivered over to "destruction at the hand of Belial" (8:2; 19:14). All of this implies a dualistic understanding of history, even though Belial is not paired with an angelic counterpart but is simply the opponent of God.

Belial, however, is not mentioned in the passage in CD that most closely resembles the Instruction on the Two Spirits. This is CD 2:2–13(italics indicate phrases that correspond to phrases in the Instruction):

> *God loves knowledge* (cf. 1QS 3:15); He has established wisdom and counsel before Him; discernment and knowledge are at His service; patience is His and abundance of pardon to atone for persons who repent from wickedness; however, strength and power and a great anger with flames of fire by the hand of all *the angels of destruction* (1QS 4:12) against those who turn aside from the path and abominate the precept, *without there being for them either a remnant or survivor* (1QS 4:14). For *God did not choose them* (1QS 4:22) at the beginning of the world, and before they were established he knew their deeds (1QS 4:25) … And He knew *the years of their existence, and the number and detail of their ages* (cf. 1QS 4:13), of all those who exist over the centuries, and of those who will exist, until it occurs in their ages throughout all the everlasting years (1QS 4:16). And in all of them He raised up men of renown for Himself … but those He hates, He causes to stray.

This text obviously stands in some tension with other sections of CD. The bold statement that God causes those He hates to stray contrasts with the emphasis on free will in the following passage (2:14–16). Yet we have noted similar tensions already in Ben Sira. The close verbal parallels between this text and the Instruction on the Two Spirits require some literary relationship. Lange (1995: 242) assumes that CD has been influenced by the Instruction on the Two Spirits. Davies, in contrast, emphasizes the differences between the two documents (Davies 1983: 72–3). The CD text makes no reference to spirits of light and darkness. It is difficult to imagine why the author of the CD passage would have omitted such a central feature of the 1QS text if he had it before him. For this reason, it is probably simpler to suppose that the CD passage influenced the Instruction, rather than vice versa. In this case, we should view the Instruction as the culmination of a process of reflection on the problem of evil, in which the emerging dualism of the sect was finally given a systematic form, with the help of some concepts that were ultimately derived from Zoroastrianism. The entire process, however, would seem to have taken place relatively early in the history of the sect. The manuscript of 1QS is dated palaeographically to the first half of the first century BCE. The Instruction on the Two Spirits may well have been composed in the second century BCE. (cf. the early date of the manuscript of 4QAmram). The relative chronology of these documents, however, and the redactional stages of their composition, are very tentative, and there is not at present any consensus of scholarship on the subject. The fact that the Instruction on the Two Spirits is missing from some of the later copies of the Community Rule should warn us that ideas of dualism did not necessarily develop in a straight line in one direction.

One other evocation of Persian dualism in CD should be noted. In the Gathas, the opponents of Zoroaster are "the followers of the Lie," and the evil spirit is "He who is of the Lie" (Yasna 30:3–6; 32:3–5 from Zaehner 1961: 42–3). In CD, the opponent of the Teacher is "the man of the Lie" (CD 8:13; 19:26; 20:15; see also 1QpHab 2:1–2; 5:9–12; 10: 9; 4QpPs 37 1:18; 4:14). The occurrence of this designation in documents which lack the explicit contrast of the two spirits, and which are largely concerned with the early history of the sect, suggests that the sectarian writers were already looking to Zoroastrian categories to express their view of history even before the systematic exposition on the two spirits was formulated.

The role of dualism in the apocalyptic worldview of the scrolls will concern us further when we examine the Rule of the War in Chapter 6. Before we turn to that, however, it is necessary to gain a clearer view of the understanding of history in the sectarian writings.

4

THE PERIODS OF HISTORY AND THE EXPECTATION OF THE END

According to the Instruction on the Two Spirits, humanity is divided between the spirits "for their generations," "for all the periods of ages" (*l^ekol qiṣṣê 'ôlāmîm*), for God established (them) in equal measure until the final period (*qēṣ 'aḥ^arôn*). . . . But in the mysteries of His understanding and in His glorious wisdom, God has ordained an end (*qēṣ*) for injustice, and at the time of the visitation He will destroy it forever" (1QS 4:15–19). Entailed by this passage are two of the most typical features of apocalyptic writings of the historical type: the division of history into periods and the expectation of a definitive end, when God will intervene and banish evil forever. It should be noted that the same Hebrew word, *qēṣ*, is used for both "period" and for "end." The translation is determined by the context. In the scrolls, we find allusions to the periodization of history in several literary genres, but especially in exegetical works (pesharim and midrashim). There is, moreover, a Serek, or Rule, devoted to "the end of days" (1QSa).

THE PERIODIZATION OF HISTORY

In the apocalyptic writings of the Hellenistic age, history is often divided into ten generations (cf. the Apocalypse of Weeks) or four kingdoms (Daniel 2 and 4). Both these schemata are found in the Sibylline Oracles Book 4, and can be traced back to Persian sources (Flusser 1972; see also Widengren 1995). One of the most influential schemata, however, is distinctively biblical. This is the schema of seventy weeks of years, found in Daniel 9. Jeremiah had prophesied that Jerusalem would lie desolate for seventy years (Jer 25:11–12;

29:10). The angel Gabriel now informs Daniel that the seventy years are really seventy weeks of years, or 490 years. This period could also be interpreted as ten jubilees. According to Leviticus 25:1–55, a jubilee or seven weeks of years (forty-nine years) was the longest period that land could be alienated from its ancestral owners or that a person could be kept in indentured slavery. The apocalyptic literature often divides history, or a segment thereof, into ten periods (Yarbro Collins 1984: 1242–4). Daniel puts these two motifs together to come up with the seventy weeks of years or ten jubilees.

Daniel does not attempt to fill in a full chronology of events for each of the seventy weeks, but we are given a few points of reference. The starting point is "the time that the word went forth to restore and rebuild Jerusalem." The reference here is to the divine word, rather than to the decree of the Persian king, and so the starting point is at some time during the Exile. Daniel's vision is dated to the first year of Darius the Mede, which cannot be correlated with any actual historical date. (No such person is known to history; see Collins 1993: 30–1). The first seven weeks end with the coming of an anointed prince, who is usually identified as either Zerubbabel or the high priest Joshua, about the year 520 BCE. Then sixty-two weeks pass without comment, until "an anointed one shall be cut off," a reference to the murder of the high priest Onias III, about 171 BCE. For the seventieth week, "the prince who is to come" (Antiochus IV Epiphanes) will make a strong covenant with many, and for half a week the temple cult will be disrupted by "the abomination that makes desolate."

As a calculation of the period from the Babylonian Exile to Antiochus IV Epiphanes, Daniel's 490 years is impossibly long, by any known chronology, ancient or modern. (By modern calculations, it is about seventy years too long.) But Daniel was not interested in the chronology of the whole period, only in its conclusion. The last week of years, or seven-year period was initiated by the murder of the high priest Onias, and the mid-point in the last week was marked by the installation that makes desolate in the temple, an event that is usually dated to December 167 BCE. The conclusion to be drawn from Daniel's prophecy, then, is that the "end" would come three and a half years after the profanation of the temple, some time in the summer of 163 BCE. The same chronology is implied in Daniel 7:25, which gives the length of the persecution as "a time, times and half a time."

A similar division of history is found in the Apocalypse of Weeks in 1 Enoch. Here, as in Daniel, history is divided into "weeks," presumably weeks of years. The prophecy grows more detailed towards the end. At the end of the seventh week, "the chosen righteous from the eternal plant of righteousness will be chosen" but history does not come to an end. In the eighth week a sword is given to the righteous, to execute judgment. In the ninth, "the righteous judgment will be revealed to the whole world . . . and the world will be written down for destruction." Finally in the tenth week there will be a great judgment, the old heaven will be taken away and a new heaven revealed. Thereafter "there will be many weeks without number, forever." Like Daniel, this apocalypse passes rapidly over large periods of history, and is primarily concerned with the end of history. Even though it envisages an end of this world, however, the "end" is not exactly a fixed point. Rather we have an eschatological scenario in which there is a series of "ends" as the old order passes away and is replaced by the new. This gradual unfolding of the "end" is also significant for the end of history in the scrolls.

PERIODIZATION IN THE SCROLLS

Only rarely in the scrolls are the periods of history spelled out as they are in the apocalypses, but several references show that this way of understanding history was widespread. The references are found especially in exegetical texts. 4Q180 is introduced as a "Pesher concerning the periods made by God, (each) period to complete [all that is] and all that will be. Before He created them, He set up their works . . . each period in its period, and it is engraved on the tablets [of heaven]". J. T. Milik suggested that "this text is a commentary on a very early work which enjoyed an authority among the Essenes equal to the prophetic books, the Psalter, etc. for which pesharim were composed " (Milik 1976: 251–2). This authoritative work would have set forth the division of history that is presupposed in the various parts of 1 Enoch, the Testament of Levi, and other apocalyptic texts. The suggestion that this book had quasi-canonical authority lacks textual support and has not won acceptance (Huggins 1992) but the text is indicative of a strong interest in periodization nonetheless. Unlike the other pesharim, which interpret specific texts, this pesher appears to be an exposition of the subject of periods (Dimant 1979: 96). The subject matter for such an exposition could be drawn from such texts as Daniel 9 and the Apocalypse of Weeks. The Damascus Document also refers to "the Book of the Divisions of the Times into their Jubilees and Weeks" (CD 16:4). It is usually assumed that this is the Book of Jubilees, although periodization is not a conspicuous feature of that book.

The division of history into jubilees plays a crucial role in another eschatological midrash, 11QMelchizedek (Kobelski 1981). There are ten jubilees, just as ten "weeks" are enumerated in the Apocalypse of Weeks. The duration is 490 years, equivalent to the seventy weeks of years in Daniel 9. In fact, the Melchizedek document cites Daniel 9 explicitly in 11QMelch 2:18: "and the herald i[s the one an]ointed of the spir[it about] whom Dan[iel] said: [. . . " (The reference is usually identified as Daniel 9:25: "until the time of an anointed prince there shall be seven weeks." It is possible that the reference is to Daniel 9:26: "after the sixty-two weeks, an anointed one shall be cut off.") The Melchizedek document, however, is not concerned with all periods of history, but with the events that begin to unfold "in the first week of the jubilee after [the n]ine jubilees" (2:7). Specifically, "the D[ay of Expia]tion i[s the en]d of the tenth [ju]bilee when expiation (will be made) for . . . the men of the lot of Mel[chi]zedek" (2:8). Melchizedek is portrayed in this document as a heavenly figure, and is even identified as the "god" (*'elōhîm*) to whom Psalm 82 refers when it says "God has taken His place in the divine council; in the midst of the gods He judges." Melchizedek and his lot are pitted against Belial and his lot, just as the Angel of Light is pitted against the Angel of Darkness in the Instruction on the Two Spirits, and Michael against Belial in the War Scroll. The tenth jubilee is identified as the time when Melchizedek will exact the vengeance of God's judgments on Belial and the spirits of his lot (2:12–13). The time in question is also identified as "the end of days" (*'aḥarît hayyāmîm*; 2:4).

A chronology based on the seventy weeks of years, or 490 years, also seems to be implied in the Damascus Document, at least in its final redaction. In CD 20:14 we are told that "from the day of the ingathering of the unique teacher until the destruction of all the men of war who turned back with the man of lies there shall be about forty years." This calculation is evidently related to the figures found in column 1 of the same document. The time from the Exile to the emergence of the sect is 390 years (a figure derived from Ezek 4:5). Then the first members wander in blindness for twenty years until the arrival of the Teacher of Righteousness. If we allow the stereotypical figure of forty years for the Teacher's career, this brings us to 450 years. Forty years after his death would then bring us to 490 years, the time stipulated in the book of Daniel (Vermes 1981: 147–8). We shall see that this manner of calculation played a significant role in the eschatological expectation of the sect.

THE END OF DAYS

The phrase *'aḥărît hayyāmîm* or end of days probably originally meant "in the course of time, in future days" (Steudel 1993). A cognate expression is found with this sense in Akkadian. The phrase appears already in the Pentateuch in Genesis 49:1 (the blessing of Jacob) and Numbers 24:14 (Balaam's oracle). Both of these passages contain archaic prophetic texts, which originally referred to the future, in an unspecified but limited sense, but were reinterpreted and given an eschatological sense in the post-exilic period, so that they were now understood to refer to a final, definitive, phase of history. The phrase "end of days" is part of the prose introduction to the poetry in both passages, and may have been added relatively late, with the eschatological sense already implied. The phrase occurs in Deuteronomy with reference to future turning points in Israel's history, in relation to the observance of the covenant (Deut 4:30; 31:29). In the prophets, the "end of days" implies a definitive transformation of Israel in the distant future. Usually, the reference is to the time of salvation. A famous oracle that appears both in Isaiah 2 and Micah 4 says that in the end of days the mountain of the Lord's house will be exalted above all mountains and all the peoples will stream to it. In Ezekiel and Daniel, however, the concept was broadened to include not only the age of salvation but also the drama that leads up to it. In Ezekiel 38, the end of days is the time when Gog invades Israel, and so it is a time of distress, but one that culminates in the destruction of the invader. In Daniel chapter 2 the Aramaic equivalent of the phrase is used with reference to Nebuchadnezzar's dream of the four kingdoms and the final, everlasting, kingdom of the God of heaven. We will find this broader usage, including both distress and salvation, continued in the Dead Sea scrolls.

The expression "end of days" (*'aḥărît hayyāmîm*) occurs more than thirty times in the Dead Sea scrolls (Steudel 1993: 225–46). The so-called Halakhic Letter, 4QMMT, declares that "this is the end of days," and 1QSa, one of the supplements to the Community Rule, is introduced as "the rule for all the congregation of Israel in the end of days." There are two references in the Damascus Document. The great majority of the occurrences, however, are found in exegetical literature, in the pesharim, and midrashic texts such as the Melchizedek Scroll and especially the so-called "Eschatological Midrash" (4Q174, the Florilegium, + 4Q177, the Catena) which contains approximately one third of the references. Surprisingly, the phrase does not occur in the Community Rule, the Hymns (Hodayot) or the War Rule.

The end of days in the scrolls has two aspects. It is a time of testing, and it is a time of at least incipient salvation. The time of testing is explicit in the Florilegium (4Q174), which explains Psalm 2: "Why do the nations conspire and the peoples plot in vain against the Lord and against his anointed one," by saying that the nations conspire against the elect of Israel at the end of days. The next column continues: "it is a time of refining which co[mes . . .] . . . as is written in the book of Daniel, the prophet: The wicked [act wickedly . . .] and the just [. . . shall be whi]tened and refined and a people knowing God will remain strong." The passage weaves together two passages from Daniel, 12:10 and 11:35. In the context of Daniel, the time of refining is the period immediately before Michael rises in victory, although it may arguably continue into the time of distress that follows Michael's rise in Daniel 12:1. Several other passages corroborate the view of the end of days as a time of testing. 4Q177 (the Catena) which may be part of the same document (see Steudel 1994: 127–51), speaks of testing and refining the men of the community at the end of days. The pesher on Habakkuk refers to traitors and ruthless ones at the end of days (1QpHab II 5–6; cf. 4QpNah 3–4 ii 2).

But the end of days also has positive aspects. It includes the dawn of the messianic age. The Florilegium refers to the Branch of David who will arise with the Interpreter of the Law at the end of days, and the "Messianic Rule," (1QSa) describes a banquet at the end of days at which the messiah of Israel will be present. We shall discuss the messianic expectations of the sect at length in Chapter 5. The end of days will also see the construction of a new, purified temple. In the course of an exposition of 2 Samuel 7:10, the Florilegium says: "That is the house which [he will build] for him at the end of days, as it is written in the book of [Moses], "The Sanctuary of the Lord which thy hands have established . . . And foreigners shall not make it desolate again, as they desolated formerly the sanctuary of Israel because of their sin. And he said to build for him a human sanctuary (or: a sanctuary of Adam) for there to be in it for him smoking offerings."

Scholars are divided as to whether the "human sanctuary" or "sanctuary of Adam" is a real temple or simply an expression for the Qumran community (for a synopsis of the discussion see Wise 1991: 107–10). In either case, it stands in contrast to the temple which the Lord will establish with His own hands. It is an interim structure, until God builds His own temple in the end of days. Similarly in the Temple Scroll, column 29, we read that God "will dwell with them for ever and will sanctify my [sa]nctuary by my glory. I will cause my glory to rest on it *until the day of creation on which I shall create my sanctuary, establishing it for myself for all time* . . ." (author's italics). From this it seems that the temple to which large sections of the Temple Scroll are devoted (cols 3–48) is also an interim arrangement, but that God will create a permanent, eschatological temple "on the day of creation."

EXCURSUS ON THE TEMPLE SCROLL AND NEW JERUSALEM TEXT

The Temple Scroll is primarily a synthetic edition of laws from Deuteronomy and Leviticus, presented as a revelation of God to Moses. It is exceptional among the scrolls insofar as God is the speaker, and so a very strong claim to divine authority is implied. It is often taken to be a law for the "end of days" (e.g. Wise 1990a, 1990b) but this does not appear to be the case. As we shall see in Chapter 5, the king envisaged in the Temple Scroll is not a messiah, and is not envisaged as the fulfillment of messianic prophecy. The Temple Scroll must be taken as a reformist document for this age rather than for the eschatological future, and is comparable to the Book of Jubilees, which also rewrites the biblical text with reformist intentions. Both Jubilees and the Temple Scroll lay claim to divine revelation, but the claim of the Temple Scroll is stronger insofar as it dispenses with the angelic mediator who plays a standard role in apocalyptic revelation and is retained in Jubilees.

Much of the Temple Scroll is taken up with the interim temple, which is to last until the day of the new creation but is not itself the eschatological temple. This temple is distinguished by its gargantuan size; it is about three times the size of the Herodian enclosure (Broshi 1987) and by the strictness of its purity laws and ritual observance. It is evidently a utopian temple, and it never actually existed. Nonetheless it is a temple for this age rather than for the eschatological future. The scroll makes some limited compromises with the necessities of real life – e.g. the distance of the latrine from the city is disproportionately short in relation to the width of the city (Wise 1990b: 84). It envisages a temple of human construction, however hyperbolic it may seem (Maier 1990).

Whether this scroll was a product of the Dead Sea sect remains uncertain. It is unique among the scrolls in claiming that God was its author, and several scholars suppose that it was an older document inherited by the sect, just like the books of Enoch and Jubilees (Stegemann 1993: 137; Schiffman 1994: 258). The idea of an ideal temple, prior to the new creation with its eschatological temple, is rare in the scrolls, but is found in one other important document, the New Jerusalem text.

The fragmentary Aramaic New Jerusalem text existed in at least six copies at Qumran (1Q32; 2Q24; 4Q554; 4Q555; 5Q15; 11Q18). Since the beginning of the document is lost, we cannot be sure of its literary genre, but it is evidently modeled on the vision of an ideal or eschatological temple in Ezekiel 40–8. Occasional statements that "he showed me . . . " suggest that this text too was a vision in which the seer was given a guided tour by an angel. As such, the New Jerusalem text is arguably one of the few apocalypses found in the scrolls, although it is too fragmentary to permit certainty (Stegemann 1983: 517–18).

The relationship between this text and the Temple Scroll is disputed. (Wise 1990b: 64–86 argues that the New Jerusalem text was a source for the Temple Scroll; García Martínez 1992: 180–213 denies the relationship, and sees the New Jerusalem text as a later product of the Qumran community.) Both texts stand in a tradition of speculation about the ideal temple, which is implicitly critical of the actual Second Temple structure. The fragmentary state of the New Jerusalem text does not permit us to say with confidence whether the temple in question is the final, eschatological one, or an interim arrangement. It should be noted, however, that this text also makes reference to an eschatological finale, which mentions Kittim, Edom, Moab and the Ammonites, and Babylon, and says that "they shall oppress your descendants until the time that . . . " (4Q554 fragment 2, col. 3, lines 15–22; Eisenman and Wise 1992:46; García Martínez 1994: 131). The final lines of the fragment mention a kingdom, and say that "the peoples shall ser[ve] them . . . " (Or: "do with them"; the Aramaic verb 'bd normally means to do, but in Hebrew it means to serve, and it may be used in its Hebrew sense here.) This passage most probably refers to the eschatological conflict between Israel and the nations, and must be located at the end of the New Jerusalem text. (Column 2 of the same fragment gives various temple measurements.) It would seem, then, that at least in one manuscript the description of the ideal temple precedes the eschatological conflict. This would suggest that it corresponds to the temple of the Temple Scroll, and is an idealized temple for this age, not a heavenly temple and not something to be revealed in the new creation.

The Temple Scroll and the New Jerusalem text are not necessarily products of the Dead Sea sect. They may have been preserved simply because they implied a strong critique of the Hasmonean temple cult. The Qumran Community Rule seems to regard the community itself as a substitute temple, which should atone for the land in the interim until the final deliverance. According to 1QS 8: 5–15, the community

> shall be an everlasting plantation, a house of holiness for Israel, an assembly of supreme holiness for Aaron. . . . They shall be the elect of goodwill who shall atone for the land and pay to the wicked their reward. . . . It shall be a most holy dwelling for Aaron, with everlasting knowledge of the covenant of justice, and shall offer up sweet fragrance. . . . And they shall be an agreeable offering, atoning for the land and determining the judgment of wickedness.

The "temple of men" in the Florilegium may well refer to the community too (Steudel 1994: 165). In that case, we should not assume that the kind of temple described in the Temple Scroll and New Jerusalem text was widely expected by the Dead Sea sect. It is clear from the Florilegium, however, that the Dead Sea sect shared with the Temple Scroll the expectation that God would build a definitive eschatological temple in the end of days.

The positive aspects of the end of days are clearly still in the future from the perspective of the authors of the scrolls. There is no suggestion anywhere that the messiah has already come. Many scholars hold, however, that the time of testing was already being experienced in the history of the sect (Brooke 1985: 206–9; Steudel 1993: 226–31). The language of the scrolls is often ambiguous. So, for example, the phrase "a time of refining which co[mes . . .]" in the Florilegium can mean, grammatically, either that the time has come or that it is coming. Annette Steudel has argued that it must mean that the time has already come (Steudel 1993: 228–9). The pesher on Psalms speaks of attempts to lay hands on the Teacher of Righteousness at the time of refining, and she assumes that the Teacher was already dead when the pesher was written. This is very likely, although there is nothing explicit in the text to that effect. If Steudel is right, we must assume that the end of days entailed two phases, the time of testing and the coming of the messiahs, and that the first phase had already begun.

Only one text in the Qumran corpus says explicitly that the end of days has already begun. This is the Halakhic Letter, 4QMMT, but its presentation of the end of days is exceptional in a number of respects. 4QMMT C 13–15 cites Deut 30:1–3: "And it is written 'and it shall come to pass, when all these things [be]fall you', at the end of days, the blessings and the curses, ['then you will take] it to hea[rt] and you will return unto Him with all your heart and with all your soul', at the end . . . " (Qimron and Strugnell 1994: 59–61). The text goes on to say that "we know that some of the blessings and the curses have (already) been fulfilled as it is written in the book of Moses," but the reference is apparently to the "blessings" experienced under David and Solomon and the "curses" experienced from the time of Jeroboam to the Babylonian exile. The fulfillment of these curses and blessings, then, is not itself part of the end of days and is hardly proof that the end of days is at hand. Nonetheless, the Letter continues: "And this is the end of days when they will return to Isra[el]." The point is not that signs of the eschaton have already begun to appear, as is sometimes implied in apocalyptic texts, but that the time of decision is now. It is time to usher in the end of days by returning to the covenant. 4QMMT is exceptional among the Dead Sea scrolls insofar as it is addressed to someone outside the sectarian community. Consequently it makes no attempt to argue from the experience of the sect that prophecy is being fulfilled, since the recipient of the letter could not be expected to accept such an argument. Instead, the Letter is framed in terms that might in principle be persuasive to any Jew, appealing primarily to the Law of Moses. The statement that "this is the end of days," however, is asserted rather than argued, and is made for the purpose of calling the addressee of the Letter to decision.

The precise limits of the end of days are never clearly defined in the scrolls. The ambiguity of the situation may be illustrated with reference to the opening column of the Damascus Document.

There we are told that at the time of the Babylonian exile God saved a remnant from Israel. Then "in the age of wrath, 390 years after having delivered them up into the hands of Nebuchadnezzar, king of Babylon, He visited them, and caused a plant root to spring from Israel and from Aaron." (On the problems of interpretation presented by this passage see Davies 1983: 61–9.) It is not clear, however, whether the whole 390 years qualify as "the age of wrath" or whether that age only begins after 390 years. The phrase, "age of wrath" (Hebrew *qēṣ ḥārôn*) involves a word-play on "the last age" (*ḥaqqēṣ hā'aḥᵃrôn*) a phrase that we meet in the pesharim, and which can scarcely be distinguished from the end of days, and must also be related to "the last generation (*dôr 'aḥᵃrôn*) of CD 1:12. It is hardly possible that the end of days was thought to begin as early as the Exile. (4QDib Ham, 4Q504 fragments 1–2, col. 3.13–14, is exceptional in seeming to include the Exile in the "end of days," but this text is probably not a product of the Dead Sea sect, but part of its wider literary heritage. See Chazon, 1992.) The beginning of this period could well coincide, however, with the emergence of the sect. As we have noted already, the period extends to the coming of the messiahs, which clearly remains in the future in all the Dead Sea scrolls.

The period of "the end of days" that follows the coming of the messiahs is the subject of the so-called "messianic rule," 1QSa (Schiffman 1989). It would appear from this document that the conditions of human existence are not greatly altered by the coming of the messiahs. Provision must still be made for the education of children, and for community meals and regulations. One of the tasks of the princely messiah was to wage war on the Kittim, the Gentile enemies of Israel (Collins 1995: 49–73). This war is included in the end of days in the pesher on Isaiah (4QpIsaᵃ). The phrase is never applied, however, to the conditions that ensue after the eschatological war. We should perhaps allow for some variation in the way the motif is used in the different texts, but in general we may agree with Steudel that the end of days is "the last period of time, directly before the time of salvation" (Steudel 1993: 231). This period includes the time of testing and eschatological distress. It includes the dawning of the era of salvation, with the coming of the messiahs, and at least in some sources it extends to the final war. It does not, however, include the final salvation that is to follow the eschatological battle.

THE CALCULATION AND RECALCULATION OF THE END

There was another development in the book of Daniel of momentous importance for later tradition. Here for the first time we find an attempt to calculate the time of the end. The expectation of an end is found in the prophets with reference to a specific, decisive event, the day of judgment. When the prophet Amos proclaimed that "the end has come upon my people Israel" (Amos 8:2) he spoke of the end of Israel as an independent kingdom, not of the end of the world. He also spoke of this event as "the day of the Lord," which would be darkness and not light (Amos 5:18–20). Other prophets expanded this occasion into a day of cosmic judgment. So we read in Isaiah 13: "the day of the Lord comes, cruel, with wrath and fierce anger, to make the earth a desolation and to destroy its sinners from it. For the stars of heaven and their constellations will not give their light; the sun will be dark at its rising and the moon will not shed its light. . . . Therefore I will make the heavens tremble and the earth will be shaken out of its place at the wrath of the Lord of hosts, in the day of His fierce anger" (Isa 13:9, 10, 13; cf. Isa 2:10–22; Zeph 1:14–16. See Hiers 1992: 82–3). The motif of the day of the Lord usually places the emphasis on destruction, but it is understood that "the Lord alone is exalted on that day" (Isa 2:11) and the exaltation of the Lord brings with it deliverance for the faithful. The double aspect of the day of the judgment is clear in the book of Daniel: "At that time Michael, the great prince, the protector of your people shall arise. There shall be a time of anguish, such as has never occurred since nations first came into existence. But at that time your people shall be delivered, everyone who is found written in the book" (Dan 12:1). Deliverance in Daniel entails resurrection of the dead.

Daniel makes several specific attempts to calculate the precise number of days until the "end." According to Daniel 8:14 the time that the cult would be disrupted is given as 2,300 evenings and mornings, or 1,150 days. At the end of the book two further figures are given: "From the time that the regular burnt offering is taken away and the abomination that makes desolate is set up, there shall be 1,290 days. Happy are those who persevere and attain the 1,335 days" (Dan 12: 11–12). Each of these figures is close to three and a half years, the final half-week of years of the seventy weeks of years of Daniel 9. In Daniel 12, however, two things are remarkable. First, we are given two different numbers side by side. Both may be regarded as approximations of three and a half years, but the fact that two different figures are given strongly suggests that the second calculation was added after the first number of days had passed (Collins 1993: 400–1). The phenomenon of recalculation is well known in later apocalyptic movements such as the Millerite movement in nineteenthth-century America (Festinger et al. 1956: 12–23; Boyer 1992: 81–2). Second, Daniel is not specific as to what will happen when the specified number of days has passed. Since the days are calculated from the time that the temple cult was disrupted, we might expect that the expected "end" is simply the restoration of that cult, and this would seem to be the implication in Daniel 8:14 and 9:24. But, according to 1 Maccabees 1:54; 4:52–4, Judas purified the temple three years to the day after it had been polluted, so both numbers in Daniel 12 point to a date after that restoration. At least, the last date must have been added after the purification had taken place. Presumably, the author of Daniel did not think that the restoration under Judas was satisfactory. But there is probably more at stake here. The numbers in Daniel 12 follow the prophecy of the victory of Michael and the resurrection of the dead. In Daniel 12:13 Daniel is told that he will rise from his rest at the end of the days. The end, then, is the time when the archangel Michael intervenes and the resurrection takes place, roughly what later tradition would call the end of the world.

THE CALCULATION OF THE END IN THE SCROLLS

There are indications in the scrolls that the Dead Sea sect also envisaged a specific end-point, which would be the occasion of divine intervention, although precisely what would happen remains elusive. In the words of the Community Rule, "God, in the mysteries of His knowledge and in the wisdom of His glory, has determined an end to the existence of injustice and on the occasion of His visitation He will obliterate it forever" (1QS 4:18–19). This "end" was not in the vague and distant future, but was expected at a particular time in the sect's history. There are primarily two pieces of evidence that point to such a specific expectation: one passage in the pesher on Habakkuk and another at the end of the Damascus Document.

The pesher on Habakkuk comments on Hab 2:3 as follows:

"For there is yet a vision concerning the appointed time. It testifies to the end-time (*qēṣ*), and it will not deceive. The interpretation of it is that the last end-time (*haqqēṣ hā'aḥᵃrôn*) will be prolonged, and it will be greater than anything of which the prophets spoke, for the mysteries of God are awesome. If it tarries, wait for it, for it will surely come, and it will not be late. The interpretation of it concerns the men of truth, those who observe the Law, whose hands do not grow slack in the service of the truth, when the last end-time is drawn out for them, for all of God's end-times will come according to their fixed order.

(1QpHab 7:6–13; Horgan 1979: 16)

This passage from Habakkuk was cited several times in Daniel, to make the point that the vision will only be fulfilled at its appointed time (Dan 8:17; 10:14b; 11:27, 35). Habakkuk was concerned with the fulfillment of the vision: "the vision is still for the appointed time." Daniel is concerned with the assuredness of the "end": "there is still an end at the appointed time" (11:27, cf. 35). A further allusion to Habakkuk can be seen in Daniel 12:12, where the final prediction of the number of days is introduced: "blessed is he who waits and comes to 1,335 days" (Cf. Hab 3:2b: "if it tarries wait for it"). In the latter case it is clear that the "end" is delayed, and Daniel finds in Habakkuk a prophetic text that envisages such an eventuality.

The situation is similar in the pesher from Qumran. The prolongation of the end-time is not merely a theoretical possibility. It is the experience of the community, for which the author seeks an explanation in the prophetic text. It is reasonable to infer, then, that the "end" was expected shortly before the pesher was written. While we do not know the exact date of the pesher, all indicators point to the middle of the first century BCE. The manuscript is dated on palaeographic grounds to the early Herodian period (Cross 1995: 120, n.20) but it is not an autograph, as it contains copyist errors (Horgan 1979: 3; Stegemann 1993: 175). The Kittim in this document are clearly the Romans, who "sacrifice to their standards" (1QpHab 6:3–4). The prediction that the wealth and booty of the "last priests of Jerusalem will be given into the hand of the army of the Kittim" (9:6–7) suggests that the conquest of Jerusalem by the Romans (63 BCE) either was imminent or had already taken place. The pesher on Nahum refers to events in the early first century, down to the time of Hyrcanus II and Aristobolus II (67–63 BCE). If we may assume that these pesharim were written about the same time, a date around the middle of the century is plausible (Stegemann 1993: 176).

Our other witness to the expectation of an end at a specific time, the Damascus Document, also points to a date towards the middle of the first century. As we have already seen, CD 20:14 says that "from the day of the ingathering of the unique teacher until the destruction of all the men of war who turned back with the man of lies there shall be about forty years." Since this figure seems to be part of a more complex calculation, based on the Danielic "seventy weeks of years," it appears then that the Dead Sea sect expected the fulfillment of Daniel's prophecy about forty years after the death of the Teacher. Unfortunately we do not know when this took place. A date around the end of the second century BCE seems likely, but we must allow a generous margin of error. If the Teacher died about 100 BCE, this would point to an "end" about 60 BCE, which would be highly compatible with the evidence of the pesher on Habakkuk.

Some scholars believe they can reconstruct the date at which the end was expected with greater specificity (Steudel 1993: 233–40). Fundamental to any such attempt is the assumption that the figure of 390 years in CD column 1, for the period from the Exile to the rise of the sect, is reliable chronological information. Two possible calculations have been proposed. Modern chronology dates the beginning of the Exile to 587/6 BCE. If we count 390 years from that date, we get the year 197/6 for the emergence of the plant root from Aaron and Israel, and 177/6 for the advent of the Teacher, according to CD 1 (Wacholder 1983: 180–1. Wacholder has the emergence of the Teacher coincide with that of the "plant root" at the earlier date.) It has been pointed out, however, that some ancient Jewish authors calculated a later date for the Exile and a shorter post-exilic period. The Jewish chronographer Demetrius, who wrote in Egypt in the late third century, calculated that there were 338 years between the Exile of Judah (587/6 BCE) and Ptolemy IV (222 BCE) rather than 364/5 as modern historians reckon (Laato 1992: 605–7). This chronology would bring the dates down by twenty-six years, so that the Teacher would have emerged about 150 BCE, shortly after the usurpation of the high priesthood by Jonathan Maccabee, which many scholars have supposed to be the occasion for the secession of the Qumran sect. (Puech 1993: 506, n. 29, arrives at a date of 152 BCE, by assuming that CD follows a chronology attested in 2 Baruch.) If we then allow forty years for the career of the Teacher and a further interval of forty years after his death, we arrive at the conclusion that the "end" was expected about 70 BCE (Stegemann 1993: 174; Steudel 1993: 236–9 gives the date as 72 BCE, following Puech).

While these suggestions are intriguing, and are not impossible, in my view they are not reliable. Although there is evidence for speculation on biblical chronology, such as we find in Demetrius, in such documents as Jubilees and the Aramaic Levi Apocryphon, there is no actual evidence that the chronology of Demetrius is presupposed in the Damascus Document. The argument is simply that this chronology would support the popular hypothesis that the origin of the Dead Sea sect was related to the usurpation of the high priesthood by Jonathan Maccabee in 152 BCE. Despite its popularity, however, that hypothesis is far from established fact (see Collins 1989: 159–78). When the sectarian documents discuss the reasons for separation, especially in 4QMMT and CD, the high priesthood is never mentioned. Besides, the chronological data attributed to Demetrius are confused and contradictory. (The calculation of the period from the exile of the northern tribes to Ptolemy IV is about seventy years too long, and cannot be reconciled with Demetrius' own calculation of the exile of Judah.) The figure of forty years for the career of the Teacher is only a round number. The same must be said for the 390 years of CD 1, which is a symbolic number for the duration of the desolation, derived from Ezekiel 4:5. The attempt to derive chronological information from it rests on a shaky foundation. It is no more likely to be accurate than the 490 years in Daniel 9. The same objections apply to any attempt to derive chronological information from the system of jubilees in the Melchizedek document.

This is not to deny that the sectarians of Qumran had a specific time in mind for the coming of the eschaton. In order to arrive at that date, however, they did not need to verify every stage of the chronology. It was sufficient that they remember how much time had passed since the death of the Teacher. Even CD did not claim that the divine intervention would come exactly forty years after that event, but an approximate number was enough to fuel a lively expectation. There is no evidence that anyone at Qumran ever counted the days, in the manner of the book of Daniel, or that their expectation ever focused on a specific day, or year. Consequently, it does not appear that they ever encountered the trauma of disappointment that the Millerites experienced in nineteenth-century America, when the appointed day passed and "we wept and wept till the day dawn" (Boyer 1992: 81). Nonetheless, as the years passed, they were aware that the end-time was prolonged. "About forty years" could not be extended indefinitely. The lack of a specific date, however, mitigated the disappointment, and made it easier for the community to adapt to the postponement of their expectations.

THE NATURE OF THE END

But what exactly was expected to happen forty years after the death of the Teacher? The Damascus Document still expected the coming of the messiahs, so this is one obvious possibility. Their coming is described as "the age of visitation" when the unfaithful will be put to the sword (CD 19:10). CD speaks explicitly of the destruction of the men of war who turned back with the men of the lie. It does not indicate, however, how long the judgment will take. The Community Rule speaks of "an end to the existence of injustice" (1QS 4:18). The Melchizedek Scroll says that after the tenth jubilee is the time for "Melchizedek's year of favor" when he will exact "the ven[geance] of E[l's] judgments" (11Q Melch 2:13). It is also "the day [of salvation about w]hich [God] spoke [through the mouth of Isa]iah the prophet" (2:15). From these passages it is clear that the community expected a day of judgment, as foretold by the prophets. Other passages, however, indicate that a lengthier process was envisaged. The day of salvation in the Melchizedek Scroll is the occasion of the arrival of the herald, the "anointed of the spirit" or eschatological prophet. We might expect that he would be followed by the messiahs of Aaron and Israel (cf. 1QS 9:11) and then by the eschatological war, which takes forty years according to the War Rule.

It is not apparent, however, that all these texts were ever synthesized into a coherent system. The Melchizedek Scroll does not speak of messiahs (except the anointed of the spirit), and the Community Rule does not mention the tenth jubilee. Different texts provided different models for the end-time, or highlighted different aspects of it. What is clear is that the "end" that was expected forty years after the death of the Teacher was supposed to inaugurate a new phase in the eschatological drama, and mark some dramatic advance towards the extermination of evil. It also appears that both the period before this "end" and some of the events that would follow it directly could be included in "the end of days."

THE PERSISTENCE OF ESCHATOLOGICAL EXPECTATION

The expected "end" forty years after the death of the Teacher came and went. The community does not seem to have suffered any major disruption, as far as we now know. It is true that the site of Qumran was abandoned for some period towards the end of the first century BCE, but the abandonment is usually explained as the result either of the earthquake of 31 BCE or of a violent destruction and fire about 9 or 8 BCE (Magness 1995: 58–65; a Parthian raid about 40 BCE is sometimes entertained as a possibility). There is no evidence that it was related to the disappointment of eschatological hope, or that the occupants had changed their views when the site was resettled. The pesharim, and indeed much of the distinctively sectarian literature was produced in the early or middle first century BCE. Steudel has argued that there was an upsurge in the production of pesharim when the "end" failed to come, as the sectarians sought to assure themselves that it was at hand (Steudel 1993: 241– 2). It is also possible, however, that many of the pesharim were composed before the anticipated "end," to show that prophecy was indeed in the process of being fulfilled. Only the pesher on Habakkuk betrays any anxiety about the delay. The War Rule continued to be copied in the Roman period, so it appears that eschatological expectation did not cease when the "end" failed to materialize. This should not surprise us. The book of Daniel had offered far more specific calculations of an "end" than anything found at Qumran. These dates also passed without event. Nonetheless, Daniel was acknowledged as scripture within a generation, and Josephus held that Daniel surpassed the other prophets in his ability to predict the times when events would take place (Josephus, *Ant* 10.266; Collins 1993: 85).

We do not know whether any further attempt was made to predict divine intervention at Qumran. The fact that the Qumran site showed signs of military destruction has often led to speculation that the community may have joined in the great revolt. The Community Rule contains a profession of quietism: "I shall not repay anyone with an evil reward . . . for to God (belongs) the judgment of every living being . . . I shall not be involved at all in any dispute with the men of the pit *until the day of vengeance*" (1QS 10:17–19; author's italics). But it is quite possible that the members of the community decided that the day of vengeance had come when the revolt against Rome broke out. The role of militant action in the end-time is a question that will concern us further in Chapter 6.

5

MESSIANIC EXPECTATION

One of the recurring features of the "end of days" is that it is marked by the coming of the messiah or messiahs. Allusions to messianic expectation are scattered across several literary genres. There are references in both the Community Rule and the Damascus Document, a fact that reflects the authoritative roles that the messiahs were expected to fill in the future of the community. The so-called "Messianic Rule" (1QSa) is introduced as "the rule for all the congregation of Israel at the end of days," but the second column of the rule provides for an occasion "when God will bring (or beget; the reading is disputed) the messiah with them." It is now apparent that the Davidic messiah has a role in the War Rule (4Q285). The exegetical Florilegium, 4Q174, identifies the figure of whom God says "I shall be his father and he shall be my son" (2 Sam 7:14) as "the Branch of David who will arise with the Interpreter of the Law in Zion at the end of days." Exegetical bases for messianic expectation are also set forth in the Testimonia (4Q175), which strings together biblical passages with eschatological implications, and in the pesher on Isaiah (4QpIsa^a). The Scroll of Benedictions (1QSb) provides a blessing for the messianic "Prince of the Congregation," "that God may raise up for him the kingdom of his people" (1QSb 5:21). A poetic passage in the Hodayot provides the earliest occurrence of the motif of "the birth pangs of the messiah," by which the upheavals that precede the coming of the messiah are compared to the labor of a woman giving birth: "for amid the throes of death she shall bring forth a man-child and amid the pains of Sheol there shall spring from her child-bearing crucible a marvellous mighty counselor and a man shall be delivered from out of the throes" (1QH 11:9–10 [formerly 1:9–10]; cf. Isa 9:6). The expectation of a messiah, or messiahs, was widespread in Judaism around the turn of the era (although the intensity of the expectation varied from time to time and from group to group). The Dead Sea sect shared the common expectations to a degree, but also had its own distinctive ideas on the subject. (For a more detailed discussion of this topic, see Collins 1995.)

THE IDEA OF A MESSIAH

It is necessary at the outset to define our terms. The Hebrew word *māšîaḥ* means simply "anointed." It is used some thirty times in the Hebrew Bible with reference to kings, but it can also refer to other figures, especially the anointed high priest. In the Dead Sea scrolls, it is sometimes used with reference to the prophets of Israel (CD 2:12; 6:1; 1QM 11:7). The English word "messiah," however, has a more restricted meaning in common usage and refers to an agent of God in the end-time, who is said somewhere in the literature to be anointed. Not all eschatological agents are messiahs. (E.g. the archangel Michael and Melchizedek are never called *māšîaḥ*). It is important to recognize, however, that messiahs can be referred to by titles other than *māšîaḥ*. So, for example, the Branch of David is simply another way of referring to the Davidic messiah, even when the word *māšîaḥ* is not used (Collins 1995: 213–27; on the definitional issue see also Oegema 1994: 26–7). Even in the eschatological sense of the word, messiahs may be of various kinds. In the Dead Sea scrolls, we are principally concerned with two messianic figures. The royal, Davidic, messiah may also be referred to as the messiah of Israel, the Branch of David, the Prince of the Congregation, or even, although the matter is disputed, the Son of God. The priestly messiah is the messiah of Aaron, but he is also known as the Interpreter of the Law, and may be described on occasion without the use of a specific title. One may also speak of a prophetic messiah, but the role of the eschatological prophet is somewhat elusive. Finally, one may speak of a heavenly messiah, such as the heavenly judge who is called both messiah and Son of Man in the Similitudes of Enoch. Heavenly agents (Michael, Melchizedek, the Prince of Light) play a prominent part in some of the scrolls, but they are not called *māšîaḥ* or said to be anointed, and so we shall not consider them as messianic figures here.

THE ORIGIN OF MESSIANIC EXPECTATION

The primary form of messianic expectation in ancient Judaism focuses on the restoration of the Davidic line. Nathan's oracle in 2 Samuel 7 promised David

> that the Lord will make you a house. When your days are fulfilled and you lie down with your ancestors, I will raise up your offspring after you, who shall come forth from your body, and I will establish his kingdom. He shall build a house for my name, and I will establish the throne of his kingdom forever. I will be a father to him, and he shall be a son to me. When he commits iniquity, I will punish him with a rod such as mortals use, with blows inflicted by human beings. But I will not take my steadfast love from him, as I took it from Saul, whom I put away from before you. Your house and your kingdom shall be made sure forever before me; your throne shall be established forever.
>
> (2 Sam 7:11–17)

In the Psalms, the king is sometimes given a superhuman status. Psalm 2, which refers to the king as the Lord's anointed, tells of the decree of the Lord: "You are my son; today I have begotten you. Ask of me, and I will make the nations your heritage, and the ends of the earth your possession. You shall break them with a rod of iron, and dash them in pieces like a potter's vessel." Psalm 110 bids the king sit at God's right hand, and tells him that he is a priest forever after the order of Melchizedek. An oracle in the book of Isaiah announces the birth of a royal child, who is named "Wonderful Counsellor, Mighty God, Everlasting Father, Prince of Peace" (Isa 9:6; cf. 1QH 11:9–10). These three texts, Psalms 2 and 110 and Isaiah 9, have all been plausibly related to enthronement ceremonies in ancient Judah. An oracle in Isaiah 11 predicts that "a shoot shall come out of the stump of Jesse" in whose wonderful reign the wolf shall live with the lamb and the leopard lie down with the kid. It is uncertain whether this oracle was uttered by Isaiah while the Davidic line was still intact, or whether it was composed later after it had been dethroned by the Babylonians.

The Babylonian exile, and the subsequent restoration of Judah as a Persian province without its own king, created a glaring discrepancy between God's promise to David and historical reality. The concern for the fulfillment of prophecy is apparent in Jeremiah

33:14–16: "I shall establish the good word which I proclaimed to the house of Israel and the house of Judah. In those days and at that time I will cause a righteous Branch to spring up for David." (The "good word" refers to an earlier prophecy in Jeremiah 23:5–6.) The passage continues emphatically:

> For thus says the Lord: David shall never lack a man to sit on the throne of the house of Israel. . . . If any of you could break my covenant with the day and my covenant with the night, so that day and night would not come at their appointed time, only then could my covenant with my servant David be broken, so that he would not have a son to reign on his throne.

The historical failure of the promise led to the hope that it would be fulfilled at some time in the future.

THE SECOND TEMPLE PERIOD

Despite the clear biblical basis for a messianic hope, however, there is little evidence for such expectation for much of the Second Temple period. There is reason to believe that the prophets Haggai and Zechariah regard Zerubbabel, the governor at the time of the Persian restoration, as a figure who would fulfill the promises and restore the Davidic line. Haggai, speaking in the name of the Lord, refers to Zerubbabel as "my servant" (often a royal title in the ancient Near East), and promises to make him like a signet ring (Hag 2:21–4). Zechariah refers to him as "my servant, the branch" (Zech 3:8, a reference to the prophecy of Jeremiah). While we do not know what eventually happened to Zerubbabel, it is clear that the prophets' hopes were disappointed.

Messianic oracles are rare in post-exilic prophecy. There is a famous messianic prophecy in Zechariah 9 ("Lo, your king comes to you; triumphant and victorious is he, humble and riding on a donkey, on a colt, the foal of a donkey"; cf. Matt 21:5). This oracle has often been related to the campaign of Alexander the Great in 333 BCE, because of a reference to "your sons, O Greece" in 9:13; but the reference is suspect on grounds of meter and parallelism and can easily be explained by dittography. The provenance of the oracle is quite uncertain. Remarkably, we find no messianic references in the literature from the time of the Maccabean revolt. The book of Daniel uses the word *mašiah* with reference to Joshua, the high priest of the Persian period (Dan 9:25) and again with reference to the murdered high priest, Onias III (9:26), but it makes no mention of a messianic king. The savior figure to which it looks is the archangel Michael (Dan 12:1) who comes on the clouds like a human being (7:13; see Collins 1993: 304–10). Neither is there any clear reference to a messiah in the books of Enoch from this period (although 1 Enoch 90:37, which refers to a white bull in the eschatological period, is sometimes interpreted as messianic. See Tiller 1993: 20, 384. The bull is better explained as a new Adam.) The absence of messianic expectation in the apocalyptic writings of the early second century BCE is a strong indication that such expectation was dormant in this period. Apart from the Dead Sea scrolls there is only one clear messianic passage in the literature of the last two centuries BCE. This is in the Psalms of Solomon, from the middle of the first century BCE.

MESSIANISM IN THE HASMONEAN PERIOD

Despite the dearth of messianic references in the early Hellenistic period, we find several allusions in the scrolls, specifically in the authoritative rule books, that treat messianic expectation as a well-known phenomenon that requires no explanation. Several of these allusions are also remarkable for the fact that they mention more than one messiah. The best-known reference is found in the Community Rule, which prescribes that the members of the community should abide by their original precepts "until there shall come the prophet and the messiahs of Aaron and Israel" (*mᵉšîḥê 'ahᵃrôn wᵉyiśrā'ēl*, 1QS 9:11). The Damascus Document contains several references to the "messiah of Aaron and Israel" (CD 12:23; 14:19; 19:10; *mᵉšîaḥ 'ahᵃrôn wᵉyiśrā'ēl*; cf. CD 20:1 "a messiah from Aaron and from Israel"). These passages say little about the messiahs except that they are expected to come. They do however imply that these figures were readily intelligible to the community, and that messianic expectation was well established. This is not to say that it was fundamental to the existence of the sect. Neither 4QMMT nor the Damascus Document lists messianic expectation as a factor that led the group to split off from the rest of Israel. It is possible that the reference to the messiahs was a secondary addition to the Community Rule (Charlesworth 1994: 41). It would seem, however, that messianic expectation arose early and came to be taken for granted in the community, so that passing allusions to it would suffice.

75

On any reasonable reckoning, these rule books were composed somewhere in the century between the Maccabees and Pompey. Presumably, then, there had been a revival of messianic expectation in this period. This was also the time of the Hasmoneans, the descendants of the Maccabees, who had established a Jewish monarchy, even though they could not claim Davidic descent. There is good reason to believe that the revival of hope for a messiah, or messiahs, was a reaction to the kingship of the Hasmoneans, which some Jews of the time viewed as illegitimate.

The anti-Hasmonean implications of the hope for a messiah from the Davidic line are expressed clearly in the Psalms of Solomon, which are not found at Qumran and have often been associated with the Pharisees (Schüpphaus 1977: 127–37). The seventeenth psalm complains bitterly about "sinners," who "took possession with violence," and "set up in splendor a kingdom in their pride. They laid waste the throne of David in the arrogance of their fortune." These sinners are overthrown, however, by "a man that is foreign to our race." It is clear, then, that they are not foreigners, but Jewish kings who were not of the Davidic line, that is, the Hasmoneans, who were overthrown by the foreigner Pompey. The first Hasmonean ruler to use the title "king" on his coins was Alexander Jannaeus (103–76 BCE). Josephus claims that the predecessor of Jannaeus, Aristobulus (104–103 BCE), "saw fit to transform the government into a kingdom . . . and he was the first to put a diadem on his head" (*Ant* 13.301). His father, John Hyrcanus (135/4–104 BCE), according to Josephus, "was accounted by God worthy of three of the greatest privileges, the rule of the nation, the office of high priest, and the gift of prophecy" (*Ant* 13.300). Hyrcanus' father, Simon Maccabee had been recognized as leader and high priest by popular decree, and the Maccabean appropriation of monarchic power could be traced back to Jonathan Maccabee in 152 BCE. The fact of Hasmonean rule, even before the adoption of the title "king," could have caused traditionalists to look for a restoration of the Davidic line. Moreover, the fact that all the Hasmoneans, beginning with Jonathan, combined political rule with the exercise of the high priesthood, provides the backdrop for the distinctive notion of two messiahs, one of Aaron and one of Israel, that we find in the scrolls.

MESSIAHS OF AARON AND ISRAEL

Perhaps the most distinctive aspect of the messianic expectation of the Dead Sea scrolls lies in the fact that the royal "messiah of Israel" is often linked with the priestly "messiah of Aaron." Ever since the publication of the Community Rule, the expectation of two messiahs has been thought to be standard at Qumran (Vermes 1979: 2.550–4; Talmon 1989: 273–300; VanderKam 1994). The quasi-normative character of this expectation has been called into question in recent years, on the ground that 1QS 9 is the only passage that speaks unambiguously of two messiahs (Wise and Tabor 1992; see the discussion by Abegg 1995). The objection, however, cannot be sustained. In part it rests on the interpretation of the phrase "messiah of Aaron and Israel," in CD. The phrase can be interpreted as referring to only one messiah. But then we must wonder why this formulation is used. Should not a priestly messiah be simply the messiah of Aaron (Cross 1992: 14)? It is hardly conceivable that this phrase was coined to describe one messiah, and later was found conveniently suitable for two. One could suppose that the phrase originally referred to two messiahs, and was then adapted to refer to only one messiah in CD (presumably the priestly messiah since he will atone for the the the guilt of the people in CD 14:19). But then we find that the fragments of CD column 7 preserved at Qumran interpret Balaam's oracle in terms of two figures, one of whom is the Prince of the Congregation, which is a title for the Davidic messiah (4QD[b] fragment 3, col. 4; see Wacholder and Abegg 1991: 8). So we should have to suppose either that the references to a single messiah of Aaron and Israel are secondary in CD, or that CD merged the messiahs of Aaron and Israel into one, but then at a later stage reintroduced the royal, warrior messiah (Brooke 1991: 215–30). It is surely simpler to suppose that the phrase "messiah of Aaron and Israel" envisaged two messiahs throughout.

In any case, the question of dual messianism cannot be reduced to the occurrence of the expression "messiah(s) of Aaron and Israel." The issue is really whether there is another figure who enjoys authority equal to or greater than the Davidic messiah. Several texts among the scrolls indicate that the priest would take precedence over the king in the end-time. In the Temple Scroll, the king was expected to defer to the authority of the high priest (TS 58:18–19). Similarly in the pesher on Isaiah, the biblical phrase "He shall not judge by what his eyes see" is taken to mean that the messiah will defer to the teachings of "the priests of renown." A priest is said to command in 4Q285, and the high priest has a prominent role throughout the War Rule. In the "messianic rule" (1QSa) the priest takes precedence over the messiah of Israel at the common table. In the Scroll of Blessings, the blessing of the high priest precedes that of the Prince of the Congregation. In the Florilegium, the Branch of David is accompanied by the Interpreter of the Law. Also in CD 7:18 the Prince of the Congregation is linked with the Interpreter. In short, all the major rule books support the bifurcation of authority in the messianic era. We need not insist that every document found in the caves conforms to this structure. It would be unreasonable to expect each document to present its messianic expectations in full in any case. But at least we find strong attestation for the notion of two messiahs, especially in the core sectarian documents. The bifurcation of authority cannot be dismissed as an aberration.

Talmon has argued at length that the dual messianism of the scrolls reflects the political ideas of the early post-exilic community of the late sixth century BCE (Talmon 1989: 290–3). The obvious precedent is found in the prophet Zechariah's symbolizing of Zerubbabel and the high priest Joshua as "two sons of oil," or anointed ones (Zech 4:14). Against this, it must be said that Zechariah 4 (unlike Numbers 24 or Isaiah 11) is not a prominent messianic proof-text at Qumran (VanderKam 1988: 365). To my knowledge it is only cited once, in a fragment of the pesher on Genesis, 4Q254 (García Martínez 1993:177; Tov and Pfann 1993: 38, lists this text as 4Q253). The fragment is too small to provide a context, but another manuscript of the same work (4Q252) contains a well-known reference to "the messiah of righteousness, the Branch of David," with reference to Genesis 49:10, and it is reasonable to expect a messianic interpretation here too (Brooke 1994). Some further indirect support for Talmon's thesis might be found in 4Q390 ("Pseudo-Moses"), which exempts the first ones who came up from the land of their exile to build the temple from the general charge of wrong-doing against the Israelites (Dimant 1992: 414, 418). Yet it must be said that there are remarkably few references to the prophecy of Zechariah or the early post-exilic situation. The bifurcation of authority in the scrolls is more likely to be a reaction to the combination of royal and priestly offices by the Hasmoneans than an attempt to preserve any memory of the post-exilic community.

The scrolls do not provide us with a systematic explanation of their messianic hopes. We have several passages that ground these hopes by reference to specific biblical verses, but none that relate them to the historical developments that may have triggered them. A rare window on historical circumstances may be provided by the Testimonia. This text strings together quotations from Exodus 20:21 (Samaritan recension = Deut 5:28b–29 + Deut 18:18–19, the prophet like Moses), Numbers 24:15–17 (Balaam's oracle), and Deuteronomy 33 (the blessing of Levi). These passages are generally taken as the basis for the expectation of a prophet and the messiahs of Aaron and Israel (Brooke 1985: 309–10). The series concludes, however, with a passage of no messianic significance, from the Psalms of Joshua. It begins with a citation of the curse on Jericho from Joshua 6:26: "Cursed be the man who rebuilds this city! At the cost of his firstborn he will found it, and at the cost of his youngest son he will set up its gates. Behold, an accursed one, a man of Belial." It now appears, from the excavations conducted by E. Netzer in 1987–8, that the man who rebuilt Jericho was none other than John Hyrcanus (Eshel 1992: 409–20). Hyrcanus was said to combine the rule of the nation, the office of high priest, and the gift of prophecy. The Testimonia, in contrast, lays out the biblical basis for three distinct figures: king, priest, and prophet. The citation from the Psalms of Joshua becomes intelligible if the author saw the fulfillment of Joshua's curse in the death of Hyrcanus' sons, Antigonus and Aristobulus I, in 103 BCE, within a year of their father's death.

It is likely then that the revival of messianic expectation in the Hasmonean era represented a critique of the Jewish rulers of the day. Some traditionalists deemed them illegitimate kings because they were not from the line of David. Others also objected to their combination of the offices of high priest and king. The messianic expectations represented the dissidents' view of the proper order of society. In the Psalms of Solomon, the emphasis is on Davidic lineage. In the sectarian scrolls, the emphasis is on the separation of the offices of priest and king.

An objection might now be raised against the view that Qumran messianism was anti-Hasmonean on the basis of 4Q448, which speaks of Jonathan the King and has been interpreted as a prayer for King Alexander Jannaeus (Eshel *et al.* 1992: 199–229). This is the only document found at Qumran that can be described as pro-Hasmonean, whereas several are decidedly critical of the dynasty. To say that the text was not a sectarian composition scarcely relieves the problem, since no other pro-Hasmonean literature has been found in the caves, regardless of original provenance. But neither does the text prove that the Qumran community, or whoever hid the scrolls in the caves, was not generally anti-Hasmonean. It only proves that they were not consistent. We do not know the occasion of this text, but it is not difficult to conceive of situations where the Dead Sea sect might have sided even with a Hasmonean king. One such situation might be a war against the foreign enemies of Israel. Another might be conflict between Jannaeus and the Pharisees, bitter enemies of the Dead Sea sect (Stegemann 1993: 187–8). In fact the Pharisees launched an open rebellion against Jannaeus about 88 BCE and called in the Syrian king Demetrius Akairos to help them. At first Jannaeus was defeated, but then the people rallied round him. Demetrius withdrew and Jannaeus had some 800 of the rebels crucified (*Ant* 13.372–83). This incident is noted in the pesher on Nahum, where Jannaeus is called "the lion of wrath" who "hangs men alive." Jannaeus appears to be censured in the pesher because of the crucifixions, but it is quite conceivable that the Dead Sea sect would have supported him in his struggle against Demetrius and the Pharisees. In any case the "Jonathan the King" text remains anomalous. Temporary support for a Hasmonean king is not necessarily incompatible with the hope that the Hasmonean dynasty would be replaced by a Davidic messiah and an Aaronide high priest.

THE ROLE OF THE DAVIDIC MESSIAH

The most complete description of the role of an ideal king in the texts from Qumran is found in the "Law of the King" in the Temple Scroll 56:12–59:21. It is not certain that the Temple Scroll was written by a member the communities envisaged in the Community Rule or Damascus Document (see the objections of Stegemann 1993: 137; Schiffman 1994: 258), but at least it must come from related circles. It throws some interesting light on the understanding of kingship which lies behind the conception of the royal messiah.

In general the scroll follows Deuteronomy in emphasizing that the king must be a native Israelite and in setting limits to his power in various ways. It elaborates the commandment that he not multiply wives: he must be monogamous. It adds a provision that he not pervert judgment. Most of the passage, however, is concerned with the conduct of war against the enemies of Israel. Even in this matter, the king is not granted independent authority: "He shall not go until he has presented himself before the high priest, who shall inquire on his behalf for a decision by the Urim and Tummim. It is at his word that he shall go and at his word that he shall come, he and all the children of Israel who are with him. He shall not go following his heart's counsel until he has inquired for a decision by the Urim and Tummim." In the matter of judgment, too, he must be guided by a council, consisting of twelve princes, twelve priests and twelve Levites. The authority of the king, then, is clearly limited in the Temple Scroll. In this respect, the scroll is heir to the criticism of the monarchy in biblical texts of the exilic period. Deuteronomy 17 prescribes that the king should have a copy of the law that is in the charge of the Levitical priests, and read in it all the days of his life. In the great vision of restored Israel in Ezekiel 40–8, the role of the "prince" (*nāśī'*) is reduced to supporting the cult, and is generally overshadowed by the interest in the temple and the sacrifices. The Temple Scroll is less restrictive than Ezekiel, and casts the king primarily in the roles of military leader and judge.

The king envisaged here is not a messianic king in the eschatological sense (despite the arguments of Wise 1990a). His rule is conditional and he is not said to be the fulfillment of messianic prophecy. Consequently the scroll should not be regarded as a law for the end of days. The nature of the king's authority, however, is quite similar to that vested in the Davidic messiah in the Dead Sea scrolls. While the full picture is not found in every individual text, the role of the royal messiah may fairly be summarized as that of military leader and judge, but subject to priestly authority.

The text chosen to represent the royal messiah in the Testimonia is Balaam's oracle of the star and the scepter, a passage well known as a messianic prophecy in later Jewish tradition, especially for its application to Bar Kokhba, the leader of the last Jewish revolt against Rome in 132 CE. There is some variation in the interpretation of this oracle in the scrolls. It is cited in column 7 of the Damascus Document from the Cairo Geniza (CD), manuscript A, in a passage also found at Qumran. (It is absent from the parallel passage in CD manuscript B from the Geniza, which has not been found at Qumran. On the complex textual history of the passage see White 1987: 537–3.) At least in this passage in CD it is understood to refer to two figures rather than one: "The star is the Interpreter of the Law who shall come to Damascus: as it is written, *A star shall come forth out of Jacob and a scepter shall rise out of Israel* (Num 24:17; author's italics). The scepter is the prince of the whole congregation, and when he comes *he shall smite all the children of Sheth*" (Num 24:17). "Prince" (*naśi'*) is the title of the lay leader of Israel in the priestly source of the Pentateuch, and for the Davidic king in the Book of Ezekiel. It is a messianic title in the scrolls. The oracle emphasizes his military role: "he shall crush the temples of Moab and destroy all the children of Sheth." This oracle is also cited in the War Rule, without interpretation. Several scholars seem to have missed the allusion, and then expressed surprise at the absence of the messiah in the War Rule (e.g. Davies 1992: 875). The role of the messianic "Prince" in the final war is now more vividly described in the fragmentary 4Q285, the so-called "dying messiah" text, which cites Isaiah 11, and narrates that the "Prince of the Congregation, the Branch of David," will kill someone, possibly the king of the Kittim (Vermes 1992a: 85–90). The Branch of David is also associated with the final battle in the pesher on Isaiah (Horgan 1979: 70–86).

The military and judicial aspects of the messiah's role are clearly evident in the blessing of the Prince of the Congregation in1QSb: "that he may establish the kingdom of His people for ever, [that he may judge the poor with righteousness and] dispense justice with [equity to the oppressed] of the land, and that he may walk perfectly before him in all the ways [of truth]." The blessing is heavily indebted to Isaiah 11. "(May you smite the peoples) with the might of your hand and ravage the earth with your scepter; may you bring death to the ungodly with the breath of your lips (Isa 11:4b); may righteousness be the girdle (of your loins) and may your reins be girded (with faithfulness)" (Isa 11:5). It goes on to pray "May he make your horns of iron and your hooves of bronze; may you toss like a young bull [and trample the peoples] like the mire of the streets." The messianic "Prince" is clearly a warrior, and like the kings of old he is charged with the administration of justice.

THE "SON OF GOD" TEXT

In my view the Aramaic "Son of God" text should also be read as a prediction of the messianic king (Collins 1995: 154–72; for the edition of the text see Puech 1992a):

> Son of God he will be called and Son of the Most High they will name him. . . . People will trample people and province, until the people of God arises and all rests from the sword. His kingdom will be an everlasting kingdom and all his ways in truth. He will judge the earth in truth and all will make peace.

The sword will cease from the earth and all provinces will worship him. The great God will be his help. He will make war for him. He will give peoples into his hand and all of them he will cast down before him. His sovereignty is everlasting sovereignty.

In this case the interpretation is disputed. Some scholars hold that the one who will be called Son of God and named Son of the Most High is a negative figure, most probably a Syrian king. (Originally the view of Milik, in an unpublished lecture at Harvard University in 1972. This interpretation is allowed as possible by Puech 1992a. It has been defended at greatest length by Cook 1995.)

The argument that the figure is negative rests on a construal of the logical progression of the text. The reference to the "Son of God" is followed by a situation where "people will trample on people and province, province, until the people of God arises (or: until he raises up the people of God)." There is a lacuna before the word "until" which strengthens the impression that this is a point of transition in the text. Those who read the text on the assumption that events are reported in chronological sequence infer that the "Son of God" belongs to the time of distress, and so must be a negative, evil figure. This inference is unsafe for two reasons. First, it is quite typical of apocalyptic literature that the same events are repeated several times in different terms. Apocalypses such as Daniel, the Similitudes of Enoch, 4 Ezra, 2 Baruch and Revelation all juxtapose multiple visions that go over the same ground with different imagery. Within the single chapter of Daniel 7, the same events are presented first in the form of a vision, then in two successive interpretations, so that the kingdom is given, in turn, to the "one like a son of man," the holy ones of the Most High, and finally to the people of the holy ones. I have argued elsewhere that 4Q246 should be read in this way, so that the coming of the "Son of God" parallels the rise of the people of God rather than precedes it (Collins 1995: 158). It is true that the repetitions in Daniel 7 are occasioned by the process of interpretation, and this is not overtly the case in 4Q246 (Cook 1995: 61). The Qumran text does, however, refer to a vision in column 1, and part of the difficulty of reading it is that we cannot be sure of its precise literary genre. We shall consider shortly the reasons for relating this text to Daniel 7. If these are accepted, the repetitions in Daniel 7 are highly relevant to our understanding of 4Q 246. Even if the parallel with Daniel 7 is not accepted, however, a second consideration should warn against the simple sequential understanding of the text. The appearance of a savior figure does not inevitably mean that the time of strife is over. In Daniel 12:1 the rise of Michael is followed by a "a time of anguish, such as has never occurred since nations first came into existence." In 4 Ezra 13, the apparition of the man from the sea is followed by the gathering of an innumerable multitude to make war on him. We should note that the statement about the people of God is ambiguous. It can be read either as "the people of God will arise ($y^e q\hat{\imath}m$)" or as "he will raise up the people of God ($y^e q\hat{\imath}m$)." If the latter reading is correct, the nearest antecedent is the one who will be called "Son of God," although it is certainly also possible that God is the subject. It is possible then that the text envisages an interval of warfare between the apparition of the deliverer and the actual deliverance. So, while the order of the text may suggest *prima facie* that the figure who appears called "Son of God" belongs to the era of wickedness, this is not necessarily the case.

Two other factors strongly suggest that the one who is called "Son of God" is accepted as a positive figure in this text. First, the title is never disputed, and no judgment is passed on this figure after the people of God arises. This would be truly extraordinary if the figure in question were an impostor. In contrast, the hubristic pretensions of Antiochus Epiphanes in Daniel 8 and 11 lead directly and very explicitly to his downfall. Second, by far the closest parallel to the titles in question is explicitly messianic. In Luke 1:32 the angel Gabriel tells Mary that her child "will be great, and will be called the Son of the Most High, and the Lord God will give to him the throne of his ancestor David. He will reign over the house of Jacob forever, and of his kingdom there will be no end." In 1:35 he adds: "he will be called the Son of God." The Greek titles "Son of the Most High" and "Son of God" correspond exactly to the Aramaic fragment from Qumran. (Note also the reference in both texts to an everlasting kingdom.) The fact that these parallels are found in the New Testament does not lessen their relevance to the cultural context of the Qumran text. No other parallel of comparable precision can be found in any other source. The use of these titles for a messianic king had a clear warrant in biblical texts such as 2 Samuel 7 and Psalm 2, and is also supported by the Florilegium (4Q174:11–12) which interprets 2 Samuel 7:12–14 ("I will be a father to him and he will be a son to me") as referring to the Branch of David at the end of days. It should also be noted that 1QSa, the so-called

Messianic Rule, has often been read to say that God will beget (*yôlîd*) the messiah, although others have read a verb meaning "bring" (*yôlîk* or *yô'ēd*; see the discussion by VanderKam 1994: 221–2). Recently, Vermes has claimed that the reading *yôlîd*, which he had previously rejected, "is confirmed by computer image enhancement" (Vermes 1995: 121). The matter remains in dispute, however. (See Puech 1994: 357–60, who reads *ytglh*, "will be revealed," and insists that *yôlîd* is out of the question.)

I have elsewhere suggested tentatively that the "Son of God" figure may be a reinterpretation of the "one like a son of man" in Daniel 7. While this suggestion cannot be proven, and must remain tentative, it is not gratuitous or without foundation. There are clear allusions to Daniel in column 2, line 5 ("its/his kingdom is an everlasting kingdom," cf. Dan 4:3; 7:27) and col. 2, line 9 ("its/his sovereignty is an everlasting sovereignty," cf. Dan 4:31; 7:14). Another possible reference to Daniel 7 is the use of the word *dwš*, trample, at column 2, line 3. The same verb is used with reference to the fourth beast in Daniel 7. Moreover, the setting of the document, where someone falls before a throne and interprets a vision, is reminiscent of Daniel. There is, then, reason to consider the possibility that the Son of God text is a reinterpretation of Daniel 7, and that the "Son of God" figure is related to the people of God as the "one like a Son of Man" is related to the people of the holy ones in Daniel 7. The suggestion remains inconclusive, however, since the Qumran text is clearly not a systematic interpretation of Daniel 7.

If the "Son of God" text is read as messianic, it fits nicely with everything we have seen about the Davidic/royal messiah in the scrolls. He functions as a warrior to subdue the Gentiles: God will make war on his behalf and cast peoples down before him. If the hypothesis is entertained that this figure also corresponds to the Danielic Son of Man, then the fusion of traditions would seem to be similar to what is found later in 4 Ezra, at the end of the first century CE. The divine origin of the figure is emphasized, but he functions on earth as a militant messiah, in a way that owes more to the traditional understanding of the royal messiah than to the imagery of Daniel.

THE PRIESTLY MESSIAH

What role was envisaged for the priestly messiah? He was to atone for the sin of the people (CD 14:19), presumably by offering the prescribed sacrifices. But more than that he was a teacher. The biblical passage chosen to represent the priestly messiah in the Testimonia is the blessing of Levi from Deuteronomy 33: "They shall cause thy precepts to shine before Jacob and thy Law before Israel. They shall send up incense towards thy nostrils and place a burnt-offering upon thy altar." The same text is cited in the Florilegium, and in Jubilees 31. The blessing of the priests in the Scroll of Blessings (1QSb) describes them as those whom God has chosen "to confirm his covenant forever and to inquire into all his precepts in the midst of all his people, and to instruct them as he commanded" (1QSb 3:23–4). The blessing prays that God may make them "an [eternal] light [to illumine] the world with knowledge and to enlighten the face of the Congregation [with wisdom]" (1QSb 4:27–8). Perhaps the most striking elaboration of the teaching office of the eschatological priest is found in 4Q541 (4QAaronA):

> He will atone for the children of his generation, and he will be sent to all the children of his people. His word is like a word of heaven, and his teaching conforms to the will of God. His eternal sun will shine, and his fire will blaze in all the corners of the earth. Then darkness will disappear from the earth and obscurity from the dry land
>
> (Puech 1992b: 449–501)

This figure, whom I take to be the messiah of Aaron, might reasonably be described as a "teacher of righteousness" for the end of days. The historical Teacher of Righteousness, who was active at the beginning of the community's history, is also called on occasion "the priest." When the Damascus Document 6:11 refers to "one who will teach righteousness at the end of days" the reference is most probably to the priestly messiah. (In the early days of research on the scrolls, the passage in CD gave rise to some wild speculation that the historical Teacher was expected to rise and come again at the end of days, a view associated especially with Dupont-Sommer and John Allegro. For a summary of the debate see Cook 1994: 130–7.) A similar ambiguity is attached to the title "Interpreter of the Law." In CD 6, he is clearly a figure of the past. In the Florilegium, however, he is expected to arise with the Branch of David at the end of days. In view of the teaching function of the priesthood, and the fact that the Teacher/Founder is described as a priest, it seems likely that the eschatological "Interpreter of the Law" is none other than the messiah of Aaron. The community conceived of the definitive, eschatological high priest in the image and likeness of the historical Teacher. (See further Collins 1995: 115, 125.)

Since the Dead Sea Scrolls are thought to span a period of more than a century and a half, it is natural to expect some development, in messianism as in other matters, over that period. The various theories of messianic development that have been proposed, however (Starcky 1963; Brooke 1991), have not proven persuasive. They typically depend on the view that the phrase "messiah of Aaron and Israel" refers to one messiah rather than two, and we have seen that this view is problematic. They also depend on assigning dates to individual documents, to a greater degree than the available evidence permits. I do not wish to deny the possibility of development during the life of the Qumran community, but I submit that in the matter of messianism the evidence does not permit us to trace it with any confidence. While we have texts that speak of an eschatological priest without reference to a king (4Q541), and others that speak of a Davidic messiah without reference to a priest (4Q246, 252, but note the reference to "two sons of oil" in 4Q254), the pattern of dual messiahship is typical, especially in the sectarian rule books, which are the documents most likely to enjoy official status in the community. Moreover, if the Book of Jubilees represents the kind of circle from which the movement described in the Damascus Document emerged, we should expect that dual messianism, rather than priestly messianism alone, was the norm from the start, since both Levi and Judah are singled out for blessing in Jubilees 31 (VanderKam 1988).

Where the relative standing of royal and priestly messiahs is in evidence, the priestly figure takes precedence. This is amply documented in the sectarian rule books. In the words of the Damascus Document: "where there are ten, there shall never be lacking a priest learned in the Book of Meditation; they shall be ruled by him" (CD 13:2–3). The Community Rule (1QS 6:3–4) has a similar provision, adding that the priest is the first to bless the food at the common meals. The so-called "Messianic Rule," 1QSa, makes clear that even when the messiah of Israel comes, the priest still takes precedence at the common table.

THE MESSIAH WHOM HEAVEN AND EARTH OBEY

Our discussion of messianic expectation would be incomplete without some discussion of the recently published text from Cave 4 that speaks of a messiah whom heaven and earth obey (Puech 1992c: 475–519). The text (4Q521) goes on to say that "the glorious things that have not taken place the Lord will do as he s[aid] for he will heal the wounded, give life to the dead and preach good news to the poor, " a passage that has a notable parallel in the New Testament, in Jesus' reply to an inquiry by John the Baptist (Tabor and Wise 1992). The opening lines of the fragment are heavily dependent on Psalm 146, which refers to the Lord "who made heaven and earth, the sea and all that is in them." The psalm, however, makes no mention of a messiah. The purpose of this innovation is not immediately apparent, as the Qumran text goes on to say that God will release captives, give sight to the blind, etc., just as He does in the Psalm. Again, at verse 12, it is God who will heal the wounded, give life to the dead and preach good news to the poor. The Lord, of course, is normally the one who raises the dead (cf. the second of the Eighteen Benedictions: "Lord, you are almighty forever who makes the dead to live"). It is surprising, however, to find God as the subject of preaching good news. This is the work of a herald or messenger.

The phrase in question is taken from Isaiah 61:1: "The spirit of the Lord God is upon me, because the Lord has anointed me; He has sent me to preach good news to the poor, to bind up the brokenhearted, to proclaim liberty to the captives and release to the prisoners; to proclaim the year of the Lord's favor, and the day of vengeance of our God." In Isaiah 61, the speaker is a prophet, but he also claims to be anointed, so he is a *mašiah* or anointed one. The anomalous reference to a messiah in the adaptation of Psalm 146 might be explained on the assumption that the acts of God are performed through the agency of an anointed agent, just as they are in Isaiah 61, although the anointed figure in Isaiah 61 is not said to give life to the dead.

The editor of this text, Emile Puech, assumes that the messiah whom heaven and earth obey is the royal messiah. If we are correct, however, that the messiah is God's agent in the remainder of the text, Puech's interpretation is unlikely to be correct. It is quite possible that God should use an agent in the resurrection, but this agent is unlikely to be the royal messiah. The resurrection is sometimes associated with the messianic age in writings of the first century CE, but the messiah is never said to raise the dead. In the New Testament, Christ is the first fruits of the resurrection, not the agent, in 1 Corinthians 15. In Revelation 20, the martyrs come to life and reign with Christ for a thousand years, but Christ is not said to raise them. In later Jewish tradition we find the notion that the dead will first come to life in the time of the Messiah (j.Ketubot 12:3), but the resurrection does not come through the royal messiah. Rather, "the resurrection of the dead comes through Elijah" (m. Sotah 9, end; j. Sheqalim 3:3). Elijah was credited with raising the dead during his historical career (1 Kings 17, cf. the story of Elisha in 2 Kings 4). So we read in Pesikta de R. Kahana 76a: "Everything that the Holy One will do, he has already anticipated by the hands of the righteous in this world, the resurrection of the dead by Elijah and Ezekiel, the drying of the Dead Sea by Moses."

I suggest, then, that the messiah whom heaven and earth obey is an anointed eschatological prophet, either Elijah or a prophet like Elijah (for more complete argumentation see Collins 1995: 117–22). Elijah's command of the heavens was legendary. In the words of Ben Sira, "By the word of the Lord he shut up the heavens and also three times brought down fire" (Sirach 48:3). The "two olive trees" in Revelation 11, who have authority to shut up the sky so that no rain may fall and to turn the waters into blood, are usually identified as Elijah and Moses. The expression "two olive trees" is an allusion to the "two sons of oil" or anointed ones announced by the prophet Zechariah.

It is not certain whether 4Q521 should be regarded as a product of the Dead Sea sect. The sectarian literature is notoriously lacking in references to resurrection, and has relatively few references to the eschatological prophet. In favor of sectarian origin, however, are several parallels in vocabulary, especially with the Hodayot and the interest in the poor, which suggest a common cultural context (Puech 1992c: 517). The question must be left open. The idea of an eschatological prophet was certainly known at Qumran, as is apparent from the famous reference to "the prophet and the messiahs of Aaron and Israel" in 1QS 9. The Melchizedek Scroll also has a role for a herald (*mᵉbaśśēr*), who is called "the anointed of the spirit, of whom Daniel spoke" (cf. Dan 9:25–6). This text also cites Isaiah 61 ("to proclaim liberty to the captives") and appears to assign to a herald the task of comforting the afflicted (11QMelch 2:20; the text is fragmentary). The Testimonia, in contrast, evokes the "prophet like Moses" of Deuteronomy 18 (the citation conforms to the Samaritan text of Exod 20:21. See Brooke 1985: 317). The role of the eschatological prophet, however, is not nearly as well attested as that of the royal and priestly messiahs.

CONCLUSION

The importance of messianic expectation in the Dead Sea scrolls should not be exaggerated. As we have noted already, there is no evidence that such expectation played a causal role in the origin of the sect. The messiahs are not the ultimate focus of the hopes of the sect, but they are role players in a larger scenario. The hopes of the sect entailed, among other things, a vision of a transformation of Israelite society. The royal messiah has an important place in this scheme of things. He was to establish the kingdom of his people, and in the process aid in the destruction of the Sons of Darkness. He is not, however, envisaged as the highest authority in the New Age. Rather, the eschatological priest, the messiah of Aaron, takes precedence, especially in his capacity as teacher. Just as the historical Teacher of Righteousness had a pivotal role in the life of the community prior to the eschaton, so there would be another to teach righteousness in the end of days. This teaching role would be augmented by the eschatological prophet, who does not, however, appear consistently in the messianic texts.

The messianic age, as a phase of "the end of days," would represent the fulfillment of what may be called the earthly strands of Jewish eschatology, which were well grounded in the Hebrew scriptures. It entailed the restoration of an Israelite kingdom. It also entailed a purified cult in a new temple and a new Jerusalem. It did not, however, represent the fulfillment of all the eschatological hopes of the sect. These hopes extended to cosmic transformation and the reward and punishment of the wicked beyond death. The cosmic aspect of the transformation figures prominently in the portrayal of the eschatological war, to which we now turn.

6

THE ESCHATOLOGICAL WAR

One of the recurring features of the "end of days" is the expectation of a final war between Israel and the Gentiles or between the
Sons of Light and the Sons of Darkness. Even this summary statement, however, alerts us to one of the problems presented by the
conception of the eschatological war: the antithesis of Israel and the
Gentiles is not identical with that of the Sons of Light and the Sons
of Darkness. The conflict between Israel and the Gentiles was traditional. We may refer to it as a nationalistic conception, insofar as the
opposition is defined in national and ethnic terms. The Dead Sea
sect, however, had an ambiguous relationship with national, ethnic,
Israel. It was patently not co-terminous with the Jewish people,
and so could claim at most to be a *remnant* of Israel, or an elect
group within Israel. Yet the sectarians also thought of themselves as
the true Israel, and hoped that the distinction would disappear in the
end of days. The "Sons of Darkness," also, were not simply the
Gentiles but evil-doers, and from the perspective of the sect many
ethnic Israelites fell into this category. Consequently, the texts vacil-
late between the traditional distinction between Israel and the Gentiles and attempts to define the opposition in non-nationalistic
terms.

THE TRADITIONAL OPPOSITION

The traditional antagonism between Israel and the Gentiles is
grounded in the political history of the ancient Near East, and the
repeated threat and experience of invasion by hostile powers.
Assyria, Babylon, Persia, Greece, Egypt, Syria, and Rome had all

sent forces into Israelite territory and held it in subjection at some time. From an early time, this experience was generalized, so that psalmists and prophets could identify the enemies of Israel not just as Babylon or Syria, but as "the nations." Psalm 2, which surely dates from the time of the monarchy, begins: "Why do the nations conspire and the peoples plot in vain? The kings of the earth set themselves, and the rulers take counsel together, against the Lord and His anointed." The Lord goes on to promise the king: "Ask of me and I will make the nations your heritage, and the ends of the earth your possession. You shall break them with a rod of iron, and dash them in pieces like a potter's vessel."

After the catastrophic Babylonian invasion in the early sixth century BCE, the antagonism of the Gentiles is imagined on an even grander scale. In Ezekiel 38–9, Gog from the land of Magog is identified as the enemy of whom the prophets of Israel had spoken. (The name may have been suggested by that of King Gyges of Lydia, a king who was remote from Israel and had no historical contact with it. It is used simply as representative of Gentile power.) God will cause Gog to invade Israel: "I will turn you around and drive you forward, and bring you up from the remotest parts of the north, and lead you against the mountains of Israel" (Ezek 39:2). But he is brought for his own destruction: "You shall fall upon the mountains of Israel, you and all your troops and the peoples that are with you; I will give you to birds of prey of every kind and to the wild animals to be devoured" (39:4). This scenario is evoked again in the Maccabean period in Daniel 11, which predicts that Antiochus Epiphanes would meet his end "between the sea and the holy mountain" (Dan 11:45; Epiphanes actually died in Persia).

One of the most extreme formulations of the antagonism between Israel and the nations is found in the book of Joel, in a passage that has no clear historical reference but dates from some time in the post-exilic period. The prophet calls on God to stir up the nations so that they will gather themselves and come to the valley of Jehoshaphat, where they will be judged on the day of the Lord (Joel 3:9–16).

In the apocalypses of the Maccabean period, the war with the Gentiles is again prominent. The Animal Apocalypse of 1 Enoch 85–90 concludes with a massacre of the hostile nations (90:19). The book of Daniel does not dwell upon human slaughter, but envisages a nationalistic conflict nonetheless. In Daniel 10 the angel Gabriel explains that he is opposed in a heavenly conflict by "the prince of the kingdom of Persia," with no one to help him except "Michael, your prince." Later "the prince of Greece" will come. The princes in question are the angelic patrons of the nations, the successors of the gods of the nations in polytheistic mythology. (Cf. Deuteronomy 32:8 where the Most High divides the nations according to the number of the sons of God, and Isaiah 36:18; 37:12, where the king of Assyria asks whether any of the gods of the nations was ever able to thwart him.) Daniel puts his trust in the victory of the archangel Michael rather than in the forces of the Maccabees, but the heavenly victory ensures the earthly supremacy of Israel. While the "one like a son of man" to whom dominion and glory and kingship is given in Daniel 7:14 should be identified as Michael, the "people of the holy ones of the Most High" (Israel) receive "the kingship and dominion and greatness of the kingdoms under the whole heaven" (7:27; see Collins 1993: 304–10; 313–17). The Gentiles are still subjugated, even if the warfare is between angelic powers.

THE ESCHATOLOGICAL WAR IN THE SCROLLS

Allusions to the final conflict are found in several documents in the scrolls. The Florilegium cites Psalm 2:1 ("Why do the nations rage . . . ") and relates it to the "time of trial" at the end of days. A pesher on Isaiah (4Q161) refers to "the war of the Kittim" and mentions Magog in a fragment that also speaks of the Branch of David. The Damascus Document identifies the Prince of the Congregation as the scepter of Balaam's oracle who will smite all the children of Sheth (CD 7:20–1). The Hodayot refer to "the war of the heavenly warriors" which fills the earth in the time of the wrath of Belial (1QH 11:35, formerly 3:35). By far the most important account of the eschatological war, however, is found in the remarkable Rule of the War of the Sons of Light against the Sons of Darkness which is preserved in an almost complete copy from Cave 1 (1QM) and in several fragmentary copies from Cave 4. (Stegemann 1993: 145, counts at least ten manuscripts in all.)

This remarkable document is a "rule" or Serek, which purports to give instructions for the various phases of the battle. Its purpose is not to disclose what will happen, as is usually the case in an apocalypse, but to prescribe the appropriate actions in the light of what is known to be at hand. It suggests, then, a greater immediacy than is usual in apocalyptic references to a final battle. This is a conflict for which one may prepare and rehearse. The actions prescribed are heavily ritualistic, and great attention is paid to prayer. The War Rule resembles apocalypses such as those of Enoch and Daniel in the role assigned to supernatural agents and the sense that the outcome of the battle is determined by God and the angels rather than by human endeavor. The Qumran document does, however, spell out an active role for human participants in far greater detail than was the case in any of the apocalypses.

Even before the publication of the Cave 4 fragments, it was clear that the War Rule was a complex document in which different sources and traditions were combined. The contents of 1QM may be summarized as follows:

Col 1: Programmatic outline of a war in seven lots between the Sons of Light and the Sons of Darkness.

Col 2:1–14: Overview of a war of forty years, with regard to the conduct of the temple service and the division of the fighting into campaigns against various peoples;

Cols 2:15–9:18: mobilization for battle;

2:15–3:11: disposition of the trumpets;

3:12–4:17: disposition of the banners;

5:1–2: the shield of the Prince of the Congregation;

5:3– 9:18: the battle formations;

Cols 10–14: prayers related to the battle;

Cols 15–19: a more detailed review of the seven-stage war envisaged in column 1 (See Yadin 1962: 3–17).

While a few scholars (notably Yadin) have defended the unity of this composition, most have recognized that the conception of the war in columns 1 and 15–19 is fundamentally different from that of columns 2–9 (van der Ploeg 1959; von der Osten-Sacken 1969; Davies 1977). The framing chapters are primarily concerned with the metaphysical dimensions of the war, while columns 2–9 are concerned rather with human organization. Column 1 envisages a war of seven lots, which appears to conclude with the definitive victory of God. Yet column 2 begins by discussing the cultic arrangements that are to be made in a sabbatical year, and proceeds to outline "the remaining thirty-three years of the war," against the nations enumerated in Genesis 10, the descendants of Shem, Ham, and Japheth. It seems reasonable to infer that two different documents have been combined, or alternatively that one document has been expanded and supplemented on the basis of a different tradition. As a result of the combination, the seven phases of the war described in column 1 appear as the first seven years of a forty-year war. In this phase, the enemies are Israel's neighbors and traditional enemies (Edom, Moab, Ammon, Philistia) together with the Kittim and the violators of the covenant. Since the sons of Japheth are also mentioned in column 1, however, the assignment of nations to the different phases of the war involves some repetition, and is not simply complementary. This lends credence to the view that columns 1 and 2 are not the products of a single author. The prayers in columns 10–12 draw heavily on older biblical material. In contrast, columns 13 and 14 have a dualistic character and are related to columns 1 and 15–19, although they may reflect different redactional stages in the growth of the Rule (see Davies 1977: 91–112).

The picture is complicated by the fragments from Cave 4, which often contain readings that have no parallel in 1QM (Baillet 1982; Duhaime 1995). Even where there are parallels, there are numerous variants. The most extensive parallels with 1QM are found in 4Q491, which overlaps with columns 5–7, 9 and 12–17, and 4Q496, which overlaps with columns 1–4, 9 and possibly 19 (Duhaime 1995: 82–3). The most important additional text is found in 4Q285, which is identified as part of the War Rule on the basis of vocabulary, and which accords the Davidic messiah a more prominent role than he enjoys in the extant fragments of 1QM (Abegg 1994; this text is not included in the edition of Duhaime 1995). In all, these fragments show that the War Rule had a history of development. 1QM has been dated on palaeographic grounds to the second half of the first century BCE (Cross 1995: 138). 4Q496 is somewhat older. The editor, Baillet, dated it before the middle of the first century BCE (Baillet 1982: 58). Since 4Q496 contains parallels to both column 1 and column 2, the essential structure of the Rule had probably taken shape by the middle of the first century BCE, even though the text continued to change and evolve for some time after that.

THE REGULATIONS FOR WARFARE IN 1QM 2–9

The general outline of the war against the nations in column 2 is followed by the disposition of the trumpets (2:15–3:11), the disposition of the banners (3:12–5:2) and the disposition of the troops for battle (5:3–9:18). The latter section bears a general similarity to Hellenistic military manuals (Duhaime 1988). Yadin has noted some features that specifically suggest Roman influence: the use of "gates of war" (the Roman *intervalla*; spaces within and between the lines from which skirmishers issued forth) and the use of reserve columns (Yadin 1962: 147, 174–5). The use of reserves was noted as a difference between the Roman legion and the Macedonian phalanx by Polybius (book 18) in the second century BCE, and was employed notably by Julius Caesar. The knowledge of military tactics was presumably derived from the experience of Hasmonean and Herodian armies, and the observation of foreign armies, such as the Roman.

But the regulations in this section of the War Rule also have a strongly ritualistic character and draw heavily on biblical tradition, especially on the organization of the tribes in the wilderness as depicted in the book of Numbers. (The forty-year duration of the war obviously recalls the wilderness period.) The organization of the assembled multitude is reflected in the section on banners (1QM 3:12–5:2). The banner at the head of the whole people bears the names "people of God," "Israel," and "Aaron." Banners are used to distinguish the various organizational units: camp, tribe, myriad, thousand, hundred, fifty, ten. This manner of organization has its basis in Exodus 18, where Jethro instructs Moses to organize the people in units of thousands, hundreds, fifties and tens. Judas Maccabee is said to have organized his army in this manner (1 Macc 3:55) but we find the same kind of organization in the sectarian rulebooks (1QS 2: 21–2; CD13:1–2; 1QSa 1:12–15; 1:29–2:1). The use of banners has its biblical mandate in Numbers 2:2: "The Israelites shall camp each in their respective regiments, under ensigns by their ancestral houses." (Cf. also Numbers 17:2–3, where Moses is told to bid the Israelites get a staff for each ancestral house and write each man's name on it.) Banners (*signa*) were a prominent feature of the Roman army. The Roman worship of standards is noted in the pesher on Habakkuk (1QpHab 6:4). In contrast, they play no role in either Greek or Jewish armies in the books of Maccabees (Yadin 1962: 62–3). It would seem that a feature of biblical organization in the wilderness period found new relevance in the light of Roman practice.

The use of trumpets has its biblical basis in Numbers 10:1–10, where they are used to assemble the people for various occasions, including festivals and war. The use of the trumpets is reserved to the sons of Aaron. In the War Rule, trumpets are also used to summon the assembly, but we find a complex, differentiated use of trumpets in battle (the "trumpets of withdrawal," the "trumpets of pursuit," the "trumpets of ambush," the "trumpets for the fanfare of the slain," etc., see Yadin 1962: 92–109). Parallels to some aspects of this usage can be found in the books of Maccabees. In 1 Maccabees 7:45, the Judean army sounded an alarm while pursuing the remnant of Nicanor's army. 1 Maccabees 9:12 mentions the use of trumpets by both Greek and Jewish forces on going forth to battle at Elasa. 2 Maccabees 15:25,26 says that Nicanor's army used trumpets but that Judas and his men did not. It seems clear enough that the Maccabean use of trumpets had developed beyond the biblical precedents, but this may have been a phenomenon of Hellenistic warfare more generally. The Romans also had a complex system of trumpet signals (Yadin 1962: 112). The Jewish use of trumpets, however, was distinctive in its religious character, and this emphasis is very pronounced in the War Rule.

The ritualistic character of the War Rule is clearly in evidence in column 7, which provides for the purity of the camp:

> No young boy and no woman shall enter their encampments when they go forth from Jerusalem to go to battle, until their return. Any one halt or blind or lame, or a man in whose body is a permanent defect, or a man affected by an impurity of his flesh, all these shall not go forth to battle with them. All of them shall be volunteers for battle and sound in spirit and flesh, and ready for the day of vengeance. Any man who is not pure with regard to his sexual organs on the day of battle shall not join them in battle, for holy angels are in communion with their hosts. There shall be a space between all their camps and the place of the "hand", about two thousand cubits, and no unseemly evil thing shall be seen in the vicinity of their encampments.
>
> (1QM 7:3–7; cf. 4Q491 frags 1–3, lines 6–8, which represents a different recension of this material. See Duhaime 1990)

There is no biblical law that prohibits women and children from going to battle, although Numbers 1:2–3 specifies those who are able to go to war as "every male individually, from twenty years old and upwards." The scroll is concerned to avoid any situation that might cause a person to become impure by reason of sexual activity. There was an old taboo in this regard associated with holy war: cf. the refusal of Uriah the Hittite to sleep with his wife while the army was on campaign (2 Sam 11:11). The reason is made explicit here: holy angels are mingled with the host. Communion with the angels is also emphasized in column 12, and it is more generally a feature of the theology of the Dead Sea sect, especially in the Hodayot. We shall consider it further in Chapters 7 and 8. The closest parallel to the War Rule on this point is found in the "Messianic Rule," 1QSa: "No man smitten in his flesh, or paralysed in his feet or hands, or lame, or blind, or deaf, or dumb, or smitten in his flesh with a visible blemish; no old and tottery man unable to stay still in the midst of the congregation; none of these shall come to hold office among the congregation of the men of renown, for the angels of holiness are [with] their [congregation]" (1QSa 2:4–10). The exclusion of such people from the military campaign is not a matter of fitness, but of purity. The kind of purity originally associated with the temple is extended here to the assembled congregation of Israel. These eschatological rules continue and develop a tendency found already in the Temple Scroll, which prohibits anyone who has had a nocturnal emission or sexual intercourse from entering the city of the sanctuary for three days, and specifies that latrines should be a distance of 3,000 cubits from the city (11QT 55–6).

The ages assigned for various functions also suggest that the regulations are dictated by ideological rather than practical concerns. Whereas Numbers gave the age of mobilization as twenty years, the youngest group in the scroll is twenty-five to thirty, and these are assigned to despoil the slain, collect the booty and cleanse the land. If practical military considerations took precedence, we should expect this age group to be involved in skirmishing, or in some military task where agility was important.

The forty years of the war are punctuated by five sabbatical years. The first of these, in 1QM 2, provides the occasion for a discourse on the organization of the temple service. Most notable here is that the scroll provides for 26 priestly courses, rather than 24, thereby implying a year of 52 weeks or 364 days as in Jubilees and elsewhere in the Dead Sea scrolls. Prayers of exhortation and thanksgiving are provided for various occasions during the war. A string of such prayers is collected in columns 10–14, but they are also interspersed with the battle accounts in columns 15–19 (Yadin 1962: 207–28). Many of these prayers are assigned to the high priest. There are biblical precedents for the role of priests in the time of battle. Deuteronomy 20:2 stipulates that "before you engage in battle, the priest shall come forward and speak to the troops." The Deuteronomic speech for this occasion is incorporated in 1QM 10:2–5.

Exhortations before battle are also common in the Maccabean books (1 Macc 4:9; 4:30; 7:41; 2 Macc 12:15). Typically they recall glorious incidents from biblical history where the enemy was defeated against great odds, such as the victory of David over Goliath and the destruction of Sennacherib. Several of these incidents are also invoked in the War Rule (1QM 11:1–3, 9–10; Yadin 1962: 214). It is significant, however, that in the Maccabean books Judas recites the prayers and delivers the exhortations. In the War Rule, these tasks are reserved to the priests. Consequently, the War Rule is much more ritualistic than the Maccabean battles, and is reminiscent of the role of the priests in the miraculous conquest of Jericho in Joshua 7.

Some scholars have argued for a close affinity between 1QM 2–9 and Maccabean warfare, so that this section of the War Rule should be viewed as a relatively early source that is not distinctively sectarian (Davies 1977: 66). The books of Maccabees are our primary source for Jewish warfare in the Hellenistic period, and so it is inevitable that there should be some parallels with the War Rule. The parallels, however, are of a general kind. The overall picture of warfare that we get from the scroll is very different from that presented by 1 Maccabees, because of its ritualized character and the prominent role of the priests. Even the descriptions of military formations in the scroll have more noteworthy parallels with Roman tactics than with those of the Maccabees, as Yadin has shown. These parallels suggest a time of origin in the first century BCE rather than earlier. Moreover columns 2–9, as they are found in 1QM, have a distinctly sectarian character, which is especially evident in the purity rules of column 7, but also in references to "sons of darkness" in 1QM 3:6, 9, and mention of Belial in 4:2. Those who see columns 2–9 as a purely traditional, nationalistic document have to posit "ethical" and "dualistic" additions by a later scribe (Davies 1977: 32). There is no doubt that columns 2–9 represent a different stream of tradition from column 1, but the Dead Sea sect was heir to multiple traditions that were not strictly consistent with each other but were woven together nonetheless.

THE DUALISTIC FRAMEWORK

The programmatic account of the war in 1QM 1 is dominated by motifs that are barely represented in columns 2–9. Here "the first engagement of the Sons of Light" is to attack "the lot of the Sons of Darkness, the army of Belial." This opening account draws heavily on the book of Daniel, especially Daniel 11:40–12:1 (see von der Osten-Sacken 1969: 30–4). The Sons of Darkness are associated with "the troop of Edom and Moab and the sons of Ammon" (cf. Dan 11:41), as well as the dwellers of Philistia (cf. Isa 11:14 where all these peoples are named) and the Kittim. The name Kittim derives from Citium in Cyprus, and is applied at various times to Greeks and Romans. According to 1 Maccabees 1:1, Alexander the Great came from "the land of Kittim." In Daniel 11:30, however, the Kittim are clearly the Romans, who forced Antiochus Epiphanes to withdraw from Egypt in 168 BCE. The Kittim are also the Romans in the pesharim. There are further echoes of Daniel in 1QM 1:4, "in his time he shall set out with great wrath" (cf. Dan 11:40) and 1:5: "a time of deliverance for the people of God" (cf. Dan 12:1). These allusions, however, are built into a conception of the war that is very different from what we find in Daniel.

As we have noted above, Daniel 10 views human conflict in the context of a heavenly battle between the angelic "princes" of the various nations. Michael, "prince" of Israel, fights in turn against the angelic "princes" of Persia and Greece. He does not, however, encounter a Prince of Evil at large, or a Prince of Darkness. The closest Daniel comes to describing a demonic force is in chapter 7, where he sees four great beasts coming up out of the sea. The sea, *yamm*, had a venerable mythological history. In Canaanite mythology, it was one of the adversaries of the god Baal, and had to be subdued in conflict. In poetic passages in the Hebrew Bible it is an unruly force that is subdued by God in the course of creation. It is also the home of chaotic monsters, Rahab and Leviathan, that God has either slain at creation or must kill in the eschatological future (cf. Job 26:12; Isa 51:9 [Rahab]; Isa 27:1 [Leviathan]. See Collins 1993: 287–9). In Daniel, however, neither God nor Michael does battle directly with the sea. The beasts are interpreted allegorically, as four kings or kingdoms, which are eventually subjected to the judgment of God and replaced by the kingdom of the holy ones of the Most High. Insofar as these beasts rise from the sea, they have a demonic quality, but Daniel has no role for a personified Satanic figure. Moreover, the beasts are portrayed as forces of rebellion, who rage against the Most High, much as the nations rage against the Lord and His anointed in Psalm 2. They are not allotted a role in the structure of creation, as the Prince of Darkness is in the Instruction on the Two Spirits in the Community Rule.

While the War Scroll incorporates several motifs from Daniel, the structure of the war is quite different. The imagery of light and darkness immediately brings to mind the Instruction on the Two Spirits, and also the tradition of Persian dualism. In the Instruction, the Prince of Darkness was given no personal name. In the War Rule, the Sons of Darkness are identified as "the army of Belial." In the Hebrew Bible, the word Belial is used predominantly in a construct relationship with "man" or "men" (von der Osten-Sacken 1969: 73–8). People of Belial are worthless, deceitful or wicked people. In most cases, Belial appears to be an abstraction, roughly equivalent to evil. In Psalm 18:5 (= 2 Sam 22:5), however, Belial is clearly associated with the netherworld: "the breakers of Death encompassed me, the torrents of Belial overwhelmed me. The cords of Sheol surrounded me, the traps of Death confronted me." (The "torrents of Belial" appear again in 1QH 11:29, formerly 3:29.) The etymology of the name is uncertain, but the two most plausible explanations also point to the netherworld: b^ely $ya'al$ = (the place from which) one does not go up; or a derivation from bl', to swallow, a verb often associated with Mot, Death, in Canaanite texts. (Cf. also Isa 25:7, where it is said that God will swallow up Death forever.) The name, then, derives from Hebrew and Canaanite tradition and associates Belial with the netherworld. He is integrated here into the dualism of light and darkness that we have already encountered in the Instruction on the Two Spirits.

We have already seen something of the Persian background of this dualism in Chapter 3. The closest parallel to the War Rule, however, is provided by a passage in Plutarch, who cites as his source Theopompus, who wrote about 300 BCE:

But they (the Persians) also relate many mythical details about the gods, and the following are instances. Horomazes is born from the purest light and Areimanius from darkness, and they are at war with one another ... Theopompus says that, according to the Magians, for three thousand years alternately the one god will dominate the other and be dominated, and that for another three thousand years they will fight and make war, until one smashes up the domain of the other. In the end Hades shall perish and men shall be happy; neither shall they need sustenance nor shall they cast a shadow, while the god who will have brought this about shall have quiet and shall rest, not for a long while indeed for a god, but for such time as would be reasonable for a man who falls asleep.

(*Isis and Osiris*, 47; Gwyn Griffiths 1970: 46–7)

As a document of Persian religion, this passage presents many problems that go beyond the scope of this discussion. We do not know where Theopompus got his information, or what form of Persian religion it represents. Moreover, the passage is unclear on some crucial points. It is not certain whether the god who brings about the resolution of the conflict should be identified with Horomazes (Ahura Mazda) or with a higher god. In early Zoroastrianism, as reflected in the Gathas, Ahura Mazda was the supreme god, and Spenta Mainyu and Angra Mainyu were the good and evil spirits. Later Ahura Mazda became identified with the good spirit, Spenta Mainyu, and the two spirits were regarded as primordial powers. Later again a Zoroastrian "heresy" arose, called Zervanism, according to which Ahura Mazda and Ahriman were the twin sons of infinite time, Zurvan. Various scholars have related Plutarch's account to early Zoroastrianism, Zervanism or even to an idiosyncratic, deviant form of Zoroastrianism. (For a summary of the debate, see Kobelski 1981: 86–7.) The chronology of the conflict also admits of different interpretations. In the classical Pahlavi sources, which are several centuries later, history is divided into twelve millennia, but a shorter chronology of nine millennia is also found. The passage in Plutarch can be read as requiring nine millennia, if the phrase "3,000 years alternately" is read to mean that each god dominates for 3,000 years (as in Kippenberg 1978: 73). But the phrase is more naturally read to mean that they dominate in turn within a single 3,000-year period. There are also parallels for a chronology of seven millennia. The Oracle of Hystaspes, preserved in Lactantius, is said to have posited a duration of 6,000 years, after which everything would come to an end (Lactantius, *Divinae Institutiones* 7.14.8; Aristokritos, *Theosophy*; Hinnells 1973:128; Kippenberg 1978:71). The Bahman Yasht, a Pahlavi work which contains some early material, records in chapter 2 a vision in which Zarathustra sees a tree with seven branches, symbolizing seven periods that are to come. (This vision, however, seems to be a secondary elaboration of a vision of four branches, found in chapter 1.)

It is not suggested that the War Rule reproduces any Persian schema with exactitude, but only that certain motifs and ideas in the Jewish text, which are novel in a Jewish context, were prompted by an acquaintance with Persian tradition in whatever form. On any interpretation of the passage in Plutarch, it shares some distinctive features with the War Rule: two supernatural forces, symbolized by light and darkness, locked in a symmetrical battle in which each in turn holds the upper hand. If the Persian myth is interpreted in terms of seven periods, the parallel is closer still. The Jewish text ultimately envisages a supreme God and two evenly matched angelic/demonic forces (Michael and Belial, Prince of Light and Prince of Darkness), but in some passages, including 1QM 1, the battle is waged between the supreme God and Belial, and so there is a parallel with the Persian myth whichever way the latter is understood. The most important parallel concerns the structure of the conflict. Belial and the Sons of Darkness are not portrayed as rebellious forces like the beasts from the sea in the book of Daniel. Rather they are playing out a role that was allotted to them in creation. This is most clearly expressed in 1QM 13, which says that God "made Belial to corrupt, an angel of hatred" (*mal'ak maśtēmāh*), a phrase that evokes the name Mastema, the Prince of Demons in the Book of Jubilees. At the same time, the War Rule also incorporates familiar Jewish motifs, such as the day of the Lord and there is an obvious analogy between the sevenfold structure of the war and the week and sabbatical cycle. (See further Collins 1975.)

The passage in Plutarch is unclear as to how the alternating dominion was envisaged in the Persian myth. The initial account in 1QM 1 is also ambiguous: "In three lots shall the Sons of Light prove strong so as to smite the wicked, and in three the army of Belial shall recover so as to bring about the withdrawal of the lot [of Light]." In columns 15–19, however, it is clear that the opposing forces prevail in alternate lots. While some portions of the text are lost, we find:

Cols 16:3–8: the order for the first attack;
  16:9ff: the counterattack of Belial;
  17:10–16: the second attack (= third lot, 17:16);
  17:16: the counterattack of Belial, fourth lot.

The fifth and sixth lots are missing, because of lacunae at the bottom of the manuscript, but in column 18 we find the final intervention of God. It is clear then that the three lots in which Belial prevails are the second, fourth, and sixth.

The battle envisaged in column 1 involves two levels, "the congregation of angels and the assembly of men" (1:10). This passage makes no mention of a leader of the forces of light other than God, who eventually decides the battle. The text does not say, however, that Belial prevails over God in the alternate lots, only that the Sons of Light are forced to withdraw. Again in column 12 the deity appears to be the leader of the angelic host: "Migh[ty men and] a host of angels are among those mustered with us, the Mighty One of War is in our congregation, and the host of His spirits is with our steps" (12:8). In column 13, however, we read: "Thou didst appoint from of old the Prince of Light to assist us . . . and all the spirits of truth in his dominion. And thou wast the one who made Belial to corrupt." It has been argued that this passage (1QM 13: 9b–12) is an interpolation, which gives "a dualistic tone to a text in which there was previously none" (Duhaime 1987:45; cf. Duhaime 1977). But the passage goes on to say that God has appointed from of old a day for the destruction of all the sons of darkness (13:16) and so it assuredly had a dualistic tone. The point at issue is whether the dualism originally had a role for an angelic Prince of Light under God, as it has in the Instruction of the Two Spirits. Immediately after the reference to the Prince of Light and Belial we read: "Who is like unto Thee in strength, O God of Israel, and yet Thy mighty hand is with the poor. What angel or prince is like unto the help of [Thy face] . . . ." In fact, the authors of the War Rule were heirs to conflicting traditions on this matter. According to Deuteronomy 32:9, when the Most High divided the nations according to the number of the gods, he kept Israel as his own portion (cf. Sir 17:14). Jubilees 15:31–2 declares emphatically: "there are many nations and many peoples and all are his, and he has set spirits over all of them to lead them astray from him. But over Israel he appointed no angel or spirit, for he alone is their ruler." Yet Jubilees gives a prominent role to the angel of the presence in thwarting Mastema in the story of the Exodus (Jubilees 48). As we have already seen, Daniel casts the archangel Michael in the role of Prince of Israel. 1QM 13 affirms an angelic helper called the Prince of Light, but qualifies his role immediately by insisting that no angel can compare with God. There may have been some controversy, even within the Dead Sea sect, about the degree of prominence that should be accorded to a super-angel, such as the Prince of Light. The angelic helper of Israel is identified as Michael in 1QM 17:6–7: "He hath magnified the authority of Michael through eternal light . . . so as to raise amongst the angels the authority of Michael and the dominion of Israel amongst all flesh." (Duhaime 1977 also regards this passage as an interpolation.)

The fact that the Prince of Light is identified with Michael underlines again that the War Rule stands, in part, in the tradition of Daniel. Echoes of Daniel are especially prominent in column 1, as noted above. In view of Michael's prominence in Daniel, it seems unlikely that he was a secondary addition to the War Rule. Even in the final redaction of 1QM, the victory clearly belongs to God. Michael is only God's agent and subordinate. The balanced structure of the war, where Belial is victorious in alternate phases, also suggests that the forces of light have a subordinate commander under God.

The dualism of the War Rule differs from that of the Instruction on the Two Spirits only in its emphasis. The Instruction is more comprehensive in its scope, addressing the creation and attributes of the two spirits as well as their eschatological destiny. The War Rule, as we should expect, focuses on the final conflict, although it does note, in 13:11, that God "made Belial to corrupt."

It now appears that the War Rule also had a place for a human leader, in the person of a Davidic messiah. The presence of this figure was only alluded to in passing in 1QM. The section devoted to the banners of the congregation concludes the shield of the Prince of the Whole Congregation, whom we have seen in Chapter 5 to be a messianic figure (1QM 5:1). In 1QM 11:6–7, Balaam's oracle of the scepter and the star is cited without interpretation. More explicit discussion of the messiah's role is now available in 4Q285. The relation of this document to the War Rule is shown by the common vocabulary, including mention of Michael, Gabriel, the Prince of the Congregation, war, and the Kittim (Abegg 1994: 82–3). The fragmentary text has been reconstructed to reveal the following events. In fragment 1, the high priest blesses God before the assembly. Fragments 6 and 4 describe a campaign beginning on the mountains of Israel. The final battle is fought on or by the sea. The enemy is routed with angelic help, and the leader is brought before the Prince of the Congregation for judgment. He is found guilty and put to death (fragment 5). The high priest orders the cleansing of the land from the corpses of the Kittim (fragment 5:6; see further Abegg 1994: 86). There was a short-lived controversy about fragment 5, because it was claimed that it referred to the death of the messiah. (Line 4 was read as "they will kill the Prince of the Congregation, the Br[anch of David]".) It is now apparent, however that the Prince is the one who does the killing in this passage. The whole passage is based on the prophecy about the shoot from the stump of Jesse in Isaiah 11. (There is a clear mention of the Branch of David in 4Q285 line 3.) In Isaiah, the messianic figure is supposed to kill the wicked with the breath of his lips. This passage is found in a pesher on Isaiah (4Q162), which clearly casts the messiah in militant and victorious role: "he shall rule over all . . . and his sword shall judge the peoples." The passage in Isaiah is never interpreted to say that the messiah is killed. Consequently, there can be no doubt that the messiah is the subject and not the object of the killing in 4Q285. (See further Collins 1995: 58–60.)

4Q285 clearly describes an eschatological war. It is related to the War Rule, and was probably part of the same composition. (It was first so identified by Milik 1972b: 43.) It does not overlap with 1QM but it may have been part of the end of the document which is not preserved in the Cave 1 manuscript.

THE DEVELOPMENT OF THE WAR RULE

The Davidic messiah belongs to the complex of traditions associated with the nationalistic conflict between Israel and the nations, rather than to the cosmic war between the forces of light and darkness. The discovery of 4Q285 raises the possibility that the War Rule may have been significantly longer than the text preserved in 1QM, and may have gone on to describe the course of the thirty-three-year war against the nations that was outlined in column 2. Even in the redaction represented by the extant text of 1QM, the cosmic war and the war against the nations are viewed as complementary. Nonetheless, the two traditions are sufficiently different from each other for many scholars to believe that at least two different documents have been editorially combined.

Attempts to reconstruct the redactional formation of the War Rule have not attained consensus. P. R. Davies argued for a complex history of redaction, beginning with "traditions that arose during and immediately after the Maccabean wars" in columns 2–9. The dualistic seven-stage war against the Kittim, in this reconstruction, was only introduced in the final stage, for which Davies suggested a date in the first half of the first century CE (Davies 1977: 124). The latter date is shown to be impossible by the manuscripts from Cave 4, which were still unpublished when Davies wrote. 4Q496, which contains fragments both of column 1 and of columns 2–9 is dated to the middle of the first century BCE on paleographic grounds. Moreover, we have seen little reason to associate columns 2–9 specifically with the Maccabean wars, while they are clearly related to other sectarian writings. Conversely, several scholars have argued that the dualistic frame represented by column 1 is early. P. von der Osten-Sacken argued that the sharpness of the dualistic antithesis reflected the situation of Israel at the beginning of the Maccabean period (von der Osten-Sacken 1969: 85). Such a specific dating is gratuitous. The use of the book of Daniel in 1QM 1 already requires a post-Maccabean date. References in 1QM 1 to "the Kittim of Asshur" and "the Kittim in Egypt" suggest that the name "Kittim" is not reserved to the Romans here, but includes in its purview the Seleucids and Ptolemies. Such an interpretation, however, does not require a date any earlier than the middle of the first century BCE. In short, while two different traditions about the eschatological war are combined in the War Rule, it is not possible to establish either that columns 2–9 were composed before columns 1, 15–19 or vice versa. Neither is it possible to show that any part of the War Rule is older than the first century BCE. The entire War Rule, combining both traditions, continued to be copied and reworked down into the first century CE. The fact that 1QM was hidden carefully in Cave 1 indicates that it was valued as an important document by the Qumran community.

THE WAR RULE AND THE DEAD SEA SECT

The question of date is closely bound up with the relation of the War Rule to the Dead Sea sect. Since the early days of research on the scrolls, a strand of scholarship, mainly German, has persistently argued that the War Rule, at least in part, is older than the Dead Sea sect (Rost 1955; von der Osten-Sacken 1969; Stegemann 1993: 145–8). It lacks the distinctive sectarian terminology of the other rule books. The word *yaḥad* is used as an adverb ("together with"), not as a noun ("commune, community"). God is referred to as "the God of Israel," *'ēl yiśrā'ēl*, a designation found rarely in the other scrolls. The War Rule presupposes participation in the temple cult, and its militant attitude contrasts with the quietism of the Community Rule. Some of the features of the War Rule, such as the analogy with the Israelite camp in the wilderness, which are also important for the sect, are integrally related to the war context, and may have been taken over by the sect from the War Rule. Most fundamentally, it is argued, the War Rule is a document for all Israel, not an elite group within it. References to a remnant in 1QM 14:8–9 appear to be secondary, since they are not found in a parallel fragment from Cave 4 (4Q491; Hunzinger 1957).

There is certainly tension in the War Rule between the pan-Israelite perspective and the sectarianism implied in the dualism of light and darkness. The tension, however, admits of another explanation. The so-called "Messianic Rule," 1QSa, is introduced as "the rule for all the congregation of Israel in the last days, when they shall join . . . according to the law of the sons of Zadok the priests and of the men of their covenant, who have turned aside [from the] way of the people." The hope, in short, is that all Israel will rally to the sectarian community in the end of days. The War Rule, accordingly is a rule for all Israel but the Israel it envisages is an entity of the eschatological future. Even the eschatological Israel can be reasonably described as a remnant, since the violators of the covenant, at least, will have been weeded out. The endorsement of the temple cult must also be seen in this context. The Rule envisages a cult that is regulated by a calendar of 52 weeks or 364 days, the sectarian calendar that was not observed in the Jerusalem Temple and was one of the main factors that led to the secession of the Dead Sea sect. The temple that is endorsed is not the actual temple of Maccabean or Hasmonean times, but the purified temple of the eschatological era.

Most intriguing of all is the relation between the militancy of the War Rule and the quietism of the Community Rule. As noted above at the end of Chapter 4, the Community Rule is pacificistic only up to a point: "I will not grapple with the men of perdition *until the day of revenge*." The *maskil* is described as "a man zealous for the precept, whose time is for the day of revenge," who entertains "everlasting hatred in a spirit of secrecy for the men of perdition" (1QS 9). It is well known that the settlement at Qumran was destroyed by military assault during the revolt against Rome, and was apparently defended (see Cross 1995: 60–2). While it is impossible to prove who the defenders were, the simplest hypothesis is that they were the same people who had inhabited the site for a century and a half. While the war anticipated in the War Rule has many fantastic qualities, it also shows some knowledge of realistic military tactics. The preparation of such an elaborate War Rule strongly suggests that the community was prepared to implement it, if the members believed that the appointed time had arrived. That time may very well have arrived in the war against Rome.

If the Qumran community expected the war against Rome to follow the course set forth in the War Rule, it was bitterly disappointed. As we have seen, even the more realistic parts of the Rule have a ritualistic character, and attach great importance to sacrifices, banners and prayers. The hope of the Sons of Light depended on the belief that "mighty men and a host of angels are among those mustered with us, the mighty one of war is in our congregation, and the host of his spirits is with our steps, and our horsemen are [like] rain-clouds and like clouds of dew covering the earth" (1QM 12:7– 8). There are some ill-fated analogues to such belief in modern colonial history. One is the Ghost Dance movement, embraced by the Sioux and other native American tribes in 1890 (La Barre 1970: 227–33). Another is the cattle-killing movement of the Xhosa people in South Africa in 1856–7 (Peires 1989; the cattle-killing was supposed to purify the earth to make way for new herds in the general resurrection). In both cases, the believers expected imminent help from the spirit world, in the form of the return of the dead ancestors. Both movements had ritual devices (ghost shirts in the case of the native Americans) which were supposed to render them invulnerable. Both movements ended in catastrophe and the near annihilation of the people involved.

We do not know for sure that the Dead Sea sect actually went into battle believing that the day of vengeance had come. Insofar as we know, however, the Qumran community disappeared at the time of the Roman invasion of Judea. (This does not necessarily mean that the entire sect disappeared. See Charlesworth 1981: 228–32). It is reasonable to suppose that they were wiped out by the Roman army, the accursed Kittim of the scrolls. Apocalyptic hopes and expectations may have given the Essenes hope and courage in their hour of danger. They could not, however, change the brutal realities of political and military power.

7

RESURRECTION AND ETERNAL LIFE

The belief in the judgment of individuals after death is one of the crucial elements that distinguish apocalyptic writings from earlier biblical tradition. The standard view in the Hebrew Bible was that, while the dead had a shadowy existence in Sheol or the Netherworld, it was devoid of satisfaction and they lacked the power even to praise God (Cf. Pss 6:5; 30:9; 115:16–17). Qoheleth echoed the dominant view of the Hebrew tradition when he asserted that "all go to one place; all are from the dust, and all turn to dust again" (Qoh 3:20). Ben Sira, a near contemporary of Enoch and Daniel, could still state confidently that "whether life lasts for ten years or a hundred or a thousand, there are no questions asked in Hades" (Sirach 41:4). It is in the apocalyptic writings of Enoch and Daniel, in the early second century BCE, that the belief in a judgment after death first gains currency in Jewish tradition.

BIBLICAL PRECEDENTS

There were however two strands of thought in the Hebrew Bible that were conducive to belief in a meaningful life after death. One strand, found primarily in the Psalms, concerns the desire for lasting enjoyment of the presence of God. We read in Psalm 73: "I am continually with you; you hold my right hand. You guide me with counsel and afterward you will receive me with honor (or: in glory)" (trans. New Revised Standard Version). Again Psalm 16:9–10 declares: "Therefore my heart is glad and my soul rejoices; my body also dwells secure. For thou dost not give me up to Sheol, or let thy godly one see the Pit." In light of passages such as these, some scholars hold that the hope for a beatific afterlife was known in ancient Israel, even though it was not widely shared (Spronk 1986: 315–38; Puech 1993: 37–73). The evidence, however, is ambiguous at best. The Psalmist is chiefly concerned with the presence of God in this life, as an experience that transcends time. (Compare Ps 84:10: "For a day in your courts is better than a thousand else-where.") In poetic language, "everlasting" may mean only that no end is in view. Rescue from Sheol may mean the postponement of death, or may even be a metaphor for rescue from distress. A some-what stronger case can be made for the immortality of the king, in light of Ugaritic parallels, but even here the language is evasive. When Psalm 21:4–5 says "He asked life of thee; thou gavest it to him, length of days for ever and ever," it is not clear whether the reference is to eternal life or simply to a long and fulfilling life in this world.

The second strand of biblical thought that is pertinent to this discussion uses the language of resurrection with reference to the restoration of the people of Israel. The classic example here is provided by the vision of a valley full of dry bones, in Ezekiel 37. The vision is explicitly metaphorical: "these bones are the whole house of Israel" (Ezek 37:11). Hosea 6:2 ("After two days He will revive us; on the third day He will raise us up, that we may live before Him") is also metaphorical. The speakers are stricken, but not dead. A more difficult case is presented by Isaiah 26:29: "Thy dead shall live, their bodies shall rise. O dwellers in the dust, awake and sing for joy!" Many scholars accept this passage as a reference to individual resurrection (e.g. Nickelsburg 1972: 18; Puech 1993: 66–73). The context, however, involves a contrast between the "other lords" who have ruled over Israel, who are now dead and will not live, and the nation that the Lord has increased (Isa 26:14–15). Isaiah 26 can be read by analogy with Ezekiel 37: Israel was dead in the Exile, and its restoration is as miraculous as the resurrection of the dead, while the power of Babylon is gone forever. All of these passages clearly assume that God has the power to raise the dead should He choose to do so. The biblical authors may have been familiar with the idea of resurrection, from various sources. (A Canaanite background has been proposed for Hosea 6 and Isaiah 26; a Persian analogue for Ezekiel 37.) Nonetheless, there is no undisputed attestation of a belief in resurrection in the Hebrew Bible before Daniel 12 (see further Collins 1993: 394–5).

111

THE EARLY APOCALYPSES: RESURRECTION OF THE SPIRIT

The resurrection is described as follows in Daniel 12:1–3:

> At that time Michael will arise, the great prince who stands over your people. There will be a time of distress such as had not been from the beginning of the nation to that time. At that time, your people will be delivered, everyone who is found written in the book. Many of those who sleep in the dusty earth will awake, some to everlasting life and some to reproach and everlasting disgrace. The wise will shine like the splendor of the firmament, and those who lead the common people to righteousness will be like the stars forever and ever.

Several features of this account should be noted. The resurrection is not universal. It is the destiny of the very good and the very bad, who are raised for reward and punishment respectively. Daniel uses the metaphor of sleep and awakening to indicate the transition that is in question. The text does not envisage unbroken immortality, but a resurrection of the dead. It is not clear, however, that the resurrection is corporeal in form, or that it involves a restoration to life on earth. The "dusty earth" where the dead sleep is probably Sheol, or the netherworld (cf. Job 17:16, where Sheol and "the dust" are used in parallelism). Daniel is not explicit about the form of the resurrected life, except that the wise *maśkilim* will be like the stars. In apocalyptic idiom, the stars are the host of heaven, or the angels (cf. 1 Enoch 104, p. 113 below). In the case of the wise teachers, at least, the resurrection appears to take the form of elevation from the netherworld to the angelic realm. Discussions of life after death in this period are often framed by the alternatives of immortality of the soul or resurrection of the body. These alternatives are not adequate for the early apocalyptic literature, which, at least in some cases, envisages resurrection of the spirit, or what St Paul would later call a "spiritual body" (1 Cor 15:44).

This is also true of the early Enoch literature. The Enochic Book of the Watchers arguably contains the oldest Jewish reference to a differentiated life after death in 1 Enoch 22, where the souls of the dead are separated into four chambers to await the day of judgment. (There is a textual corruption in 1 Enoch 22:9, which gives the number as three.) This passage is a peculiar mix of Babylonian and

Greek traditions (see Wacker 1982). The location of the abodes of the dead inside a mountain reflects Babylonian myth. The location of the souls of the righteous by a spring of water on which there is light is indebted to Greek, Orphic, traditions. The passage as a whole, however, is exceptional in Jewish sources and has little influence on subsequent tradition. More significant for our purposes are the references in the Epistle of Enoch (1 Enoch 91–105). 1 Enoch 90:10 predicts that "the righteous will rise from sleep," as also predicted by Daniel. The destiny to which they rise is spelled out in 1 Enoch 104: "you will shine like the lights of heaven and will be seen, and the gate of heaven will be opened to you . . . for you will have great joy like the angels of heaven . . . for you shall be associates of the host of heaven" (1 Enoch 104: 2,4,6). Here again we are dealing with resurrection, not an unbroken state of immortality. But there is no mention of bodily resurrection or of return to life on earth. What is envisaged is the resurrection of the *nepes* or spirit and its transformation to an angelic state.

Another witness to this kind of "resurrection of the spirit" is found in Jubilees 23. As in Daniel and Enoch, the resurrection is an eschatological event, that comes at a predetermined time in the future, when "the Lord will heal his servants, and they shall be exalted and prosper greatly, and they shall drive out their adversaries." Then: "the righteous shall see it and be thankful, and rejoice with joy for ever and ever; and they shall see all the punishments and curses that had been their lot falling on their enemies. And their bones shall rest in the earth, and their spirits shall have much joy" (Jub 23:30–1). Here again we have a notion of resurrection that is neither immortality of the soul, in the Greek sense, nor resurrection of the physical body.

The notion of physical resurrection was certainly known in Judaism in the second century BCE. The clearest testimony is found in 2 Maccabees 7, where the martyrs sacrifice their limbs in full confidence that they will get them back again at the resurrection. But it is by no means the case that Jews always thought of resurrection in bodily terms. As we have seen, the prevalent notion in the early apocalypses of Daniel and Enoch is better described as resurrection of the spirit. (On the range of Jewish conceptions of the afterlife see further Nickelsburg 1972; Cavallin 1974.)

JOSEPHUS ON THE ESSENES

Nonetheless, the antithesis of bodily resurrection/immortality of the soul has dominated discussions of afterlife in the Dead Sea scrolls. This is due in large part to Josephus, who described the eschatology of the Essenes as follows:

> It is a firm belief among them that although bodies are corruptible, and their matter unstable, souls are immortal and endure for ever; that, come from the subtlest ether, they are entwined with the bodies which serve them as prisons, drawn down as they are by some physical spell; but that when they are freed from the bonds of the flesh, liberated, so to speak, from long slavery, then they rejoice and rise up to the heavenly world. Agreeing with the sons of the Greeks, they declare that an abode is reserved beyond the Ocean for the souls of the just; a place oppressed neither by rain nor snow nor torrid heat, but always refreshed by the gentle breeze blowing from the Ocean. But they relegate evil souls to a dark pit shaken by storms, full of unending chastisement. The Greeks, I think, had the same idea when they assigned their valiant ones, whom they call "heroes" and "demi-gods", to the Islands of the Blessed, and the souls of the bad to Hades, the place of the wicked, where according to their mythology, certain people such as Sisyphus, Tantalus, Ixion and Tityus, undergo their torment. A belief of this kind assumes in the first place that souls are eternal; next, it serves to encourage virtue and deflect from vice. Indeed, the good will become better during their lives if they hope to be rewarded, even after their end; whilst the wicked will restrain their instincts out of fear if they expect to suffer eternal punishment after their dissolution even though they escape while they live.
>
> (Josephus, *Jewish War* 2.154–6; trans. Vermes and Goodman 1989: 47)

Josephus, or his source, is evidently at pains to make the beliefs of the Essenes intelligible in Greek terms. But even if we allow for some exaggeration in this respect, he paints a very clear picture of a belief in judgment after death that does not require the resurrection of the body.

A very different account of Essene eschatology is found in Hippolytus of Rome, a Christian bishop who flourished about 200 CE:

The doctrine of the resurrection has also derived support among them, for they acknowledge both that the flesh will rise again and that it will be immortal, in the same manner as the soul is already imperishable. They maintain that when the soul has been separated from the body, it is now borne into one place, which is well ventilated and full of light, and there it rests until judgement. This locality the Greeks were acquainted with by hearsay, calling it Isles of the Blessed. But there are many tenets of these men which the wise of the Greeks have appropriated and thus have from time to time formed their own opinions ... for they affirm that there will be both a judgement and a conflagration of the universe, and that the wicked will be eternally punished.

(Refutation of all Heresies, 27; trans. Vermes and
Goodman 1989: 73)

The relationship of the account of Hippolytus to that of Josephus is disputed, but most probably the two are based on a common source, and Hippolytus did not draw on Josephus directly. Some of the differences between the two accounts are due to confusion on the part of Hippolytus (e.g. he identifies the Essenes with the Zealots) or to editorial censure (he deleted apparent references to sun worship). On the subject of eschatology, however, it is quite possible that Hippolytus has preserved some authentic details that were omitted by Josephus. The mention of "a conflagration of the universe" seems to find striking confirmation in 1QH 11:29–36 (formerly 1QH 3), which describes how "the torrents of Belial will overflow their high banks like a fire which devours ... the bases of the mountains shall burn and the roots of flint rock become streams of lava. It consumes right to the great deep." Some scholars have argued that Hippolytus also gives the more accurate account of the beliefs of the Essenes on the subject of resurrection (so notably Puech 1993:703–69). The majority view, however, holds that the account of Josephus is essentially accurate, although it is distorted by the imposition of Hellenistic categories on the beliefs of the sect.

THE EVIDENCE OF THE RULE BOOKS

The major sectarian rule books leave no doubt about the importance of reward and punishment after death in the ideology of the sect. In the Instruction on the Two Spirits in the Community Rule, the visitation of those who walk in the spirit of light "will be for healing, plentiful peace in a long life, fruitful offspring with all everlasting blessings, eternal enjoyment with endless life, and a crown of glory with majestic raiment in eternal light" (1QS 4:6–8). Some scholars have expressed doubts as to whether this passage refers to the afterlife, rather than to the blessings of this life (Duhaime 1985). These doubts should be dispelled by the corresponding retribution of the wicked. The visitation of those who walk in the spirit of darkness

> will be for a glut of punishments at the hands of all the angels of destruction, for eternal damnation for the scorching wrath of the God of revenge, for permanent error and shame without end with the humiliation of destruction by the fire of the dark regions. And all the ages of their generations they shall spend in bitter weeping and harsh evils in the abysses of darkness until their destruction, without there being a remnant or a survivor among them.
>
> (1QS 4:11–14; trans. García Martínez)

There is no language of resurrection here. The punishments of the wicked in a place of darkness are quite reminiscent of Josephus' account of the eschatology of the Essenes.

Nonetheless, this account of the "visitation" of the children of light and darkness is not without its ambiguity. Puech (1993:434) argues that the term "visitation" refers to the final judgment, on the day of the Lord. The term is certainly used with reference to a final, global, judgment, even within the Instruction on the Two Spirits. According to 1QS 3:18, God placed within humanity two spirits to "walk with them until the appointed time of his visitation" (*mo'ed p'qûdātô*). 1QS 4:18–19 says that "God, in the mysteries of his knowledge and in the wisdom of his glory, has determined an end to the existence of injustice and on the occasion of his visitation he will obliterate it forever." God's "visitation" is clearly a public, eschatological event, the day of judgment. Since the visitation of each spirit seems to follow automatically from their conduct, the passage lends itself more readily to the view that this "visitation" awaits each individual after death, in the sense of that which is appointed for them. (The verb *paqad* can mean "appoint" as well as "visit;" cf. 1QM 13:10, where the verb is used with reference to the appointment of the Prince of Light.) There is still a final judgment by which God puts an end to wickedness, but neither the Instruction nor any of the clearly sectarian texts says that the dead are raised or brought back for that judgment. Rather, people seem to go directly to their rewards or punishments. Some of the rewards of the righteous would seem to require a corporeal state, but the body in question may be a spiritual rather than an earthly body, to use the distinction drawn by St Paul. This conception is rather different from the Greek notion of immortality of the soul, and it is entirely in keeping with traditional Hebrew anthropology, whereby the *nepeš* survives the body in the netherworld. Insofar as there is no mention of resurrection of the body, it is not difficult to see how this conception could be confused with immortality of the soul by a Hellenized observer.

There is another passage in the Community Rule, however, that puts the question of life after death in a new perspective. The long hymn in 1QS 10–11 is a formally discrete unit within the scroll, and should be regarded as an independent composition. Generically, it is akin to the Thanksgiving Hymns, or Hodayot. Nonetheless, the fact that it is included in the same scroll as the Instruction on the Two Spirits and other components of the Community Rule suggests that it was accepted as representative of the community. It is reasonable to assume that the various components of the scroll were read in light of each other in the community, even if they had been composed separately. The passage in question is found in 1QS 11:5–8:

> My eyes have gazed on that which is eternal, on wisdom concealed from men, on knowledge and wise design (hidden) from the sons of men; on a fountain of righteousness and on a storehouse of power, on a spring of glory (hidden) from the assembly of flesh. God has given them to His chosen ones as an everlasting possession, and has caused them to inherit the lot of the holy ones. He has joined their assembly to the Sons of Heaven to be a Council of the Community, a foundation of the Building of Holiness, and eternal Plantation throughout all ages to come.
>
> (trans. Vermes 1995: 87)

This passage introduces a theme that we will meet repeatedly in the Hodayot: the fellowship of the elect with the angels. In the Epistle of Enoch, this fellowship was the destiny of the righteous after death. The Hodayot claim that it is already experienced in the life of the community (H.-W. Kuhn 1966; Nickelsburg 1972: 144–69). Puech (1993: 425) objects that the glory is anticipated and not realized. The community still lives among sinful humanity. But while the glory remains to be realized, the fellowship has already begun. This is apparent not only from the use of the perfect tense but also from the fact that the fellowship is constitutive of the council of the community. God has joined their assembly to the Sons of Heaven and thereby constituted them as the council of the community. This fellowship with the angels sheds new light on the question of life after death. The glory that the elect hope to enjoy is a continuation of something that they already experience. This may explain why passages like the Instruction on the Two Spirits do not use the language of resurrection, and why death does not appear as a problem in these texts. The members of the council of the community believed that they had made the transition to angelic, eternal life while still living in this life.

As noted in Chapter 3, CD 2:3–13 has several verbal parallels to the Instruction on the Two Spirits, although it lacks the underlying dualism of light and darkness. The destiny of the wicked is described in terms that are very similar to 1QS 4:12: "great flaming wrath by the hand of all the Angels of Destruction . . . without remnant or survivor." Like the Community Rule, CD teaches that those who hold fast to the covenant "are destined to live forever and all the glory of Adam shall be theirs" (CD 3:20; cf. 1QS 4:23). Both these rule books envisage a public, communal judgment when God will put an end to wickedness (1QS 4:18), and when the wicked "will have a visitation for destruction at the hand of Belial. This is the day when God will make a visitation" (CD 8:3–4). But they also specify the destiny entailed by the behavior of individuals, without any indication that all reward and punishment is deferred to the day of judgment, and rather implying that it is implemented immediately after the death of the individual.

Because of the manifest influence of the book of Daniel on the War Rule, Puech (1993:498) has argued that the eschatology of the Qumran document should be understood in the light of the biblical apocalypse. A key passage is found in 1QM 12:1–5, where the text unfortunately has several lacunae. Puech (1993: 451) reads as follows:

> For the multitude of holy ones [is] impatient (?) in the heavens
> and the hosts of angels are in your holy abode to ce[lebrate]

your [fideli]ty. The elect of the holy people you have placed for yourself in the l[ight? and the bo]ok of the names of all their host is with you in your holy abode and the n[umber of the holy o]nes is in your glorious residence.

This passage is reminiscent of Daniel at several points. The holy ones figure prominently in Daniel 7. In Daniel 12, the elect are written in a book and are destined to shine like the angels in light. (The reference to light is questionable in 1QM 12.) The association of the elect with the angels or holy ones goes to the heart of the problem of the understanding of the blessed afterlife in the scrolls. In Daniel, the assimilation of the wise teachers to the stars is clearly future, and only comes about after a resurrection, described as an awakening from sleep. There is no resurrection language in the War Rule. (1QM 14:11 says that God has raised up the fallen, but the point is that He has revived those who were defeated in battle.) Instead, the heavenly host mingles with the elect in the eschatological battle: "Migh[ty men and] a host of angels are among those mustered with us, the Mighty One of War is in our congregation, and the host of his spirits is with our steps" (1QM 12:8, trans. Yadin 1962: 314). Here, as in 1QS 11, the elect community claims to experience before death the fellowship with the angels that was reserved for the resurrected life in Daniel and Enoch. To be sure, the glory is not yet complete. The elect are still subjected to the attacks of Belial. But the eschatology of the War Rule, and of all the Qumran rule books, is different from that of the older apocalypses, because it involves a degree of participation in the angelic life even before death.

THE HODAYOT

The most controversial evidence on the subject of afterlife in the scrolls is found in the Thanksgiving Hymns or Hodayot. The most complete manuscript, 1QH[a], dates from the second half of the first century BCE, but the other manuscripts (1QH[b] and several manuscripts from Cave 4) are older, and none of these manuscripts are autographs. One cluster of hymns (the "Teacher hymns") is commonly ascribed to the Teacher of Righteousness (Jeremias 1963: 168–267). There does not appear, however, to be any significant difference between these hymns and the remainder ("Community hymns") on the subject of life after death.

The theme of fellowship with the angels and present participation in the eschatological state emerges clearly in 1QH 11:19–23 (formerly 1QH 3:19–23, a Teacher hymn):

> I thank you, Lord, because you saved my life from the pit, and from Sheol and Abaddon you have lifted me up to an everlasting height, so that I can walk on a boundless plain. And I know that there is hope for someone you fashioned out of clay for an everlasting community. The corrupt spirit you have purified from the great sin so that he can take his place with the host of the holy ones, and can enter into communion with the congregation of the sons of heaven.
>
> (trans. García Martínez 1994: 332)

The hymn goes on to dwell on the helplessness and unworthiness of the human condition. But the author has been rescued from this state. Life in the community already anticipates the heavenly assembly. Even though the floods of Belial still rage on earth, the author has found his place of refuge. He has been lifted up from Sheol to the "everlasting height," which is to say that he has already experienced the resurrection predicted for the wise in Daniel 12.

Again in 1QH 19: 10–14 (formerly 1QH 11: 10–14; a hymn of the community) the hymnist thanks God "because you have done wonders with dust, and have acted very mightily with a creature of clay." The hymn goes on to say that

> for your glory, you have purified man from sin so that he can make himself holy for you from every impure abomination and blameworthy iniquity, to become united with the sons of your truth and in a lot with your holy ones, to raise from the dust the worm of the dead to an [everlasting] community, and from a depraved spirit, to your knowledge, so that he can take his place in your presence with the perpetual host and the [everlasting] spirits, to renew him with everything that will exist, and with those who know in a community of jubilation.

In both of these passages, membership of the sectarian community admits the hymnist to the fellowship of the angels, which is the reward of the righteous dead in the apocalypses. While he is still surrounded by the trials of this world he can claim, in the words of the Gospel of John (5:24), to have already passed from death to life. Consequently the hymnist feels no need to speak of death and resurrection. The closest parallel to the scrolls in an ancient Jewish text, apart from the Gospel of John, is found in the Wisdom of Solomon. There we are told that "the souls of the righteous are in the hand of God and no torment will ever touch them. In the eyes of the foolish they seemed to have died . . . but they are at peace" (Wis 3:1). The Wisdom of Solomon was written in Greek in Alexandria, probably in the early first century CE, and the author was certainly familiar with the Greek concept of the immortality of the soul. The opening section of Wisdom, however (chapters 1–5, the Book of Eschatology) has notable parallels with the scrolls, and seems to be based on a Semitic source. The destiny of the righteous in Wis 5:5 is very close to the language of the Hodayot: "why have they been numbered among the children of God? and why is their lot among the saints?" Such phrases as "children of God" and "a lot among the saints, or holy ones" reflects Semitic idiom, not the language of Greek philosophy. The Wisdom of Solomon shows, however, how the apocalyptic notion of the elevation of the spirit to the angelic realm could be adapted in a Hellenistic context and assimilated to a belief in the immortality of the soul.

Some scholars, nonetheless, find in the Hodayot a belief in the resurrection of the body. The passage just cited from 1QH 19 is one of the main pieces of evidence for this view. God is said to "raise the worm of the dead from the dust." The same phrase (*twl't mtym*) occurs in 1QH 14:34 (= 6:34, a Teacher hymn): "Hoist a banner, you who lie in the dust; raise a standard, worm of dead ones." There is an allusion here to Isaiah 26:19, which refers to those who *dwell* in the dust. There is also an allusion to Isaiah 41:14: "do not fear, worm of Jacob, men of Israel." (The Hebrew for "men" here is *mty*, a rare word that occurs only in the construct plural in the Hebrew Bible, and which has the same consonants as the more familiar word for "dead ones.") In Isaiah 41, the addressees are in a lowly state, but they are not dead. Analogously, the phrase "worm of the dead" in the Hodayot may indicate metaphorically the abject state of unaided human nature. Just as the hymnist claims to be lifted up from Sheol or the netherworld, he claims that the dead are raised from the dust to become members of the community and so enter into fellowship with the holy ones. It is not necessary to suppose that the author has actual corpses in mind.

The interpretation of these passages is not only a matter of deciding whether the language is literal or metaphorical. It also involves the contexts in which the passages occur. The passage in 1QH 14 (=6) is preceded by a passage describing the eschatological battle and judgment:

> And then at the time of judgment the sword of God shall hasten, and all the sons of His truth shall awake to [overthrow] wickedness; all the sons of iniquity shall be no more. The Hero shall bend his bow; the fortress shall open on to endless space and the everlasting gates shall send out weapons of war. They shall be mighty from end to end [of the earth and there shall be no escape] for the guilty of heart [in their battle]; they shall be utterly trampled down without any [remnant, There shall be no] hope in the greatness [of their might], no refuge for the mighty warriors for [the battle shall be] to the Most High God. . . . Hoist a banner, you who lie in the dust; raise a standard, worm of dead ones.
>
> (1QH 14: 29–33 [= 6:29–33])

The call to those who lie in the dust, then, comes at the end of the eschatological battle, precisely where we should expect a reference to resurrection, by analogy with the apocalypses (Puech 1993: 361–3).

The point is not conclusive, however. Those who lie in the dust could be those who are downcast during the dominion of Belial, or who have been defeated in one of the phases of the eschatological battle. A reference to resurrection is possible here, but it is not certain. The possibility is more remote in 1QH 19 (= 11), where "the worm of the dead" is lifted up to commune with the children of truth. (The verb is *yhd*.) Even though this communion participates in the lot of the holy ones, it is most probably located in the *yahad* or community of the sect. Compare the passage cited above from 1QS 11: "He has joined their assembly to the Sons of Heaven to be a Council of the Community."

The Hodayot frequently refer to the final cosmic war (see especially 1QH 8 = 1QH 3). It is not unreasonable to expect that this war would culminate in the resurrection of the dead. Nonetheless there are no unambiguous references to resurrection in the Hodayot, and even possible references are very rare. (Puech 1993:413 finds another reference in 1QH 5:29 [= 13:12] which seems to indicate a new creation, but not a resurrection of the dead.) We have noted a similar lack of resurrection language in the sectarian rule books. This does not necessarily mean that there was no place for resurrection in the eschatology of the Dead Sea sect. But it does mean that the hopes of the sectarian community were not formulated in terms of resurrection. Rather, the focus was on sharing the angelic life within the community and thereby transcending death and continuing that life in heaven. In its Hebraic formulation, this idea is very different from the Greek immortality of the soul, but it is not difficult to see how it might have served as the basis for the account of Essene eschatology in Josephus. The primary sectarian texts, such as the rule books and the Hodayot, provide no clear evidence, however, in support of the claim of Hippolytus that the Essenes believed in bodily resurrection.

THE BURIALS AT QUMRAN

One other kind of evidence has been adduced in support of the belief in bodily resurrection at Qumran. This concerns the burials in the cemetery at the site. In all but a few cases, these are individual tombs, but their most distinctive characteristic is their orientation. In the great majority of the tombs, the orientation is south–north. (The head is to the south and the feet to the north). There are a few burials with a west–east orientation, and one tomb, on the periphery of the cemetery, that is east–west. The absence of family tombs argues in favor of a celibate life-style at Qumran, but there are some burials of women and children, which are problematic on that hypothesis. Celibacy, however, is not the issue that concerns us here, but the significance of the preponderant south–north orientation.

J. T. Milik proposed that the reason for this orientation was that Paradise was situated in the north. The Essenes were buried in this way so that they would rise facing north and march directly to Paradise (Milik 1958: 77; Puech 1993: 700–1). Milik found support for this view in the Book of the Watchers in 1 Enoch, where Paradise was supposedly located in the north. The evidence of Enoch on this question, however, is far from clear. The mountain where the abodes of the dead are located is clearly in the west (1 Enoch 22:1). In 1 Enoch 24–5, Enoch sees a mountain with the divine throne and the tree of life, but its location is not clearly indicated. In chapter 32, he sees seven mountains to the north, but he goes over the summits of these mountains "far away to the east" in order to come to the Garden of Righteousness, where the tree of wisdom is located. The eternal abode of the righteous, however, would seem to be in proximity to the tree of life, as described in chapters 24–5. In view of the mythical importance of Mount Zaphon, the mountain of the north in the Hebrew Bible (cf. Ps 48:3; Isa 14:13), a strong case can be made for locating that mountain in the north, but the case is inferential, and another inference is required to reach the conclusion that the geography of Enoch was normative at Qumran. Finally, even if the people at Qumran were buried facing Paradise, this does not necessarily imply a belief in bodily resurrection. The bodies might have been oriented towards the divine throne even if no resurrection were expected.

Milik's explanation of the orientation of the tombs at Qumran is ingenious, and not impossible, but it involves many inferences that are not required by the available evidence. The archaeological data are mute, and require a theory about the beliefs of the sect to explain them. They cannot themselves provide that theory, in the absence of written evidence.

RESURRECTION IN SCROLLS THAT ARE NOT CLEARLY SECTARIAN

Despite the lack of clear references to resurrection in the major sectarian texts, traditions about resurrection were certainly known at Qumran. The books of Enoch and Daniel were obviously well known and influential. In addition, references to resurrection have been identified in several texts that were not known before the discovery of the scrolls but which are not clearly of sectarian origin. In his exhaustive search for references to resurrection in the scrolls, Emile Puech has adduced several pseudo-prophetic texts as evidence for the currency of the belief. We shall review six of these texts here. Two of the passages in question do not appear to be addressing the question of resurrection at all; two clearly envisage reward and punishment after death but not necessarily resurrection; and finally two speak clearly of resurrection.

The texts in the first category are Pseudo-Daniel (4Q245) and the Words of the Heavenly Luminaries (4Q504). Neither of these texts gives any clear indication of sectarian origin (on 4Q504 see Chazon 1992). As noted in Chapter 2 above, 4Q245, which contains the putative reference to resurrection, most probably does not belong to the same document as the other Pseudo-Daniel fragments, 4Q243–4. The putative reference to resurrection hangs on a single word *yqwmwn*, "they will arise." While the context is clearly eschatological (line 2 of the fragment has the words "to put an end to wickedness") the verb "to arise" does not necessarily connote resurrection. The passage has been compared to Daniel 12 because it contrasts two groups ("these will wander in blindness . . . but these will arise"). The contrast with wandering here suggests that those who arise find the true way, and that the reference is to the emergence of an elect group, as in CD 1 or the Apocalypse of Weeks, and not to the resurrection of the dead. The following line has the word *ytwbwn*, they will return, which also suggests that the reference is to the rise of a group rather than to resurrection.

The Words of the Heavenly Luminaries (4QDibHam, 4Q504–6) is a prayer in the Deuteronomic tradition, similar to Daniel 9, devoid of sectarian characteristics. The manuscript is dated to the mid-second century BCE. The argument that it implies resurrection rests on a possible allusion to Daniel 12 in fragments 1–2, col. 6, lines 13–14: "free your people Isr[ael from all] the countries, both near and far . . . All that is written in the book of life." According to Daniel 12:1: "your people will be rescued, all that are found written in the book." In Daniel the reference is to resurrection, and Puech argues that a similar reference is entailed here by the mention of the book of life (Puech 1993:565). It is quite possible, however, that 4QDibHam is older than Daniel. The reference to the book of life can be understood as an allusion to Isaiah 4:3: "Whoever is left in Zion and remains in Jerusalem will be called holy, everyone who has been recorded for life in Jerusalem." In that case, those who are found written in the book may be those who are destined to share in the restoration of Israel, and there may be no reference to resurrection here at all.

The Testaments of Qahat and Amram clearly envisage reward and punishment beyond death, but do not clearly use the language of resurrection. These are Aramaic documents that are dated no later than the second century BCE on palaeographic grounds. We noted the Testament of Amram in Chapter 3, because of its developed dualism, which is similar to what we find in the Instruction on the Two Spirits. While it is often thought to be pre-Essene because of the palaeographic dating, the dualism is a distinctive characteristic of the Dead Sea sect, and the Testament must at least come from kindred circles. The passage that concerns us here is found in 4QAmram^f fragment 1 ii 1–16 (Puech 1993: 537–40):

> [The sons of light] will go to the light, to [everlasting] happiness, [to rejoicing;] and all the sons of dark[ness will go to the

shades, to death] and to annihilation. [. . .] There will be light for the people and they shall live.

(trans. García Martínez 1994: 275)

Puech reconstructs a reference to "the great judgment" instead of "rejoicing" ("the sons of light will go to the light . . . at the time of the great judgment") but the text is very fragmentary at this point. He also translates "they shall be resuscitated" instead of "they shall live." (The verb is *ḥyw*). The eschatology of this passage, however, seems to be very similar to that of the Instruction on the Two Spirits. It outlines the respective destinies of the sons of light and the sons of darkness. Since these destinies seem to follow naturally from their characters, we should expect them to be actualized on the death of the individuals. Puech's reading implies that the reward and punishment are deferred to the time of "the great judgment," and that a resurrection is entailed. While the text is very clear about eternal reward and punishment, however, the notion of resurrection is at best implicit.

The Testament of Qahat (1 ii 2–8) also clearly envisages reward and punishment after death. The wicked are punished "in fire and in the abysses." The descendants of Qahat are told that "you will rise to execute judgment" (*tqwmwn lmdn dyn*) and see the punishment of sinners. Whether this is a reference to resurrection is by no means "sans doute" (Puech 1993: 541). Since they are to take an active role in judgment, it is more likely that the passage means that they will rise up to execute judgment on their enemies. (Compare 1 Enoch 91:12 where a sword is given to the elect to execute judgment, *lm'bd dyn*.) Neither Testament Amram nor Testament Qahat necessarily counts as direct evidence for the eschatology of the Dead Sea sect, but in fact they seem to be quite compatible with what we have found in the sectarian documents.

The clear instances of resurrection are found in 4Q521 (the "Messianic Apocalypse") and 4Q385 (Pseudo-Ezekiel). The account of resurrection in Second Ezekiel might be considered debatable, since it is a paraphrase of Ezekiel 37, where the resurrection of the dry bones serves as a metaphor for the restoration of the people of Israel. It is likely, however, that the Qumran text has individual resurrection in view. 4Q385 fragment 2 reads as follows:

[and they will know that I am Yahweh] who redeem my people, giving unto them the covenant. [And I said: Yahweh,] I have seen many men from Israel who have loved thy Name and have walked in the ways of [righteousness, and th]ese things, when will they be, and how will they be recompensed for their loyalty? And Yahweh said to me: I will cause the children of Israel to see, and they shall know that I am Yahweh. [And He said:] Son of Man, prophesy over the bones and say: be ye joined bone to its bone and joint [to its joint. And it wa]s so. And He said a second time: Prophesy and let sinews come upon them and let them be covered with skin [above. And it wa]s s[o]. And He said again: Prophesy concerning the four winds of heaven and let the win[ds of heaven] blow [upon them and they shall revive] and a great crowd of people shall stand up, and they shall bless Yahweh Sabaoth who [has given them life again. And] I said: O Yahweh when shall these things be? And Yahweh said to m[e . . .] and a tree shall bend and shall stand erect.

In this passage, Ezekiel's vision is given in response to his query about the recompense of "many men from Israel." The logic of the question requires that they receive their own recompense, and not only that they be assured of the future restoration of Israel. Moreover, the image of the tree recalls Job 14:7–10, "there is hope for a tree, if it is cut down, that it will sprout again . . . but mortals die and are laid low." While Job contrasts the fate of human beings with that of a tree, the Qumran text may be drawing a more positive analogy. As a tree can bend and become erect again, human beings who have been laid low may be lifted up. The text does not appear to envisage a general resurrection, but only a restoration of the righteous dead of the people of Israel.

Here again, the relation of this text to the Dead Sea sect is debatable. The situation is summed up as follows by Strugnell and Dimant (1988: 58):

both the content and form of the work contain elements very close to the sectarian writings as well as elements very different from them. In fact, we do not find, in the present work, characteristic sectarian terms such as *Yahad*, nor matters related to the community. Nor do we find anything relating to the dualistic system of Light and Darkness which is a typical feature of the sectarian writings such as the *Rule of the Community* and the *Rule of the War*. But in matters relating to the People of Israel and its history we find certain terms and ideas, and a general character of thought similar to that in works such as the

Damascus Covenant. Indeed, the relation of the present work to some sectarian writings closely resembles that of other pre- or non-Qumranic works such as *Jubilees* or the *Animal Apocalypse* in *1 Enoch* 85–90.

The use of the divine name also argues against authorship within the Dead Sea sect.

We have already considered 4Q521 in Chapter 5 and suggested that the messiah whom heaven and earth obey should be identified as the eschatological prophet, either Elijah or a prophet like Elijah. This figure should then be understood as the agent through whom God will do "the glorious things that have not (yet) taken place." These works correspond to the acts of mercy mentioned in Psalm 146:7–8 and Isaiah 61:1, with the notable addition of the raising of the dead. Elijah was well known for raising the dead in his historical career, and he was associated with the eschatological resurrection in the text of Ben Sira 48:11 from the Cairo Geniza. (In view of Ben Sira's usual rejection of resurrection, it is unlikely that this passage was part of his original composition.) There is another mention of resurrection in fragment 7 of 4Q521, which refers to God as "the one who gives life to the dead of his people." Here then we have unambiguous evidence of a belief in resurrection, which involves the public restoration of the dead as distinct from the elevation of the spirit to the angelic realm at the point of death.

It is not clear, however, whether this "messianic apocalypse" is a product of the Qumran sect. Puech has noted terminological correspondences with sectarian writings, especially with reference to the spirit (*rûaḥ*) and the poor (*'anāwîm*). Especially noteworthy is the fact that, unlike Pseudo-Ezekiel, this text avoids the divine name and uses instead the substitute *adonay*, the Lord. Nonetheless, there is no reference in this text to the sectarian community, and the content on the whole is rather atypical of the sectarian scrolls. Elijah appears only very rarely in the scrolls, and the eschatological prophet, while clearly attested in 1QS 9, is not prominent. Consequently, the provenance of this text must be left open. It would be unwise to treat it as the key to the eschatology of the sect in the matter of resurrection.

CONCLUSION

As noted at the outset, the early apocalypses of Enoch and Daniel introduced into Jewish tradition not only the notion of resurrection but the idea of reward and punishment beyond death. The latter idea is quite fundamental in the sectarian literature. There can be no doubt that the sect was influenced directly by the apocalypses in this respect. The sectarian writers did not, however, follow the apocalypses slavishly, but developed their understanding in an original way. Some texts found at Qumran provide new scriptural models for an understanding of eschatological resurrection. 4Q521 uses the model of Elijah; 4Q385 that of Ezekiel. Whether these texts were composed within the Dead Sea sect, however, is uncertain. The more distinctive sectarian idea does not entail resurrection, although it places great emphasis on eternal life. In the major sectarian rule books, eternal reward and punishment seems to follow directly on the life of the individual. Hence the need for a general resurrection seems to be obviated. It is possible that the sect still believed in a general, eschatological resurrection. Such an idea was familiar from the apocalypses and is nowhere denied. But the lack of clear references to resurrection in the major sectarian writings makes this belief purely hypothetical. The "messianic apocalypse" of 4Q521 seems to reflect at most a minority belief in the sect. Hippolytus was most probably assimilating the Essenes to Christian (and much Jewish) belief when he claimed that they expected the resurrection of the flesh.

The idea of eternal life that we find in the scrolls is quite different from the Greek immortality of the soul, although the two notions were confused by Josephus (or his source). That which lives on is the spirit or *nepeš*, which is either raised up to fellowship with the angels or sent down to torture in the Pit, or netherworld. This idea of eternal life was rooted in the cultic experience of the sect, whose members believed that they were already sharing the life of the angels in their community. This experience was proleptic, to be sure. They were not yet free from the attacks of Belial and the distractions of earthly life. But it was nonetheless a transcendent experience, where the member of the community could rise above his human limitations, and where death ceased to be regarded as a problem. Those who had no safe home on earth found a refuge with the angels in heaven. The understanding of this heavenly world is the subject to which we turn in Chapter 8.

8

THE HEAVENLY WORLD

One of the features of apocalyptic literature that distinguishes it from earlier biblical tradition is its increased attention to the heavenly world. In Enoch and Daniel, angels are given names for the first time, and their number and functions multiply. Enoch initiates a tradition of otherworldly journeys, whereby the visionary is guided through the heavens or the netherworld by an angel. The hope of the righteous is to be elevated to join the angelic host after death. To a great degree, the apocalypses shift the attention of the reader to the heavenly world, either to seek an explanation of what is happening on earth or to take refuge in an alternative reality freed from worldly problems.

THE APOCALYPTIC TRADITION

The increased prominence in the heavenly world can be seen by contrasting the throne vision of Isaiah chapter 6 with the visions of Enoch and Daniel half a millennium later. Isaiah saw the Lord "sitting on a throne, high and lofty . . . Seraphs were in attendance above him; each had six wings: with two they covered their faces, and with two they covered their feet, and with two they flew." The divine figure seated on the throne receives a more elaborate treatment in Ezekiel 1, but there is no elaboration of the angelic attendants. In Daniel 7, however, "a thousand thousands served him, and ten thousand times ten thousand stood attending him." Enoch also tells us that "ten thousand times ten thousand" stood before the enthroned deity, and the holy ones who were near to him did not leave by night or day and did not depart from him" (1 Enoch 14:

22–3), but adds enigmatically that "no angel could enter, and at the appearance of the face of him who is honored and praised no creature of flesh could look" (14:21). Implicit here is a distinction between the heavenly beings that are called angels and the holy ones, who evidently hold a higher rank. In the Similitudes of Enoch, from the first century CE, we find a more differentiated hierarchy of angels in the heavenly temple:

> And round about were the seraphim, and the cherubim and the ophannim; these are they who do not sleep, but keep watch over the throne of His glory. And I saw angels who could not be counted, a thousand thousands and ten thousand times ten thousand, surrounding that house; and Michael and Raphael and Gabriel and Phanuel, and the holy angels who are in the heavens above, went in and out of that house.
>
> (1 Enoch 71:7–9)

The angels fill several roles in this literature. (For a thorough inventory, see Mach 1992.) The visionary typically encounters an angel as interpreter of his visions and mediator of heavenly secrets. In the Enoch literature, they also serve as tour guides. Angels are the attendants around the heavenly throne. In the oldest biblical throne vision in 1 Kings 22, the angels are heavenly courtiers, on the analogy of the royal court on earth. Isaiah's vision in contrast is located in the temple, and the seraphim are engaged in praising the holiness of God. The "thousand times ten thousand" who serve the Lord in Daniel 7 and 1 Enoch 14 may be taken as courtiers or as participants in a heavenly liturgy, or both. Angels are also involved in the affairs of this world. The Astronomical Book of Enoch identifies angels as leaders of the stars (1 Enoch 72; Uriel is the leader of all the heavenly luminaries). In Daniel, Michael is the Prince of Israel, who does battle with the heavenly princes of other peoples. In the Animal Apocalypse of 1 Enoch, a recording angel keeps account of the sins of the Gentiles, and the same angel helps the "ram," Judas Maccabee in his fight against them (1 Enoch 90:14). In the Book of the Watchers, the fallen angels lead humanity astray, but the archangels bring the complaint of humanity to the Lord and then execute the divine judgment on the Watchers. The intercessory role of the angels is also clear in 1 Enoch 15:2–3 where Enoch is told to tell the Watchers: "You ought to petition on behalf of men, not men on behalf of you." (The angelology of the Enoch literature is reviewed by Davidson 1992.)

131

In the Enoch literature, interest in the heavenly world also takes the form of otherworldly geography, as Enoch is shown not only the heavenly throne room but also Paradise, the abodes of the dead and the places of judgment. This interest is not paralleled in Daniel, or indeed in the Enochic apocalypses of the historical type (the Animal Apocalypse, the Apocalypse of Weeks). It has an illustrious history, however, in later Jewish apocalypses such as 2 Enoch and 3 Baruch, and in Christian apocalypses down to the Middle Ages (see Himmelfarb 1993).

Various reasons have been proposed for the upsurge of interest in the heavenly world in the apocalypses, and more generally in the Hellenistic period. According to *Berēšit Rabbāh* 48:9 (on Gen 18:1), R. Resh Laqish taught that the names of the angels had been brought back from Babylon (Bietenhard 1951:12). In modern times, Babylonian influence was posited by W. Bousset (Bousset and Gressmann 1926: 326, 499–500). Persian influence has been widely assumed especially in the literature from the late nineteenth and early twentieth centuries. It is, in fact, likely that Jewish interest in angels was stimulated by the prominence of intermediary beings in Zoroastrianism, and at least one Jewish demon, Azmodeus in the Book of Tobit, has a Persian name. The great majority of angelic names, however, are Hebrew or at least West Semitic. (Note the frequency with which they include the theophoric element *-el*: Michael, Gabriel, Raphael, Uriel, etc.) Many of the names of the Watchers in 1 Enoch 6 refer to celestial elements: Kokabiel (star of God), Baraqiel (lightning of God), Ananel (cloud of God), etc. Angelic names in later Judaism are mostly derived exegetically from the Hebrew Bible (Olyan 1993). So, for example, five names for angelic brigades in rabbinic and mystical texts are derived from Ezekiel 1 and 10: ophannim (wheels), galgallim (wheels), *Ma'asim* (creatures or structures), hashmallim (those of electrum), and the tarshishim (those of chrysolite). In light of this evidence, the development of angelology cannot be explained simply as a foreign borrowing.

Another proposed explanation for the increased interest in angels suggests that God was felt to be remote in Second Temple Judaism, and that accordingly there was a need for intermediary beings (see especially Bousset and Gressmann 1926: 319–21, 329–31; for further bibliography see Olyan 1993: 6). This theory has been widely criticized as implying a negative view of Judaism, but this is not necessarily the case. Intermediary beings are prominent throughout the

Hellenistic world, and on into Late Antiquity, and this phenomenon may well be related to the political changes that transformed the eastern Mediterranean world, beginning with the Persians. Already in the Hebrew Bible, the heavenly court was imagined by analogy with the court of the local king. (The vision of Micaiah ben Imlah in 1 Kings 22 provides a particularly clear example.) When the Great King was far away in Persia, or Antioch, or later in Rome, the religious imagination may have supposed that the Most High God was equally remote, and that one must approach Him through a complex system of intermediaries, just as one must in the case of the Great King. This should not be understood to imply an inferior spirituality. The Jews of the Hellenistic age were not less devout than their ancestors. In fact, the increased interest in intermediaries seems to have gone hand in hand with the rise of mysticism. But it does imply a new view of the world, that was grounded in a different political reality. The sources of power were more remote from the people of Judea through much of the Second Temple period than they had been in the pre-exilic era.

Another set of considerations is distinctively Jewish. Heaven, or the highest heaven, is the abode of God, and can therefore be understood as a heavenly temple. Martha Himmelfarb has argued that Enoch's ascent in 1 Enoch 14 assumes that the heavenly temple is structurally similar to earthly temples (Himmelfarb 1993: 14–15). The typical temple structure in the ancient Near East, exemplified both in Solomon's temple and in its post-exilic replacement, had three chambers, the *'ûlam*, or vestibule, the *hēkāl*, or nave, and the *dᵉbîr*, or inner sanctum. According to the Ethiopic text, Enoch passes through two houses to reach the throne of God (14:10–14, 15–17). These may be compared to the *hēkāl* and *dᵉbîr*. Before these the Ethiopic has a wall built of fire and hail. In the Greek text, this is another building, and Himmelfarb argues that it corresponds to the *'ûlam*. Be that as it may, there is at least a good measure of similarity between the heavenly abode of God and the earthly temple.

There is also some similarity between the Watchers and holy ones who attend the divine throne and the earthly priesthood. It has been suggested, with plausibility, that the account of the Watchers could serve as an allegorical criticism of the priesthood (Suter 1979). The Watchers are told that they should intercede for humanity, a priestly duty, but instead have left the high and holy heaven and become unclean with the daughters of men (1 Enoch 15:3). Accusations of fornication and improper marriage are made against priests in the Testament of Levi 14–16, but admittedly they are also made against other people in this period (cf. CD 4:12–19; Pss Sol 2:11–13; 8:9–13). It is not necessary to suppose that Enoch is also a priest in the Book of the Watchers. He is identified only as a scribe, and he is told that the Watchers should intercede for men, not men for them. If the Watchers in this passage represent the priesthood, it would seem that the apocalypse exalts the (lay) scribe over the priest, and can well be understood as a critique of the Jerusalem priesthood of the day (probably in the late third or early second century BCE). In the Book of Jubilees, Enoch takes on a more priestly character, when it is said that "he burned the incense of the sanctuary" (Jub 4:25). It is possible that he was taken to represent a strand of the priesthood that was at odds with the current Jerusalem cult (Himmelfarb 1993: 23–5).

This is not to suggest that the Book of the Watchers is opposed to temple worship as such. Criticism of the Jerusalem cult is widespread in the Second Temple period, from the prophet Malachi to the Dead Sea scrolls. But the cult in the heavenly temple remains intact. Just as dissatisfaction with the Jerusalem Temple gave rise to utopian visions of a new Jerusalem in the Temple Scroll and the New Jerusalem text, it also gave rise to depictions of a heavenly liturgy by the angels and holy ones. The heavenly liturgy does not necessarily imply a critique of its earthly counterpart. The two are often understood as complementary in both Judaism and Christianity. (For example the Roman Catholic Mass calls on the faithful to join "with angels and archangels" in reciting the chant of the Seraphim from Isaiah 6, "holy, holy, holy".) Nonetheless, the widespread dissatisfaction with the Jerusalem cult in prophetic and apocalyptic circles in the Second Temple period most probably contributed to the increase of interest in the heavenly world (cf. Gruenwald 1988: 125–44).

THE QUESTION OF MYSTICISM

The prominence of the heavenly world in the scrolls invites comparison not only with the preceding apocalyptic traditions but also with later Jewish mysticism, which is sometimes called hekalot mysticism, because of its interest in the heavenly "temples," or *hekalot*, or merkavah mysticism because of the importance attached to the vision of the *merkavah* or "throne-chariot" of God. (On the continuity between apocalypticism and merkavah mysticism see Gruenwald 1980, 1988). The study of Jewish mysticism in modern times has been shaped to a great degree by the work of Gershom Scholem. In Scholem's view, early Jewish mystics of Talmudic times focused on "the ascent of the soul to the Celestial throne where it obtains an ecstatic view of the majesty of God and the secrets of His Realm" (Scholem 1961:5). The centrality of the ascent in hekalot mysticism has been a matter of controversy in recent years (Schäfer 1986, 1992), but there can be no doubt that it is an important motif in the mystical tradition (Elior 1993: 15–16; see also the criticism of Schäfer by Gruenwald 1988: 175–89). Scholem emphasized that Jewish mystics did not aspire to the mystical union that is characteristic of mysticism in other traditions: "The mystic who in his ecstasy has passed through all the gates, braved all the dangers, now stands before the throne; he sees and hears – but that is all" (Scholem 1961:194). Elliot Wolfson, however, has argued that the major hekalot texts envisage a higher goal: "a critical part of the ascent experience is the enthronement of the *yored merkavah* [literally, the one who goes down to the chariot, or divine chariot-throne], either on the chariot itself or on a throne alongside the throne of glory . . . the heavenly ascent culminates in the enthronement of the mystic that transforms him into an angelic being" (Wolfson 1994: 193; cf. Wolfson 1993: 13–44; Smith 1990). In Wolfson's view, "the narrative description of the glory, throne, attendant angels, and the rest of the celestial realm is not in and of itself sufficient to be classified as mystical" (Wolfson 1994: 194). Such descriptions of the heavenly world are, nonetheless, commonly called mystical in current scholarship. We need not insist on the definitional issue here. Wolfson has, however, drawn attention to an important distinction: between texts that contain descriptions of the heavenly world and its inhabitants, and texts that describe the heavenly enthronement or transformation of the visionary.

THE HEAVENLY WORLD IN THE SCROLLS

When we turn to the Dead Sea scrolls we find that angels are no less prominent than they were in the apocalypses. We have already discussed the role of the Angels of Light and Darkness in shaping the destiny of humankind, and the importance of Michael and the heavenly host in the War Rule. The dualism that is typical of the sectarian scrolls is realized on both the angelic and the human levels.

One of the major functions of angels in the apocalypses, however, is absent in the sectarian scrolls. There is no role for interpreting angels or for angelic tour guides. This is a by-product of the fact that there are no examples of the literary form of an apocalypse in the clearly sectarian scrolls. There are several fragmentary texts from Cave 4 that may be apocalypses, but where the crucial opening section has not been preserved, and so we do not know how the revelation was received (4Q521, the "Messianic Apocalypse"; 4Q246, the "Son of God text"; 4Q243–4, "Pseudo-Daniel"). We also have several texts that contain visionary material (e.g. the new Jerusalem text; 4Q552–3, the Four Kingdoms text). In the major sectarian texts, however, we find a different mode of revelation. When the author of 1QS 11:5–6 claims "my eyes have gazed on that which is eternal, on wisdom concealed from men," he does not proceed to describe what he saw. The revelation takes the form of illumination, rather than the kind of pictorial imagery that we find in Enoch and Daniel: "For my light has sprung from the source of His knowledge; my eyes have beheld His marvellous deeds, and the light of my heart, the mystery that is made to be" (1QS 11:3). Similar claims of illumination are found repeatedly in the Hodayot (e.g. 1QH 17:26, formerly 9:26: "my light shall shine forth in Thy glory, for as a light from out of the darkness so wilt Thou enlighten me"). We find, however, neither visions of the type represented by Daniel 7 nor otherworldly tours of the type represented by the Book of the Watchers.

The scrolls include a number of compositions that bear some resemblance to later traditions about Jewish mysticism. These texts are hymnic in character, rather than accounts of visions or ascents. The text that has given rise to the most extensive discussion in this regard is the fragmentary composition known as The Songs of Sabbath Sacrifice (*Shirot Olat Ha-Shabbat*), pieces of which are preserved in eight manuscripts from Cave 4 (4Q400–7), one from Cave 11 and one that was found at Masada.

THE SONGS OF SABBATH SACRIFICE

The Songs consist of separate compositions for each of thirteen sabbaths. The editor (Newsom 1985) contended that these were designed for the first quarter of the year, but it is more likely that the quarter was regarded as a cultic-calendaric unit, and that the Songs were intended for the sabbaths of each quarter in turn (Maier

1992: 544). Each song begins with the formulaic heading *l^emaśkîl* followed by the number and date of a sabbath (e.g. "the first sabbath on the fourth of the first month"). The Songs proceed to call on the angels to give praise. There are also descriptive statements about the praise-giving of the heavenly beings. The Songs do not, however, give the actual words of the angels or cite any angelic hymns of praise.

The first five songs are concerned with the establishment and responsibilities of the angelic priesthood. 4Q400 fragment 1 says that God "has established for himself priests of the inner sanctum, the holiest of the holy ones." They are also "ministers of the Presence in His glorious *debir*." (The debir was the inner sanctuary of the temple.) These holy ones, who are also called "gods" (*'ēlîm*) and "angels," are associated with knowledge and teaching about holiness. They propitiate God for all who repent of sin. There is some description of the eschatological battle. 4Q402 fragment 4 line10 refers to "the heavenly beings in the war of heaven."

The sixth to eighth songs are dominated by repetitious literary structures in which the number seven appears prominently. The sixth and eighth songs detail the praises of the seven chief angels and their deputies. The seventh song, the mid-point of the cycle, calls not only on the angels but also on various parts of the heavenly temple to praise God. The ninth to thirteenth songs appear to contain a systematic description of the heavenly temple that is based in part on Ezekiel 40–8. (There are several references to the portals through which various beings go in and out.) The twelfth song opens with a lengthy description of the divine throne-chariot:

> The image of the throne-chariot do they bless (which is) above the firmament of the cherubim. [And the splendo]r of the luminous firmament do they sing (which is) beneath His glorious seat. And when the wheels move, the holy angels return. They go out from between its glorious [h]ubs. Like the appearance of fire (are) the most holy spirits round about, the appearance of streams of fire like hashmal. And there is a radiant substance with glorious colors, wondrously hued, purely blended, the spirits of living godlike beings which move continuously with the glory of the wondrous chariot(s).
>
> (4Q405 fragments 20–21–22; trans. Newsom 1985: 306)

One respect in which this passage differs from Ezekiel chapters 1 and 10 is that it introduces a role for the holy angels, the spirits of living godlike beings.

It is noteworthy that this account of the throne-chariot, or *merkavah*, does not occur in the thirteenth song, but in the penultimate twelfth. The final song refers to "the sacrifices of the holy ones," "the odor of their offerings," and "the o[do]r of their drink offerings" (11QShirShabb 8–7). It concludes by describing the splendor of the angelic high priests. (For a full account of the contents see Newsom 1990a: 101–13).

Part of this text, including the description of the *merkavah*, was published in 1960 by John Strugnell, who noted its importance as a witness to the early exegesis of Ezekiel 1. (Another paraphrase of Ezekiel's vision can be found in 4QPseudo-Ezekiel, = 4Q385 4; see Dimant and Strugnell, 1990). Scholem noted its relevance to the history of Jewish mysticism: "These fragments leave no doubt that there is a connection between the oldest Hebrew Merkabah texts preserved in Qumran and the subsequent development of the Merkabah mysticism as preserved in the Hekhaloth texts. The solemn and pompous language of the new fragments has already many ingredients of the particular style of the Hekhaloth hymns" (Scholem 1965: 128; cf. Schiffman 1982). The style to which Scholem referred is especially in evidence in songs 9 to 13, which have few finite verbs and are dominated by nominal and participial sentences, with elaborate construct chains. This style has been explained as an attempt to create an ecstatic or numinous style appropriate to the heavenly temple (Newsom 1990a: 103).

Also reminiscent of the later hekalot literature is the variety of names for the angels (gods, spirits, holy ones, princes, etc.). It is not apparent that the different names can be consistently identified with different classes of angels, but there is evidence of hierarchical ordering. There are seven angelic priesthoods in seven heavenly sanctuaries. These are presided over by seven chief princes, who are almost certainly to be identified as seven archangels, although their personal names are not given. Each of these also has a deputy prince. (See further Newsom 1985: 23–38.) The usual number of archangels in Jewish texts of this period is four. In 1QM 9:14–16, these are identified as Michael, Gabriel, Sariel, and Raphael. Usually Uriel or Phanuel is found instead of Sariel (1 Enoch 9:1; 40:9; 54:6; 71:8 and in several rabbinic texts; see Yadin 1962: 238. The Ethiopic manuscripts of 1 Enoch 9:1 read Suriel). The Greek text of 1 Enoch

20, however, lists seven: Uriel, Raphael, Raguel, Michael, Sariel, Gabriel, and Remiel, and so the seven chief angels of the Songs are not without parallel, although they are unusual.

The extant text of the Songs does not preserve the full name of any individual angel, or clearly indicate any single superior angel as the leader of the host. There are however two fragmentary passages that are most plausibly restored to yield the name Melchizedek (Newsom 1985: 37). 4Q401 11:3 reads "[Melchi]sedek, priest in the assemb[ly of God]" and 4Q401 22:3 has "[Mel]chisedek" in a line that follows a reference to the ordination of angelic priests. Other fragments of the same manuscript also refer to a single angelic figure, who is sometimes called "prince" or "chief." Melchizedek is well known from 11QMelchizedek, in which he is identified as the *'elōhîm* (god, divine being) who stands in the Council of El in Psalm 82:1. In that text he is depicted primarily as a heavenly warrior, who "will exact the vengeance of El's judgments." He is not said to be a priest, although we are told that expiation will be made for all the people of his lot on the Day of Atonement at the end of the tenth jubilee. Melchizedek was associated with priesthood in Psalm 110 ("you are a priest forever after the order of Melchizedek") and again in the New Testament in the Epistle to the Hebrews, chapters 5–7. If the restoration of his name in the Songs of Sabbath Sacrifice is correct, he was recognized there primarily as a heavenly priest. Psalm 110 also speaks of enthronement: "The Lord said to my Lord, sit at my right hand." In Hebrews, the enthronement is specifically said to be heavenly, and the one enthroned is the heavenly high priest: "we have such a high priest, one who is seated at the right hand of the throne of the majesty in the heavens, a minister in the sanctuary and the true tent that the Lord, and not any mortal, has set up" (Heb 8:1–2). The extant text of the Sabbath Songs does not refer to the enthronement of Melchizedek. In view of his role as an *'elōhîm* in 11QMelchizedek, however, Melchizedek seems to be God's principal angel or heavenly angel. He is almost certainly identified with Michael and the Angel of Light in 4QAmram (see Chapter 3 above). This role of principal angel is later filled by the Son of Man in the Similitudes of Enoch and in its most elaborate form by Metratron, the "little Yahweh," in 3 Enoch, both of whom are enthroned in heaven. (On Michael and Metatron as heavenly priests see Bietenhard 1951: 150).

The seven heavenly sanctuaries do not seem to correspond to the seven heavens of later apocalypses, despite the coincidence of number. The text gives no indication of their spatial relationship. It is reasonable to suppose that the speculation on seven heavenly sanctuaries and seven archangels was a factor that contributed to the motif of seven heavens, but that motif only becomes common in apocalypses of the Christian era (see Yarbro Collins 1995).

THE FUNCTION OF THE SABBATH SONGS

Various suggestions have been put forward as to the function of the Songs of Sabbath Sacrifice. On one view, it is a speculative exercise about the cult performed in heaven, and it is based on biblical exegesis rather than on mystical experience (Schiffman 1982: 18–19). On another, the text constructs a heavenly cult as a replacement for the invalid cult of the Jerusalem Temple (Maier 1992: 553). On this view, the text expresses traditional priestly theology, which acquires its distinctive character only because of the circumstances of the Qumran community (Maier 1964: 133). On yet another view, the text is

> a quasi-mystical liturgy designed to evoke a sense of being present in the heavenly temple. . . . Although no claim is made that the audience which recited or heard the Songs were actually transported to the heavenly realms, the hypnotic quality of the language and the vividness of the description of the celestial temple cause even the modern reader of these fragments to feel the power of the language to create a sense of the presence of the heavenly temple
>
> (Newsom 1985: 59, 72).

While each of these proposals is independent of the others, they are not mutually exclusive. The exegetical element in the text is undeniable, but exegesis is not incompatible with mystical experience. The interpretation of older Scriptures can provide the furnishings for a visionary's imagination. Again, a replacement cult would be all the more effective if it were experienced imaginatively. There is no evidence that such an elaborate construction of the heavenly liturgy was part of traditional priestly theology, before the rise of the Qumran sect. In favor of the quasi-mystical interpretation is the one statement in the Songs that reflects on the human condition: "how shall we be considered [among] them? And how shall our priesthood (be considered) in their habitations? And our ho[liness – how can it compare with] their [surpassing] holiness? [What] is the offering of our mortal tongue (compared) with the knowledge of the el[im? . . .]" (4Q400 2:5–7; Newson 1990a: 105). While this passage shows a clear distinction between human and heavenly worshipers, it reflects the aspiration of the human community to be considered with that of the angels. Similarly, the statements in the Hodayot about fellowship with the angels regularly include a confession of unworthiness, and thanksgiving for being lifted up from the Pit and cleansed from great sin.

The Songs of Sabbath Sacrifice are not in the form of an apocalypse, although the heavenly world that they describe is typical of apocalyptic revelations. Yet the experience of reading this text is similar to that of reading an apocalypse of the "heavenly journey" type. The reader is led in imagination through the various heavenly sanctuaries, even to the contemplation of the throne-chariot of God. It is true that the focus of the work is ultimately on the angels rather than on the divinity, and that there is no account of the exaltation, enthronement or transformation of a visionary. The text remains at most quasi-mystical, at least on Wolfson's definition. Yet those who see the Songs as a forerunner of merkavah mysticism are on the right track, as they seem to be written to enable the reader to experience in imagination the angelic liturgy in the heavenly world.

Most commentators have assumed that the Songs are a product of the Qumran community. The editor, Newsom, however, has expressed second thoughts on the matter (Newsom 1990b: 179–85). The Songs are non-polemical and are not concerned with defining one group over against another. There is no reference to institutional offices or structures, unless the *maśkîl* of the superscription be deemed a sectarian official. The presence of a copy of the text at Masada has also raised doubts about its sectarian provenance. Moreover, while the Songs agree with the major sectarian scrolls in avoiding the tetragrammaton, they differ from Qumran usage in their frequent use of the word *'elōhîm*.

On the other hand, the Songs have numerous parallels to other sectarian scrolls. 4Q402 4:12, "from the God of knowledge everything was made to be" is almost identical to the language of the Instruction on the Two Spirits. The Songs are especially closely related to 4QBerakot (4Q286–90). This text consists of a series of liturgical-ceremonial blessings and curses, whose liturgical function is shown by rubrics such as the concluding response, Amen, Amen. (Nitzan 1994b). Milik (1972b: 54) suggested that it is another edition of the covenant renewal ceremony found in 1QS, but the relationship between the two texts does not extend to the details. There is no doubt that 4QBerakot is a sectarian text; it refers explicitly to "the council of the community" (4Q286 10 ii 1). The points of similarity concern the description of the heavenly temple, the *merkavah* and the angelic attendants. (4Q286 1 ii begins: "the residence of your honour, and the footstool of the feet of your glory in the heights of your position, and the step of your holiness, and the chariots of your glory with their multitudes and their wheels and all their secrets, foundations of fire, flames of your lamp and brilliance of honor.") Further close parallels are found in the Songs of the *Maśkil* (4Q510–11), which praise the majesty of God "in order to frighten and terrify all the spirits of the ravaging angels and the bastard spirits" (4Q510 1; 4Q511 10). The dualistic and predestinarian language of these songs is similar to such compositions as the Instruction on the Two Spirits and the War Rule. (4Q510 1:6–7 refers to "the era of the rule of wickedness and the periods of humiliation of the sons of light.") There are also extensive parallels in language with the Hodayot. The two sets of songs share the superscription *l'maśkil*, certain terminology for praise, and even the divine epithet *'elohim*, which is rare in the sectarian scrolls. The Songs of the *Maśkil* speak of God setting aside for himself angelic priests, in language that is very similar to that of the Songs of Sabbath Sacrifice: "Among the holy ones, God makes (some) holy for himself like an everlasting sanctuary, and there will be purity amongst those purified. And they shall be priests, his holy people, his army and his servants, the angels of his glory" (4Q511 35; trans. García Martínez).

Discussions of sectarian or non-sectarian provenance have generally labored under the mistaken assumption that the Dead Sea (or Essene) sect was identical with the Qumran community or *yahad*, with the consequent expectation that sectarian texts should allude to the instutional structure known from 1QS. It is clear, however, both from CD and from Josephus' account of the Essenes, that there were many sectarian settlements, and that the sect was not hermetically closed in the manner that has often been assumed. The presence of an Essene text at Masada shows at most that some Essenes joined the resistance movement, whether in desperation or through eschatological conviction. It does not require that the whole sect joined, and it does not prove that the text in question is not sectarian. The common language shared by the Songs of the Maśkil and the Hodayot strongly suggests that the hymnic texts we are considering in this chapter come from a common milieu. The Songs of Sabbath Sacrifice were preserved at Qumran in nine copies, and the text apparently influenced other sectarian compositions such as 4QBerakot. If the Songs were not a sectarian composition, they must at least have come from circles that were highly congenial to the sect. While the 364-day calendar implied in the Songs was not unique to the Dead Sea sect, it limits considerably the circles from which it could have come. (The Book of Jubilees may be an analogous case, of a book that is not strictly a product of the sect but is nonetheless closely related.)

Newsom's original view, that a sectarian provenance is the most economical hypothesis to explain the origin of the Songs, has much to commend it. Nothing in the Songs is incompatible with such a provenance. (The unusual use of the word *'elōhîm* cannot be considered decisive.) The Dead Sea sect provides an exceptionally illuminating setting for a composition of this kind. The imaginative construction of an elaborate heavenly cult is most readily intelligible on the part of a community that had rejected the earthly cult in Jerusalem. Moreover, the interest in the angels, and the aspiration to be reckoned among them in worship, reflects the same spiritual universe that we find in the Hodayot. If the Songs are viewed in the context of the sectarian literature that we have reviewed in the preceding chapters, they are seen to express more than an alternative to the defiled cult of Jerusalem. They also depict the world in which the sectarians hoped to share after death, in accordance with apocalyptic tradition. They even made possible the imaginative participation in that world before death, by their vivid representation of the angelic liturgy and the divine throne.

A THRONE IN HEAVEN (4Q491)

The Songs of Sabbath Sacrifice never speak of the enthronement of a human being in heaven. Such an eventuality seems to be implied, however, in an enigmatic fragment found in 4Q491, fragment 11. This text is in very fragmentary condition, but some striking phrases are quite clearly preserved: "a throne of strength in the congregation of the gods . . . besides me no one is exalted . . . for I reside (or: have taken a seat, *yāšabtî*) [. . .] in the heavens . . . I am counted among the gods and my dwelling is in the holy congregation . . . for I am counted among the gods and my glory is with the sons of the king." In view of the repeated claims of exaltation and the use of the verb *yāšabtî*, it seems reasonable to infer that the author claims to occupy the "throne of strength in the congregation of the gods," and so to be enthroned in heaven.

This fragment was published as part of the War Rule by Baillet (1982:26), who placed it immediately before the account of battle in 1QM 16–17. This identification no longer seems plausible, however. By far the closest parallels are found in the Hodayot. Several words and phrases are paralleled exactly in a Hodayot manuscript, 4Q427 7 (Schuller 1993). Further parallels to both texts are found in 4Q471b, which was originally thought to be part of the War Rule but is now deemed to be an independent composition. It seems likely that these three texts, 4Q491 11, 4Q471b and 4Q427 7 are variants of the same text, although they do not correspond exactly, and the discrepancies are greatest between 4Q491 and the other two (Collins and Dimant 1994; see the synopsis of the three texts by Dimant 1994b: 157–61). The parallels between 4Q491 and 4Q427 continue in the following passages, 4Q491 11:13 and 4Q427 7:13, which use imperatives to call on the just to praise God. The claim to be ranked with the gods or angels runs through all three texts. 4Q427 and 4Q471b use the phrase "companion to the holy ones" (*rēa' liq dōšîm*), which is paralleled in 4Q471b by "beloved of the king." 4Q471b also contains a rhetorical question that is not paralleled in the other texts: "who is like me among the gods?" Neither 4Q427 nor 4Q471b, however, contains a reference to a throne in the extant fragments. 4Q491 and 4Q471b contain references to teaching. 4Q491 also contains a cryptic reference to pains or griefs (*ṣ'ārîm*), but the context is very fragmentary.

Baillet identified the speaker in 4Q491 as the archangel Michael, and dubbed the passage "the Canticle of Michael." There is no parallel for comparable boasting by a human speaker, either in the scrolls or in other Jewish texts. But neither is there any parallel for such a speech by Michael. Such boastful speech is often attributed to personified Wisdom. (Cf. Sir 24: "Wisdom praises herself, and tells of her glory in the midst of her people. In the assembly of the Most High she opens her mouth and in the presence of his hosts she tells of her glory. . . . I dwelt in the highest heavens and my throne was in a pillar of cloud.") Yet the impression given in 4Q491 is that the speaker has come to be reckoned with the gods, but was not of heavenly origin. The reference to griefs may also point to a human speaker, but much depends on how the context is restored. (If the line is read "who ta[kes away all] griefs like me" the speaker is not necessarily human.) Nonetheless, the repeated emphasis on the exaltation of the speaker suggests an exalted human being rather than pre-existent Wisdom. Since the speaker is evidently a teacher, however, the similarity to Wisdom is probably intentional.

Morton Smith claimed that this text was evidence of "speculation on deification by ascent towards or into the heavens, speculation which may have gone along with some practices that produced extraordinary experiences understood as encounters with gods or angels" (Smith 1990: 187–8). Those who ascended were thought to become like gods in form and to be enthroned in heaven. In Smith's view, this was the goal of hekalot mysticism, of which this text was an early witness. Ascents to heaven are well attested in the apocalyptic literature of the Hellenistic and Roman periods, beginning with the ascent of Enoch in the Book of the Watchers and that of Levi in the Aramaic Apocryphon of Levi.

Wilhelm Bousset argued that the ascent of the visionary anticipates the ascent of the soul after death (Bousset 1901: 136). Gershom Scholem saw it as a central element in Jewish mysticism, and identified its goal as the vision of God on His throne and knowledge of heavenly mysteries (Scholem 1961: 40–79). The paradigm case for the view that the ascent had as its goal the heavenly enthronement of the visionary is provided by Enoch in the Hebrew book of Enoch, or 3 Enoch. In that book, Rabbi Ishmael tells how he ascended to heaven and was greeted by Metatron, an exalted angelic figure who has several names, including Enoch, son of Jared. Metatron tells how he was taken up before the Flood and how "the Holy One, blessed be he, made for me (Metatron) a throne like the throne of glory" (3 Enoch 10:1; in a later passage Metatron is removed from his throne because of the controversy as to whether there were two powers in heaven). 3 Enoch is unlikely to be older than the sixth century BCE, but elements of this tradition can be found already in the Similitudes of Enoch in the first century CE. There the figure who is called "that Son of Man" (an allusion to Daniel 7) sits on the throne of glory (1 Enoch 62:5; 69:27, 29). At the end of the Similitudes, when Enoch ascends to heaven he is greeted by an angel who tells him: "you are the Son of Man who was born to righteousness." This passage is notoriously problematic, since the text had hitherto given no hint that Enoch was identical with the figure in his vision (see Collins 1995: 178–81). The identification may well be secondary, but nonetheless it is relatively early, and may date from the end of the first century CE. It does not necessarily follow that the legendary transformation of Enoch could be replicated by other human beings prior to their deaths. Several texts, however, promise heavenly enthronement as a reward for the pious after death. 4Q521 (the "Messianic Apocalypse"), fragment 2, says that God will glorify the pious on the throne of an eternal kingdom. According to 1 Enoch 108:12 God says: "I will bring out into shining light those who love my holy name and I will set each one on the throne of his glory." Several early Christian texts speak of heavenly enthronement after death (Matt 19:18; Luke 22:30; Rev 3:21; 20:4; Ascension of Isaiah 9:24–6).

Morton Smith claimed not only that traditions about heavenly ascent and enthronement were known around the turn of the era, but that Jewish mystics in this period had developed techniques for ascent. The evidence for such techniques in this period is inferential, because the relevant texts are pseudepigraphic. Enoch practices certain techniques by the waters of Dan before his ascent in 1 Enoch 13, and the later hekalot texts also give evidence of techniques. We do not, however, have any accounts of such practices by historical people around the turn of the era. But regardless of the practice of ascent in this period, neither 4Q491 nor any of the sectarian texts from Qumran provides evidence on the subject. Unlike Enoch in the Book of the Watchers, the author of 4Q491 does not describe an ascent, or provide a description of what he saw in the heavenly regions. The claim to reside or to have taken a seat in heaven has mystical implications, since it implies experience of the heavenly world. The kind of experience implied, however, is different from what we find in the accounts of ascents and also from the later hekalot texts, which give great prominence to the quasi-magical formulae to be used in the course of ascent (Schäfer 1986).

We saw in Chapter 7 that the Qumran community claimed to enjoy fellowship with the angels, even in this life. This claim is found especially in the Hodayot, in both the Teacher hymns and the Community hymns. The claims made in 4Q491, and also in 4Q471b, go beyond this general belief, and assert a level of exaltation that seems to be unique. (Cf. 4Q471b: "who is like me among the gods?") Even though 4Q427 has been classified as a "hymn of the community" (Schuller 1994: 148–9), the speaker evinces the kind of distinctive personal claims that we associate with the Teacher hymns. The vocabulary of the hymn, however, matches the profile of neither the hymns of the Community nor those of the Teacher (as distinguished by Jeremias 1971: 171). While this hymn resembles the Hodayot in several respects, it remains distinctive and seems to be independent of the rest of the corpus. The claims that it makes are the claims of an individual, and cannot be extended to the community as a whole.

I have argued elsewhere that the best parallel to the claim of the author to have occupied a throne in heaven is provided by the tradition about Moses preserved in the Hellenisitic Jewish author, Ezekiel the tragedian (Collins 1995: 144–5). The motif of teaching in 4Q491 and 4Q471b is more easily related to Moses than to other figures who are said to be enthroned in heaven at various times (e.g. David). But who is this teacher like Moses who speaks in this hymn? The most obvious candidate is the Teacher of Righteousness, who was the authoritative Interpreter of the Law (CD 6:7). But the tone of this hymn is considerably more confident than that of the Teacher hymns, whose author complains of persecution and has an acute sense of human frailty. The community expected another leader who would "teach righteousness in the end of days" (CD 6:11; cf. the Interpreter of the Law in the Florilegium, 4Q174). This eschatological teacher is often thought to be identical with the eschatological priest, the messiah of Aaron. There was a clear basis for the heavenly enthronement of the Davidic messiah in Psalm 110 ("the Lord said to my Lord, sit at my right hand."). The addressee in Psalm 110 is also said to be "a priest forever after the order of Melchizedek," and the text is related to "a high priest, one who is seated at the right hand of the throne of majesty in the heavens" in Heb 8:1–2. Since the priestly messiah usually takes precedence over the Davidic in the sectarian scrolls, we should not be surprised that a similar claim could be made on his behalf.

The problem is that nowhere else in the corpus of the scrolls do we find words placed in the mouth of either messiah, and so there is no parallel for a speech such as we find in 4Q491 by a messianic figure. Neither is there any parallel for such claims by anyone else, with the possible exception of personified Wisdom. The implied authorship remains enigmatic. Nonetheless, it seems clear that this passage must be understood in the context of the fellowship with the gods or angels that is claimed for the Qumran community in the Hodayot. The claim that is made here exceeds that of the community in general. The passage implies an exceptional individual. But the exaltation that he enjoys is exceptional in degree rather than in kind.

CONCLUSION

The interest in the heavenly world that we find in the scrolls is more intense and developed than anything we find in the earlier apocalypses, but it is also different in kind. The scrolls lack the interest of the Enoch tradition in the geography of otherworldly regions, and they contain surprisingly little visionary material of the kind we find in the apocalypses. The interest in angelic beings, however, is intense, and the hymnic literature in the scrolls enters into the cultic activity of the heavenly world with an immediacy that surpasses anything in Enoch or Daniel. (The Book of Jubilees occupies a mediating position between the apocalypses and the scrolls in this respect, since it also shows little interest in visionary material or heavenly geography, but attaches great importance to angels.)

The distinctive attention to the heavenly world in the scrolls can be attributed primarily to the priestly leadership of the Dead Sea sect. There is good reason to believe that the "council of the community" saw itself as a replacement for the cult of the Jerusalem Temple that was regarded as invalid. It was to be "a holy house for Israel and the foundation of the holy of holies for Aaron . . . to atone for the land and to render to the wicked their retribution" (1QS 8:5–6). But the scrolls also provide a more grandiose replacement for the Jerusalem cult, by describing in detail the worship of the angels in heaven. Presumably, this liturgy would go on whether the Jerusalem Temple was defiled or not, but there is no evidence that it had been imagined or described in such detail before the rise of the Dead Sea sect. The sectarians could no longer go to the temple to behold and praise the glory of God, but they could be transported in their hymns to the heavenly temple, to witness and participate in a more perfect liturgy. In the words of the Hodayot:

> The corrupt spirit you have purified from great sin so that it may take its place with the host of the holy ones and enter into communion with the congregation of the sons of heaven . . . that it may praise your name together in celebration and tell of your wonders before all your works.
>
> (1QH 11:21–3, formerly 3:21–3)

The communion with the angels was not limited to the act of praise-giving. The Dead Sea sect was heir to an apocalyptic tradition according to which the righteous would become companions to the angels and shine like the stars after death. One of the major ways in which the sect differed from earlier apocalyptic tradition was in its claim to experience that communion in this life, and so in effect to transcend death in the present. We are reminded here of Bousset's theory that the ascent of the visionary was an anticipation of the ascent of the soul after death. In this respect, the scrolls may reasonably be said to attest a form of communal mysticism, even though they do not describe ascents, or claim heavenly enthronement except in one exceptional case, and do not describe the transformation of the members into the angelic state. No doubt the sectarians were aware that the transformation was not yet complete. They were still beset by transgressions and "the snares of Belial." Nonetheless, these texts claim a degree of present participation in the angelic world that is distinctive in the apocalyptic tradition, and that may reasonably be characterized as realized eschatology.

9

THE APOCALYPTICISM OF THE SCROLLS IN CONTEXT

The preceding chapters have outlined the texts and aspects of the Dead Sea scrolls that give substance to the view that the Dead Sea sect was an apocalyptic community. While a number of fragmentary works from Cave 4, such as 4Q246, may be apocalypses of which key elements have been lost, and while some of these texts may have been products of the sect, the primary evidence is found in the major sectarian compositions such as the rule books and the Hodayot. These books are not in the form of apocalypses, but they are informed by an apocalyptic worldview, and influenced by the apocalypses of Enoch and Daniel, which were also prominent at Qumran. The sectarian texts are not without their internal tensions. The dualism of the Instruction on the Two Spirits is only faintly hinted at in CD. It is reasonable to suppose that there was some change and development in the history of the sect, even though we cannot trace it with any confidence. The sect was not organized on the basis of a creed, and there may well have been variation in what the members believed. Nonetheless, a distinctive worldview emerges from these writings that may be accepted as representative of the sect, even though the full scenario is not necessarily implicit in every sectarian text.

THE APOCALYPTIC WORLDVIEW

The key elements of this worldview are as follows. The world is divided between warring forces of good and evil. In some texts this division is described in terms of the Zoroastrian opposition of light and darkness, with emphasis on predestination and the role of angelic forces, Michael/Melchizedek on the one hand and Belial/ Melchiresha on the other. Other texts, such as CD, give greater weight to the role of the human inclination, but even these texts posit a sharp division between the forces of good and evil. The conflict between these forces plays itself out in a history that is divided into predetermined periods. There is a time when the wrath of Belial is dominant. But God has set an end to the era of wickedness. The "end of days" is the period immediately before the decisive divine intervention. It appears to have two phases: the time of testing, which was already experienced by the sect, and the messianic age, which was still to come. The messianic age would involve a final decisive war against the Gentile powers of the day (the Kittim) and the Sons of Darkness (including opposing Jewish factions). The messiah of Israel would play a key role in that conflict, but ultimately it would be decided by the power of God through the agency of Michael/Melchizedek. The texts are not as clear as we might wish on the state that would follow this final battle. The vision of a new and purified Jerusalem would presumably find its fulfillment here. We also find reference to a final conflagration, which would imply an end of this world, as we find in some apocalyptic texts. It is not clear whether a general resurrection was expected. Such an expectation is not explicitly attested in the extant portions of the major texts, and the few texts which speak of resurrection (e.g. 4Q521) may not be representative of the sect. There is a well-attested expectation of eternal life, of bliss for the righteous and torment for the damned, which seems to follow as the inevitable culmination of the life of the individual. Moreover, the righteous members of the community claimed to experience life with the angels already in the present, through communion with the heavenly liturgy. The heavenly state was not fully realized; the depredations of Belial would continue until the final battle. Yet the quasi-mystical participation in angelic life was such that death is never addressed as a problem in the sectarian scrolls.

CONTINUITY AND INNOVATION

When we compare this admittedly synthesized worldview with the apocalyptic tradition inherited from Enoch and Daniel, we find both continuity and innovation. The notion that evil on earth is due to supernatural forces was pioneered in the Enochic Book of the Watchers, and developed in Jubilees in the role of Mastema, while the archangel Michael has a prominent role in the book of Daniel. The apocalypses, however, never imagine such a systematic division of creation as we find in the Instruction on the Two Spirits. The Qumran text was influenced not only by the apocalypses but also by Zoroastrian myth and by the discussions in Jewish wisdom circles about the origin of evil. The division of history into periods is characteristic of apocalypses of the historical type, as is the expectation of a final battle. Messianic expectation, in contrast, is absent from the books of Enoch and Daniel, although it becomes prominent in later apocalypses such as 4 Ezra. The Qumran community followed the precedent of Daniel in attempting to calculate the date of the "end," but it seems to have gone further in believing that the end of days had already begun, even if the coming of the messiahs and the eschatological war were still in the future. The apocalypses are the first Jewish texts to engage in extensive speculation about angels and the heavenly world. The scrolls imagine the angelic hosts in much greater detail, but show virtually no interest in heavenly geography. They posit a more immediate kind of experience of the angelic world, which has a strongly cultic character, and must be attributed to the priestly character of the Qumran community. The apocalypses had offered the hope that after death the righteous would become companions to the angels. The scrolls claim that members of the community already experienced that companionship in this life, and consequently they pay little attention to the notion of resurrection.

The "realized eschatology" of the Dead Sea sect is also relevant to the puzzling absence of apocalypses as a literary genre among the scrolls. The visions of Daniel and Enoch imply a great gulf between the recipients of the revelation and the heavenly world. This gulf is bridged only by the mediation of ancient heroes (antediluvian in the case of Enoch) and revealing angels. The places seen by Enoch are described in tones of wonder, and Daniel's visions are veiled in strange mythological symbolism. The sectarian scrolls, in contrast, imply a more immediate experience. When the author of the Community Rule says that his eyes have gazed on that which is eternal (1QS 11:5), he does not go on to describe it. Presumably the community that already shared the lot of the holy ones did not need a description. Similarly, the War Rule only describes the course of the final battle incidentally. The primary emphasis is on giving instructions for proper participation. Here again the sense that the community is already living the angelic life renders the conventions of apocalyptic revelation superfluous. While the readers of an apocalypse might glimpse the heavenly world as through a glass darkly, the sectarians of Qumran believed that they encountered it face to face.

A second factor that rendered the apocalyptic form of revelation superfluous concerned the structure of authority in the community. The apocalypses derived their authority from the claim of visionary experience and the prestige of the pseudonymous authors (Enoch and Daniel). In the Dead Sea sect, authority was vested in the Teacher of Righteousness and his successors. He is the one in whose heart God has put the source of wisdom for all those who understand (1QH 10:18 = 2:18). To him "God has disclosed all the mysteries of the words of his servants the prophets" (1QpHab 7:4). If the prophet Habakkuk did not know the end of the age, even though he had written about it, what reason was there to look to Enoch and Daniel for further revelations? The Teacher had superseded the prophets of old. Consequently, revelation at Qumran is found, indirectly, in the rule books that regulate the life of the community, present and future, and piecemeal in the biblical commentaries (pesharim) and midrashic texts. The community's understanding of revelation can also often be gleaned from the hymns and liturgical texts in which the members expressed their beliefs. The fact that these beliefs were expressed in new forms at Qumran does not in any way lessen the apocalyptic character of the worldview they embody.

THE PLACE OF APOCALYPTICISM IN ANCIENT JUDAISM

One conclusion that follows from this comparison concerns the nature of apocalypticism in ancient Judaism. Apocalypticism cannot be identified with a single movement, or even with a single tradition. There is no reason to believe that the book of Daniel was produced in the same circles as the books of Enoch. Both Daniel and Enoch are influential at Qumran. But there are new ingredients in the Qumran texts that bespeak a provenance that is quite different from that of the apocalypses. One such element is the centrality of the Torah, which shows a common interest with wisdom schools such as that of Ben Sira. The occasional attempts of Christian scholars to create an antithesis between apocalypticism and Torah-piety (e.g. Rössler 1960) collapse in view of the evidence of the scrolls. Another distinctive factor is the priestly character of the Qumran community. It has sometimes been suggested that apocalypticism arose in opposition to priestly theology (Hanson 1975). Others have argued that the Enoch books come from priestly circles, and so that apocalypticism arose out of priestly tradition (Himmelfarb 1993: 23–8). Neither position is satisfactory; apocalypticism is not inherently tied to any one group or tradition. Even greater diversity can be found in the later apocalypses. While 4 Ezra and 2 Baruch share common themes with the scrolls (García Martínez 1991), the differences are more notable, as the later apocalypses lack the cosmic dualism and the interest in the angelic world, and have no suggestion of realized eschatology. Apocalypses that describe ascents through the heavens (3 Baruch, 2 Enoch) differ again, both from 4 Ezra and from the scrolls, and must be ascribed to quite different circles.

Apocalypticism is primarily concerned with a metaphysical framework, within which various theologies and ideologies can find meaning. What is crucial to an apocalyptic community is the belief that its way of life is in accordance with the angels in heaven, that it will be vindicated in a final judgment, and that it will lead its members to everlasting life. The actual way of life may differ from one community to another. It may center on Torah-piety, or it may be antinomian. It may be hierarchical or egalitarian. The hated opponents of the Dead Sea sect, who turned back with the "man of the lie," may have believed that a different understanding of the Law would be vindicated in the final judgment. The "apocalyptic" character of a community lies in this hope for angelic support and eschatological vindication, not in its specific practice or its understanding of the Law.

At the time that the sectarian texts were produced, the apocalyptic worldview was still relatively novel in ancient Judaism. The notions that human conduct was shaped by angelic forces, that an end of history was imminent, and that righteous human beings could be exalted to fellowship with the angels, were innovations in Jewish tradition, introduced by the authors of Enoch and Daniel. It is generally assumed that this worldview, with its hope for otherworldly salvation, arose from a state of alienation and dissatisfaction with the circumstances in which the authors found themselves. This assumption is well justified in the cases of the early apocalypses and of the Qumran community. Daniel's visions reflect the crisis of the Maccabean period. The Dead Sea sect arose from a profound disagreement with the interpretation of the Law and the regulation of the temple cult on the part of the Jerusalem authorities. Alienation from the temple was of fundamental importance, in view of the priestly character of the sect. The distinctive interest of the community in the angelic liturgy, and the belief in present fellowship with the angels, can be understood in large part as compensation for the loss of participation in the temple cult. The foreign domination of Israel by the Gentile Kittim was a further source of alienation. In later centuries, the apocalyptic worldview was assimilated to some degree in Judaism and to a greater degree in Christianity, and could also be invoked, on occasion in support of the status quo (McGinn 1979: 28–36). Yet the hope for an end to this world, and the vision of an alternative reality in the heavens, have remained powerful resources for protest on the part of the alienated down to modern times.

We do not know just how widespread the apocalyptic ideas of the scrolls were in the Judaism of their day. Our knowledge of Judaism around the turn of the era is dependent on the histories of Josephus to an unfortunate degree. Most scholars are persuaded that the sectarian scrolls from Qumran are representative of the group that Josephus identifies as the Essenes. Yet it is striking that Josephus' account of the Essenes (and also that of Philo) gives no hint that the sect had an apocalyptic character. (His account of the Essene belief in life after death comes close to what we find in the Community Rule, but that belief in itself is not enough to characterize the sect as apocalyptic.) He makes no mention of warring forces of light and darkness, of messiahs, or of an eschatological war. There is good reason to think that Josephus, or his source, omitted aspects of Essene theology that would have been either offensive or unintelligible to Hellenized readers. (The subject of purity also gets short shrift.) Hippolytus paints a more apocalyptic picture of the sect, and while his account is also problematic the motif of cosmic conflagration is corroborated by the Hodayot. Josephus notoriously omits Daniel chapter 7 in his paraphrase of the biblical book (*Ant* 10.186–281), presumably because it was understood to predict the overthrow of Rome. We should not be surprised if he also suppressed the belief of the Essenes in an eschatological war. Nonetheless, the discrepancy between Josephus' account and the evidence of the scrolls on the matter of apocalypticism should be noted. It should cause some doubts either about the identification of the sect or, more probably, about the reliability of Josephus.

Apart from the Essenes, the group with which the scrolls have most often been compared are the early Christians. The followers of Jesus of Nazareth can also be described as, among other things, an apocalyptic movement. The comparisons can be divided into two sections, those that concern Jesus as messiah and those that concern the early Church as evidenced in the Pauline epistles and the Johannine writings.

JESUS OF NAZARETH AND THE DEAD SEA SCROLLS

Much of the discussion of Jesus and the scrolls has been sensational in character. In the early days of scrolls research, the distinguished French scholar Dupont-Sommer claimed that Jesus was "an astonishing reincarnation of the Teacher of Righteousness," who had also been killed and taken up to heaven and whose second coming was also awaited (Dupont-Sommer 1950: 121–2). John Allegro, a member of the original team of editors, claimed that Jesus was one of those "hanged alive" by the Wicked Priest according to the pesher on Nahum. He continued: "When the Jewish king had left, [the sectarians] took down the broken body of their Master to stand guard over it until Judgment Day. . . . They believed their Master would rise again to lead his faithful flock (the people of the new testament they called themselves) to a new and purified Jerusalem" (*Time Magazine*, February 6, 1956, p. 88, cited by Fitzmyer 1992: 164). When Allegro first aired these views on British radio in 1956 he provoked an outcry and a letter of protest from the other members of the editorial team. The views of Allegro and Dupont-Sommer are nearly universally dismissed as far-fetched by scholars, but they were widely disseminated by the American literary critic Edmund Wilson (1955), and they have recently been resurrected by British journalists (Baigent and Leigh 1991).

In recent years, new maverick theories were put forward by Barbara Thiering and Robert Eisenman. Thiering identifies the Teacher as John the Baptist and sees the Gospels as coded Essene documents. Eisenman identifies the Teacher as James the Just, the brother of Jesus, and St Paul as "the man of the lie" who sometimes appears as his adversary. In his view the scrolls are the authentic record of early Christianity and the Gospels are later fabrications. Despite the fact that they have generated enormous publicity, these theories cannot be taken seriously by anyone who is at all familiar with the history and literature of the period. (The views of Thiering and Eisenman are summarized with appropriate comment by Cook 1994: 137–45.)

Some other supposed correspondences between Jesus and the scrolls must also be debunked. In November 1991, headlines from Los Angeles to London proclaimed that a reference to a dying messiah had been found in an unpublished fragment. The text in question was 4Q285 fragment 5. Line 4 could be construed grammatically to read "they will put to death the Leader of the Community, the Bran[ch of David]" (Eisenman and Wise 1992: 29). It is also possible, however, to construe the text so that it reads "the Prince of the Congregation, the Branch of David, will kill him." Since the fragment refers clearly to Isaiah 11, where the "shoot from the stump of Jesse" is said to slay the wicked with the breath of his mouth (a favorite messianic prophecy), it is clear that the second construal of the fragment is correct (Vermes 1992a). The passage is in accordance with the usual portrayal of the Davidic messiah in the scrolls as a warrior king in the eschatological war.

Another minor controversy has concerned the possibility that 4Q541 envisages "a suffering messiah, in the perspective opened up by the Servant poems" (Starcky 1963: 492). Here again the verdict of scholarship is negative. The passage speaks of a figure whose light will be kindled in all the corners of the earth, and will dispel the darkness. The Servant of the Lord in said to be a light to the Gentiles in Isaiah 42 and 49. The motif of light does not occur, however, in the passage that describes the Servant as a suffering figure (Isaiah 53). The figure in the Qumran text is said to endure opposition and calumny, but this is suffering of a different sort from being beaten and put to death, as the Servant is in Isaiah 53. The figure in the Qumran text is probably an eschatological teacher/priest, modeled on the historical Teacher, who also endured opposition. There is no reason to relate this passage to Isaiah 53, and none to compare it with the depiction of Jesus in the New Testament (Collins 1995: 123–6).

There are, however, two passages that have striking parallels in the Gospel accounts of Jesus. The first of these is found in 4Q246, the "Son of God" text, which we discussed in Chapter 5. The statement in this text, "'Son of God' he shall be called and they will name him 'Son of the Most High,'" finds an exact parallel in Luke 1:31–5, where the angel Gabriel says of Jesus: "he will be great and will be called the Son of the Most High and the Lord God will give to him the throne of his ancestor David. He will reign over the house of Jacob forever, and of his kingdom there will be no end . . . he will be called the Son of God." It is overwhelmingly probable that Luke borrowed these titles, either from this text or from a common tradition, to identify Jesus as the messiah. If the Son of God in the Qumran text is understood as a messiah, however, he conforms to the usual picture of the warrior-messiah in the scrolls: "The great God will be his strength. He will make war on his behalf, give nations into his hand and cast them all down before him." Luke borrows only the titles for Jesus. The career that unfolds in the Gospel is quite different from that of the warrior-messiah.

There is another parallel to the Gospels, however, which may ultimately be more illuminating for the messianic claims made in connection with Jesus. In a passage that derives from the Sayings Source Q (Matt 11:2–5; Luke 7:22) John the Baptist asks Jesus: "Are you he that is to come or are we to look for another?" Jesus answers: "Go and tell John what you hear and see: the blind receive their sight, the lame walk, the lepers are cleansed, the deaf hear, the dead are raised and the poor have good news preached to them." There is a striking parallel in 4Q521: "he will heal the wounded, give life to the dead and preach good news to the poor." (See Tabor and Wise 1992; Puech 1992c.) While the antecedent of the pronoun in 4Q521 is God, we have argued that God works through an agent, the messiah whom heaven and earth obey, and that this figure who gives life to the dead and preaches good news to the poor should be understood as a prophet like Elijah. In the Gospels, these tasks are performed by Jesus.

Jesus of Nazareth was crucified as king of the Jews, and was known as Christos, the Greek equivalent of messiah, from a very early point after his death. As we have seen, the Davidic messiah was consistently portrayed as a militant figure, not only in the scrolls but in Jewish texts from various sources in this period. But there is little basis in the Gospels for identifying Jesus as the kind of figure who would play this role. In contrast, much of his activity resembles that of a prophet, and the miracles of healing and raising the dead specifically recall Elijah. The possibility that Jesus might be Elijah *redivivus* is voiced in Mark 6:14–15, where various people identify Jesus to Herod as John raised from the dead, Elijah, or "a prophet," and again in Mark 8:27, where Jesus' question, "who do people say that I am?" receives the answer, "John the Baptist; and others, Elijah; and still others, one of the prophets."

The parallel with 4Q521 raises again the possibility that Jesus may originally have been called "messiah" as Elijah-like prophet rather than as king. There is no doubt that he was eventually identified specifically as the Davidic messiah. The scrolls throw no light on this development. We can only conjecture that the prophet who preached the coming of the kingdom was thought by his followers to be the king who would usher it in. Jesus seems to have been quite evasive about his own messianic claims. If the triumphal entry into Jerusalem is historical, it would seem to encourage such claims by evoking Zechariah 9:9, although even then Jesus is not said to have endorsed them in public. (See further Collins 1996b.)

There is nothing in the Dead Sea scrolls that would lessen the scandal of the crucifixion of the messiah. After the resurrection, however, the disciples found new ways to apply to Jesus the traditional messianic imagery. In Revelation 19, Jesus appears from heaven riding a white horse and leading the armies of heaven: "From his mouth comes a sharp sword with which to strike down the nations, and he will rule them with a rod of iron." Here is a figure who would readily have been recognized as the Davidic messiah at Qumran. But this is the Jesus of apocalyptic myth rather than the Jesus of history.

If Jesus bore little resemblance to the kingly messiah in his earthly career, he bore even less to the messiah of Aaron, since he was not a priest. But in this respect too the risen and exalted Christ took on characteristics that were not hinted at before the crucifixion. In the Epistle to the Hebrews, Jesus is portrayed as a high priest, seated at the right hand of God, a priest after the order of Melchizedek. We have already noted the parallel with the enigmatic fragment 4Q491 11, which purports to be spoken by a figure who has a throne in heaven. We have suggested that this figure is the eschatological high priest, although the identification is far from certain. If our suggestion is correct, 4Q491 provides an interesting parallel to the portrayal of Christ in Hebrews.

THE EARLY CHURCH

Many scholars have mined the scrolls for parallels to aspects of the New Testament (Stendahl 1957, 1992; Black 1961). Many of the points noted relate to the organization of the respective communities (e.g. the sharing of possessions) and their rituals (baptism, eucharist, etc.). Here we are only concerned with those parallels that bear on the apocalyptic character of the two movements.

The most fundamental point of comparison and contrast lies in the structure of eschatological expectation in the New Testament and in the scrolls. Early Christianity lived in the interval between the resurrection of Jesus and the Second Coming. Paul tells the Corinthians that "the end of the ages has come" (1 Cor 10:11). The resurrection of Jesus was not an isolated event but "the first fruits of those who have died (1 Cor 15:20). The general resurrection was near at hand. Paul could assure his readers that "we will not all die, but we will all be changed" (1 Cor 15:51) and that after the dead are raised "then we who are alive, who are left, will be caught up in the clouds together with them to meet the Lord in the air" (1 Thess 4:17). The "end of days" is inaugurated by the death and resurrection of Christ, even though its fulfillment remains in the future.

In this situation, the eschatology of the early Church has been described as "realized eschatology," or more appropriately as "inaugurated eschatology" (Allison 1985). The degree of present realization varies from one New Testament author to the other. Paul tells the Romans that "you are not in the flesh, you are in the spirit, since the spirit of God dwells in you," but the glory that is to come is firmly in the future. He also supposes that the angels of God mingle with the community in its worship (1 Cor 11:10; Fitzmyer 1990: 31–47). The Deutero-Pauline epistles go much further. According to the Epistle to the Ephesians, God "made us alive together with Christ . . . and raised us up with him and seated us with him in the heavenly places in Christ Jesus" (Eph 2:5–6). Ephesians also tells its readers: "once you were darkness, but now in the Lord you are light. Live as children of the light" (Eph 5:8). The imagery of light and darkness provides a clear point of comparison with the doctrine of the two spirits, while the language of exaltation "to heavenly places" recalls the Hodayot (K. G. Kuhn 1990; Mussner 1990). These passages have been held to show "a clear relationship with the Essene community of the Qumran texts" (Kuhn 1990: 131). It is not clear either how this relationship should be understood or how it should be explained. The language of the Dead Sea sect could presumably be used by people who were never attached to it. Even closer to the language of the scrolls is a passage in 2 Cor 6:14–7:1 that is widely regarded as an interpolation: "What partnership is there between righteousness and lawlessness? or what fellowship is there between light and darkness? What agreement does Christ have with Beliar? . . . For we are the temple of the living

God." This passage has been described as "a Christian exhortation in the Essene tradition" (Gnilka 1990: 66). Its provenance, and the source of its Qumran-like language remain obscure, but it may be cited plausibly as an instance of Essene influence on a New Testament writing.

The most thoroughly realized eschatology in the New Testament is found in the Gospel of John. John's Jesus declares: "Very truly I tell you, anyone who hears my word and believes him who sent me has eternal life, and does not come under judgment, but has passed from death to life" (5:24); or again: "the hour is coming, and is now here, when the dead will hear the voice of the Son of God, and those who hear will live" (5:25); and "those who believe in me, even though they die, will live, and everyone who lives and believes in me will never die" (11:25–6). The imagery of light and darkness also figures prominently in John. The Word is a light shining in the darkness, and the darkness does not overcome it (1:5). John 12:36 refers to "children of light." Points of similarity with the dualism of the scrolls are pervasive in the Gospel and in the Johannine epistles (Brown 1992: 183–207; Charlesworth 1990). 1 John 4:6 contrasts the spirit of truth and the spirit of error. John 14:17 refers to the spirit of truth. The "ruler of this world" (John 12:31) is reminiscent of Belial.

The parallels between the scrolls and the Johannine literature undoubtedly strengthen the case that "John has its strongest affinities . . . with Palestinian Judaism" (Cross 1995: 155). The affinities, however, should not be exaggerated. The dualism of John is not nearly so developed as that of the Instruction on the Two Spirits. John has no concept of an eschatological war between the two spirits. The realized eschatology of the scrolls is grounded in temple piety and attaches great importance to purity. The Johannine concept of eternal life has closer parallels with the wisdom tradition, and even with a Hellenized philosopher like Philo. There is no reason to suppose that John shared anything more with Qumran than a general cultural milieu and some language that was originally formulated in a sectarian setting.

The notion of an eschatological battle figures prominently in another Johannine writing, the book of Revelation, which has been characterized by one commentator as a Christian war scroll (Bauckham 1993). Revelation 12 describes the woes that attend the birth of the messiah. The only parallel to this idea in pre-Christian Jewish literature is found in the 1QH 11 (formerly 1QH 3), although the two passages show little similarity in detail (Yarbro Collins 1976: 67–9). The "birth-pangs of the messiah" become a standard eschatological motif in later tradition. Revelation 12 depicts a heavenly battle between two angelic forces, one led by the archangel Michael and the other by "the dragon." Much of this imagery recalls Daniel rather than the War Rule, but it is noteworthy that the adversary is a Satanic figure rather than the angelic prince of a particular people. The devil is said to come down to earth "with great wrath, because he knows that his time is short," an idea that recalls the "wrath of Belial," which precedes the end of days in the scrolls. Revelation, however, has no counterpart of the tactical and organizational sections of the War Rule. It attributes the victory over the dragon not to Michael but to "the blood of the Lamb," an idea that has no parallel in the scrolls. It is noteworthy that the 144,000 followers of the Lamb in Rev 14:1–5 "have not defiled themselves with women." This isolated comment evokes old purity taboos pertaining to holy war (cf. the refusal of Uriah the Hittite to sleep with his wife in 2 Samuel 11, because the army is on campaign). Josephus claims that one order of the Essenes was celibate, and while the scrolls never require celibacy they regularly adopt restrictive rulings on sexual intercourse for reasons of purity.

The vision of the new Jerusalem in Revelation 21 invites comparison with the New Jerusalem texts from Qumran (García Martinez 1992: 180–213). Both the Qumran texts and Revelation draw heavily on Ezekiel 40–8 and on the tradition that Jerusalem would be rebuilt with precious stones and metals (Isa 54:11–12). There are also significant differences (Yarbro Collins, forthcoming). The city in Revelation descends from heaven and is part of a new creation, where there is no sun or moon or night. Moreover, "I saw no temple in the city, for its temple is the Lord god the Almighty and the Lamb" (Rev 21:22). While the New Jerusalem text is fragmentary, it clearly presupposed that there would be a temple, since there are references to the ritual activities of priests.

The New Jerusalem text, like the Qumran sect in general, was critical of the actual temple cult as practiced in Jerusalem, but attached great importance to the ideal, purified temple cult. There was a fundamental difference between early Christianity and the Dead Sea sect in this respect.

There is also a fundamental difference on the subject of resurrection. The Christian movement received its impetus from the belief that Jesus had risen from the dead, and that the general resurrection was at hand. The person of Jesus acquires a central importance for Christians in a way that neither the Teacher nor the messiahs ever do in the scrolls. Christian life centers on the imitation of Christ. Essene life centers on fulfillment of the Torah. Consequently, the hope of resurrection plays a crucial role in the Christian texts. Nowhere is this more evident than in the conclusion of the book of Revelation, with its elaborate scenario of a double resurrection: first that of the martyrs, then the general resurrection. Revelation has close parallels in some Jewish apocalypses, notably in 4 Ezra 7, which also envisages a messianic reign on earth *before* the new creation and resurrection. The Qumran texts are distinctive in their relative lack of attention to resurrection, at least in the major sectarian scrolls.

Ultimately, the Dead Sea sect and early Christianity were very different movements. One was inspired by zeal for exact fulfillment of the Torah; the other was based on the life and teachings of an eschatological prophet, and even became antinomian in some of its formations. Ritual and purity were of central importance at Qumran. Christianity generally dispensed with the ritual and purity laws, although it developed rituals of its own. The Essene understanding of realized eschatology was based on participation in the heavenly cult of the angels. This idea is of minor importance in the New Testament. The strongly realized eschatology of the Gospel of John is formulated in terms that are sapiential rather than cultic.

Nonetheless, both movements framed their understanding of the world with beliefs and ideas that were heavily influenced by apocalyptic tradition. Angelic and demonic forces were seen to shape human destiny to a far greater degree than was the case in the Hebrew Bible. History was felt to be in its final stage, and God's intervention in judgment was close at hand, when the evils of the present would be swept away. Both movements were animated by the hope for a life beyond death. Each movement adapted this common tradition in its own way, and used it in the service of ethical commitments that were profoundly different. The fact that two movements that were so opposed in their ways of life could both formulate their worldviews in apocalyptic imagery is testimony to the flexibility of the apocalyptic tradition.

THE FATE OF THE SCROLLS

The Dead Sea scrolls represent a phase of Judaism that flourished before the rise of Christianity, and was contemporaneous only with the earliest stages of the younger movement. They also represent a form of Judaism before the great codifications of rabbinic religion in the Mishnah and Talmud. In recent years there has been a growing appreciation of the common interests shared by the Dead Sea sect and the rabbis in issues of purity and halakah. Since the document 4QMMT was made public in 1984, it has been clear that matters of religious law were at the root of the quarrel between this sect and its Jewish contemporaries. While the positions taken in the scrolls are often at variance with later rabbinic rulings, they at least address similar issues.

There is less continuity between the scrolls and the rabbis, however, in conceptual areas relating to apocalyptic beliefs. In the wake of the disastrous Jewish revolts against Rome in 66–70 and 132–5 CE, the rabbis seem to have turned away from apocalypticism. Of the Jewish apocalypses composed between 200 BCE and 100 CE, only the book of Daniel, which had attained the status of scripture, was transmitted by Jews in its original languages. The books of Enoch and Jubilees, and the various apocalypses in the names of Abraham, Ezra, and Baruch, owed their survival to the interest of Christians. Even within Christianity, this literature was pushed to the fringes, and most of it was only preserved in tertiary translations, in Ethiopic, Syriac and Slavonic. The sectarian compositions from Qumran that were never translated into Greek were lost to posterity. We know, from a letter written in Syriac by the Nestorian Patriarch Timotheus I of Seleucia about 800 CE, that some books were found near Jericho in the eighth century, and the tenth-century Karaite writer Al Kirkisānī refers to a Jewish sect known as the Maghariyah or "men of the cave" because their books were found in caves. (For references see Golb 1980: 3, 16–17; Kahle 1959: 16.) Two manuscripts of the Damascus Document found their way to the Cairo Geniza. It is possible that some of the scrolls were known to, and had some influence on, the Karaite sect in the Middle Ages, but they had no impact on the main lines of the development of Jewish thought. Hidden in the caves near Qumran, they were simply unknown to Jews as well as to Christians until their chance resurrection in the twentieth century.

Yet precisely because they were lost for so long the scrolls offer the possibility of fresh insight into a crucial period of Western history, especially into the nature of Judaism and the relationship between Judaism and Christianity. In the words of L. H. Schiffman: "The scrolls speak to us across the centuries about the issue of pluralism in Judaism. Through them, we gain a glimpse of an era characterized by several competing approaches to Judaism, each claiming a monopoly on the true interpretation of the Torah" (Schiffman 1994: XXV). The affinities between the scrolls and early Christianity must be seen in this context: both were competing approaches to Judaism, claiming a monopoly on divine revelation. The fate of the scrolls is a sobering reminder that such claims are never self-validating, and that the certainties of apocalyptic revelation are invariably vulnerable to the ongoing revelations of history.

BIBLIOGRAPHY

Abegg, M. (1994) "Messianic Hope and 4Q285: A Reassessment," *Journal of Biblical Literature* 113: 81–91.
—— (1995) "The Messiah at Qumran: Are We Still Seeing Double?" *Dead Sea Discoveries* 2: 125–44.
Allison, D. C. (1985) *The End of the Ages Has Come* (Philadelphia: Fortress).
Baigent, M. and R. Leigh (1991) *The Dead Sea Scrolls Deception* (London: Cape).
Baillet, M. (1982) *Qumrân Grotte 4. III (4Q482–520)* (Discoveries in the Judean Desert 7; Oxford: Clarendon).
Batto, B. F. (1992) *Slaying the Dragon* (Louisville: Westminster).
Bauckham, R. (1993) *The Climax of Prophecy. Studies on the Book of Revelation* (Edinburgh: Clark).
Bianchi, U. (1980) "The Category of Dualism in the Historical Study of Religion," *Temenos* 16: 10–25.
Bietenhard, H. (1951) *Die himmlische Welt im Urchristentum und Spätjudentum* (Tübingen: Mohr/Siebeck).
Black, M. (1961) *The Scrolls and Christian Origins* (New York: Scribners).
Bousset, W. (1901) "Die Himmelsreise der Seele," *Archiv für Religionswissenschaft* 4: 136–69, 229–73 (reprinted as book, Darmstadt: Wissenschaftliche Buchgesellschaft, 1960).
Bousset, W. and H. Gressmann (1926) *Die Religion des Judentums im späthellenistischen Zeitalter* (3rd edn; Tübingen: Mohr/Siebeck).
Boyer, P. (1992) *When Time Shall Be No More. Prophecy Belief in Modern American Culture* (Cambridge, MA: Harvard).
Brooke, G. J. (1985) *Exegesis at Qumran: 4QFlorilegium in its Jewish Context* (Sheffield: Journal for the Study of the Old Testament).
—— (1991) "The Messiah of Aaron in the Damascus Document," *Revue de Qumran* 15: 215–30.
—— (1994) "4Q254 Fragments 1 and 4, and 4Q254a: Some Preliminary Comments," *Proceedings of the 11th World Congress of Jewish Studies, Division A*, 185–92.
Broshi, M. (1987) "The Gigantic Dimensions of the Visionary Temple in the Temple Scroll," *Biblical Archaeology Review* 13: 36–7.
Brown, R. E. (1992) "The Qumran Scrolls and the Johannine Gospels and

Epistles," in K. Stendahl (ed.) *The Scrolls and the New Testament, with a New Introduction by J. H. Charlesworth*, (New York: Crossroad) 183–207.

Cameron, R. and A. J. Dewey (1979) *The Cologne Mani Codex: "Concerning the Origin of His Body"* (Missoula, MT: Scholars Press).

Cavallin, H. C. C. (1974) *Life after Death. Paul's Argument for the Resurrection of the Dead in 1 Cor 15. Part 1. An Inquiry into the Jewish Background.* (Lund: Gleerup).

Charlesworth, J. H. (1981) "The Origin and Subsequent History of the Authors of the Dead Sea Scrolls: Four Transitional Phases among the Qumran Essenes," *Revue de Qumrân* 10 (1979–81): 213–33.

Charlesworth, J. H. (ed.) (1990) *John and the Dead Sea Scrolls* (New York: Crossroad).

—— (ed.) (1994) *The Dead Sea Scrolls. Hebrew, Aramaic, and Greek texts with English translations. Volume 1. Rule of the Community and Related Documents* (Tübingen: Mohr; Louisville: Westminster).

—— (ed.) (1995) *The Dead Sea Scrolls . . . Volume 2. Damascus Document, War Scroll and Related Documents* (Tübingen: Mohr; Louisville: Westminster).

Chazon, E. (1992) "Is Divrei Ha-Me'orot a Sectarian Prayer?" in D. Dimant and U. Rappaport, (eds) *The Dead Sea Scrolls. Forty Years of Research* (Leiden: Brill) 3–17.

Collins, J. J. (1975) "The Mythology of Holy War in Daniel and the Qumran War Scroll," *Vetus Testamentum* 25: 596–612.

—— (1979) "Introduction: Towards the Morphology of a Genre," *Semeia* 14: 1–19.

—— (1984) *The Apocalyptic Imagination* (New York: Crossroad).

—— (1989) "The Origin of the Qumran Community. A Review of the Evidence," in M. P. Horgan and P. J. Kobelski, (eds) *To Touch the Text. Biblical and Related Studies in Honor of Joseph A. Fitzmyer, S. J.* (New York: Crossroad) 159–78.

—— (1990) "Was the Dead Sea Sect an Apocalyptic Community?" in L. H. Schiffman (ed.) *Archaeology and History in the Dead Sea Scrolls* (Sheffield: Journal for the Study of the Old Testament) 25–51.

—— (1991) "Genre, Ideology and Social Movements in Jewish Apocalypticism," in J. J. Collins and J. H. Charlesworth, (eds) *Mysteries and Revelations. Apocalyptic Studies since the Uppsala Colloquium* (Sheffield: Journal for the Study of the Old Testament) 11–32.

—— (1992) "Essenes," *Anchor Bible Dictionary* vol. 2, (New York: Doubleday) 619–26.

—— (1993) *Daniel* (Hermeneia, Minn.: Fortress).

—— (1995) *The Scepter and the Star* (New York: Doubleday).

—— (1996a) "Wisdom, Apocalypticism and the Dead Sea Scrolls," in A. A. Diesel, R. G. Lehmann, E. Otto, and A. Wagner (eds) "Jedes Ding hat seine Zeit . . . ", *Studien zur israelitischen und altorientalischen Weisheit Diethelm Michel zum 65 Geburtstag* (BZAW 241; Berlin: de Gruyter) 19–32.

—— (1996b) "Jesus and the Messiahs of Israel," in H. Lichtenberger, (ed.) *Geschichte – Tradition – Reflexion. Festschrift für Martin Hengel,* (vol. 3; Tübingen: Mohr).

Collins, J. J. and J. H. Charlesworth (1991) *Mysteries and Revelations. Apocalyptic Studies since the Uppsala Colloquium* (Sheffield: Sheffield Academic Press).

Collins, J. J. and D. Dimant (1994) "A Thrice-Told Hymn," *Jewish Quarterly Review* 85: 151–5.

Cook, E. M. (1994) *Solving the Mysteries of the Dead Sea Scrolls* (Grand Rapids: Zondervan).

—— (1995) "4Q246," *Bulletin for Biblical Research* 5: 43–66.

Cross, F. M. (1961) "The Development of the Jewish Scripts," in G. E. Wright (ed.) *The Bible and the Ancient Near East* (New York: Doubleday) 133–202.

—— (1992) "Some Notes on a Generation of Qumran Studies," in J. Trebolle Barrera and L. Vegas Montaner, (eds) *The Madrid Qumran Congress* (Leiden: Brill) 1–21.

—— (1995) *The Ancient Library of Qumran* (3rd edn; New York: Doubleday; Sheffield: Sheffield Academic Press; first published 1961).

Davidson, M. J. (1992) *Angels at Qumran. A Comparative Study of 1 Enoch 1–36, 72–108 and Sectarian Writings from Qumran.* (Sheffield: Sheffield Academic Press).

Davies, P. R. (1977) *1QM, the War Scroll from Qumran* (Rome: Biblical Institute).

—— (1983) *The Damascus Covenant: An Interpretation of the "Damascus Document"* (Sheffield: Journal for the Study of the Old Testament).

—— (1985) "Eschatology at Qumran," *Journal of Biblical Literature* 104: 39–55.

—— (1992) "War Rule (1QM)," *Anchor Bible Dictionary*, Vol. 6 (New York: Doubleday) 875–6.

Dimant, D. (1979) "The 'Pesher on the Periods' (4Q180) and 4Q181," *Israel Oriental Studies* 9: 77–102.

—— (1984) "Qumran Sectarian Literature," in M. E. Stone, (ed.) *Jewish Writings of the Second Temple Period* (Philadelphia: Fortress) 483–550.

—— (1992) "New Light on the Jewish Pseudepigrapha – 4Q390," in J. Trebolle Barrera and L. Vegas Montaner, (eds) *The Madrid Qumran Congress* (Leiden: Brill) 405–8.

—— (1994a) "Apocalyptic Texts at Qumran," in E. Ulrich and J. VanderKam, (eds) *The Community of the Renewed Covenant* (Notre Dame, IN: University of Notre Dame Press) 175–91.

—— (1994b) "A Synoptic Comparison of Parallel Sections in 4Q427 7, 4Q491 11 and 4Q471b," *Jewish Quarterly Review* 85: 157–61.

Dimant, D. and J. Strugnell (1990) "The Merkabah Vision in Second Ezekiel (4Q385 4)," *Revue de Qumrân* 14: 331–48.

Duchesne-Guillemin, J. (1952) *The Hymns of Zoroaster* (London: Murray).

Duhaime, J. (1977) "La rédaction de 1QM XIII et l'évolution du Dualisme à Qumrân," *Revue Biblique* 84: 210–38.

—— (1985) "La Doctrine des Esséniens de Qumrân sur l'après-mort," in G. Couturier *et al.* (eds) *Essais sur la Mort* (Montreal: Fides).

—— (1987) "Dualistic Reworking in the Scrolls from Qumran," *Catholic Biblical Quarterly* 49: 32–56.

—— (1988) "The War Scroll from Qumran and the Greco-Roman Tactical Treatises," *Revue de Qumrân* 13: 133–51.

—— (1990) "Étude comparatif de 4QMᵃ fgg. 1–3 et 1QM," *Revue de Qumrân* 14: 459–72.

—— (1995) "War Scroll," in J. H. Charlesworth (ed.) *The Dead Sea Scrolls. Hebrew, Aramaic, and Greek Texts with English Translations Vol. 2* (Tübingen: Mohr; Louisville: Westminster) 80–203.

Dupont-Sommer, A. (1950) *Apercus préliminaires sur les manuscrits de la Mer Morte* (Paris: Maisonneuve).

—— (1953) *Nouveaux apercus sur les manuscrits de la Mer Morte* (Paris: Maisonneuve).

Eisenman, R. and M. Wise (1992) *The Dead Sea Scrolls Uncovered* (Shaftesbury: Element).

Elgvin, T. (1994) "Admonition Texts from Qumran Cave 4," in M. O. Wise, N. Golb, J. J. Collins, and D. Pardee, (eds) *Methods of Investigation of the Dead Sea Scrolls and the Khirbet Qumran Site* (New York: New York Academy of Sciences) 179–94.

—— (forthcoming) "The Mystery to Come: Early Essene Theology of Revelation," in T. L. Thompson and N. P. Lemche, (eds) *Qumran between the Old and the New Testament* (Sheffield: Sheffield Academic Press).

Elior, R. (1993) "Mysticism, Magic, and Angelology. The Perception of Angels in Hekhalot Literature," *Jewish Studies Quarterly* 1: 3–53.

Eshel, E., H. Eshel and A. Yardeni (1992) "A Scroll from Qumran Which Includes Part of Psalm 154 and a Prayer for King Jonathan and His Kingdom," *Israel Exploration Journal* 42: 199–229.

Eshel, H. (1992) "The Historical Background of the Pesher Interpreting Joshua's Curse on the Rebuilder of Jericho," *Revue de Qumrân* 15: 409–20.

Festinger, L., H. W. Riecken and S. Schachter (1956) *When Prophecy Fails: A Social and Psychological Study of a Modern Group that Predicted the Destruction of the World* (New York: Harper & Row).

Fitzmyer, J. A. (1990) "A Feature of Qumran Angelology and the Angels of 1 Cor 11:10," in J. Murphy-O'Connor and J. H. Charlesworth, (eds) *Paul and the Dead Sea Scrolls* (New York: Crossroad) 31–47.

—— (1992) *Responses to 101 Questions on the Dead Sea Scrolls* (New York: Paulist).

Flusser, D. (1972) "The Four Empires in the Fourth Sibyl and in the Book of Daniel," *Israel Oriental Studies* 2: 148–75.

García Martínez, F. (1988) "Qumran Origins and Early History: A Groningen Hypothesis," *Folia Orientalia* 25: 113–36.

—— (1991) "Traditions communes dans le IVᵉ Esdras et dans les MSS de Qumrân," *Revue de Qumrân* 15: 187–301.

—— (1992) *Qumran and Apocalyptic* (Leiden: Brill).

—— (1993) "Messianische Erwartungen in den Qumranschriften," *Jahrbuch für biblische Theologie* 8: 171–208.

—— (1994) *The Dead Sea Scrolls Translated* (Leiden: Brill).

García Martínez, F. and A. S. van der Woude (1990) "A 'Groningen' Hypothesis of Qumran Origins and Early History," *Revue de Qumrân* 14: 521–41.

Gnilka, J. (1990) "2 Cor 6:14–7:1: in the Light of the Qumran Texts and the

Testaments of the Twelve Patriarchs," in J. Murphy-O'Connor and J. H. Charlesworth, (eds) *Paul and the Dead Sea Scrolls* (New York: Crossroad) 48–68.

Golb, N. (1980) "The Problem of Origin and Identification of the Dead Sea Scrolls," *Proceedings of the American Philosophical Society* 124: 1–24.

Grayson, A. K. (1975) *Babylonian Historical-Literary Texts* (Toronto: University of Toronto Press).

Gruenwald, I. (1980) *Apocalyptic and Merkavah Mysticism* (Leiden: Brill).

—— (1988) *From Apocalypticism to Gnosticism* (Frankfurt: Lang).

Gwyn Griffiths, J. (1970) *Plutarch's De Iside et Osiride* (Cardiff: University of Wales Press).

Hanson, P. D. (1975) *The Dawn of Apocalyptic* (Philadelphia: Fortress).

—— (1977) "Rebellion in Heaven. Azazel and Euhemeristic Heroes in 1 Enoch 6–11," *Journal of Biblical Literature* 96: 195–233.

Harrington, D. J. (1996) *Wisdom Texts from Qumran* (London: Routledge).

Hengel, M. (1974) *Judaism and Hellenism*, 2 vols. (Philadelphia: Fortress).

Hiers, R. H. (1992) "Day of the Lord," *Anchor Bible Dictionary*, vol. 2 (New York: Doubleday) 82–3.

Himmelfarb, M. (1991) "Revelation and Rapture: The Transformation of the Visionary in the Ascent Apocalypses," in J. J. Collins and J. H. Charlesworth, (eds) *Mysteries and Revelations*, (Sheffield: Sheffield Academic Press) 79–90.

—— (1993) *Ascent to Heaven in Jewish and Christian Apocalypses* (New York: Oxford).

Hinnells, J. R. (1973) "The Zoroastrian Doctrine of Salvation in the Roman World. A Study of the Oracle of Hystaspes," in E. J. Sharpe and J. R. Hinnells, (eds) *Man and His Salvation. Studies in Memory of S. G. F. Brandon* (Manchester: Manchester University Press) 125–48.

Horgan, M. P. (1979) *Pesharim: Qumran Interpretations of Biblical Books* (Washington, DC: Catholic Biblical Association).

Huggins, R. V. (1992) "A Canonical 'Book of Periods' at Qumran?" *Revue de Qumran* 15: 421–36.

Hunzinger, C. H. (1957) "Fragmente einer älteren Fassung des Buches Milhamā aus Höhle 4 von Qumran," *Zeitschrift für die alttestamentliche Wissenschaft* 69: 131–51.

Jeremias, G. (1963) *Der Lehrer der Gerechtigkeit* (Göttingen: Vandenhoeck & Ruprecht).

Kahle, P. (1959) *The Cairo Geniza* (2nd edn. Oxford: Clarendon).

Kampen, J. (1988) *The Hasideans and the Origin of Pharisaism. A Study in 1 and 2 Maccabees* (Atlanta: Scholars Press).

Kippenberg, H. (1978) "Die Geschichte der Mittelpersischen Apokalyptischen Traditionen," *Studia Iranica* 7: 49–80.

Kobelski, P. J. (1981) *Melchizedek and Melchireša'* (Washington, DC: Catholic Biblical Association).

Koch, K. (1972) *The Rediscovery of Apocalyptic* (Naperville, IL: Allenson).

Kuhn, H. W. (1966) *Enderwartung und gegenwärtiges Heil* (Göttingen: Vandenhoeck & Ruprecht).

Kuhn, K. G. (1952) "Die Sektenschrift und die Iranische Religion," *Zeitschrift für Theologie und Kirche* 49: 296–316.

—— (1990) "The Epistle to the Ephesians in the Light of the Qumran

Texts," in J. Murphy-O'Connor and J. H. Charlesworth, (eds) *Paul and the Dead Sea Scrolls* (New York: Crossroad) 115–31.

Laato, A. (1992) "The Chronology in the Damascus Document of Qumran," *Revue de Qumrân* 15: 605–7.

La Barre, W. (1970) *The Ghost Dance. The Origins of Religion* (New York: Doubleday).

Lambert, W. G. (1978) *The Background of Jewish Apocalyptic* (London: Athlone).

Lange, A. (1995) *Weisheit und Prädestination* (Leiden: Brill).

Licht, J. (1958) "An Analysis of the Treatise on the Two Spirits in DSD," in C. Rabin and Y. Yadin, (eds) *Aspects of the Dead Sea Scrolls. Scripta Hierosolymitana 4* (Jerusalem: Magnes) 88–100.

Lücke, F. (1832) *Versuch einer vollständigen Einleitung in die Offenbarung Johannis und in die gesamte apokalyptische Literatur* (Bonn: Weber).

McGinn, B. (1979) *Visions of the End. Apocalyptic Traditions in the Middle Ages* (New York: Columbia University Press).

Mach, M. (1992) *Entwicklungsstadien des jüdischen Engelglaubens in vorrabbinischer Zeit* (Tübingen: Mohr).

Magness, J. (1995) "The Chronology of the Settlement at Qumran in the Herodian Period," *Dead Sea Discoveries* 2: 58–65.

Maier, J. (1964) *Vom Kultus zur Gnosis* (Salzburg: Müller).

—— (1990) "The Temple Scroll and Tendencies in the Cultic Architecture of the Second Commonwealth," in L. H. Schiffman (ed.) *Archaeology and History in the Dead Sea Scrolls* (Sheffield: Journal for the Study of the Old Testament) 67–82.

—— (1992) "Shîrê 'Ôlat hash-Shabbat. Some Observations on their Calendric Implications and on their Style," in J. Trebolle Barrera and L. Vegas Montaner, (eds) *The Madrid Qumran Congress* (Leiden: Brill) 543–60.

Mertens, A. (1971) *Das Buch Daniel im Lichte der Texte vom Toten Meer* (Stuttgart: Katholisches Bibelwerk).

Milik, J. T. (1956) "Prière de Nabonide' et autres écrits d'un cycle de Daniel," *Revue Biblique* 63: 411–15.

—— (1958) "Hénoch au pays des aromates (chap XXVII à XXXII): Fragments araméens de la grotte 4 de Qumrân," *Revue Biblique* 65: 70–7.

—— (1972a) "4Q Visions de 'Amram et une citation d'Origene," *Revue Biblique* 79: 77–97.

—— (1972b) "Milkî-ṭedek et Milkî-reša' dans les anciens écrits juifs et chrétiens," *Journal of Jewish Studies* 23: 95–144.

—— (1976) *Books of Enoch* (Oxford: Clarendon).

Mussner, F. (1990) "Contributions made by Qumran to the Understanding of the Epistle to the Ephesians," in J. Murphy-O'Connor and J. H. Charlesworth, (eds) *Paul and the Dead Sea Scrolls* (New York: Crossroad) 159–78.

Newsom, C. A. (1985) *Songs of the Sabbath Sacrifice: A Critical Edition* (Atlanta: Scholars Press).

—— (1990a) "He Has Established for Himself Priests': Human and Angelic Priesthood in the Qumran Sabbath Shirot," in L. H. Schiffman, (ed.) *Archaeology and History in the Dead Sea Scrolls* (Sheffield: Journal for the Study of the Old Testament) 101–20.

——— (1990b) "'Sectually Explicit' Literature from Qumran," in W. H. Propp, B. Halpern, and D. N. Freedman (eds) *The Hebrew Bible and its Interpreters* (Winona Lake, IN: Eisenbrauns) 167–87.

Nickelsburg, G. W. (1972) *Resurrection, Immortality and Eternal Life in Intertestamental Judaism* (Cambridge: Harvard).

——— (1977) "Apocalyptic and Myth in 1 Enoch 6–11," *Journal of Biblical Literature* 96: 383–405.

Nitzan, B. (1994a) *Qumran Prayer and Religious Poetry* (Leiden: Brill).

——— (1994b) "4QBerakhot (4Q286–90): A Preliminary Report," in G. J. Brooke (ed.) *New Qumran Texts and Studies* (Leiden: Brill) 53–71.

Oegema, G. S. (1994) *Der Gesalbte und sein Volk* (Göttingen: Vandenhoeck & Ruprecht).

Olyan, S. M. (1993) *A Thousand Thousands Served Him* (Tübingen: Mohr/Siebeck).

Pagels, E. (1991) "The Social History of Satan, the 'Intimate Enemy': A Preliminary Sketch," *Harvard Theological Review* 84: 105–28.

——— (1995) *The Origin of Satan* (New York: Random House).

Peires, J. B. (1989) *The Dead Will Arise* (Bloomington: Indiana University Press).

Philonenko, M. (1995) "Mythe et histoire qoumrânienne des deux Esprits: ses origines iraniennes et ses prolongements dans le judaïsme essénien et le christianisme antique," in G. Widengren, M. Philonenko and A. Hultgard, *Apocalyptique Iranienne et Dualisme Qoumrânien* (Paris: Maisonneuve) 163–211.

Puech, E. (1992a) "Fragment d'une Apocalypse en Araméen (4Q246 = pseudo-Dan^d et le 'Royaume de Dieu,'" *Revue Biblique* 99: 98–131.

——— (1992b) "Fragments d'un apocryphe de Lévi et le personnage eschatologique, 4QTestLévi (c–d) et 4QAJa," in J. Trebolle Barrera and L. Vegas Montaner, (eds) *The Madrid Qumran Congress*, vol. 2 (Leiden: Brill) 2:449–501.

——— (1992c) "Une Apocalypse Messianique (4Q521)," *Revue de Qumrân* 15: 475–519.

——— (1993) *La Croyance des Esséniens en la vie future: immortalité, résurrection, vie éternelle* (Paris: Gabalda).

——— (1994) "Préséance sacerdotale et messie-roi dans la règle de la congrégation (1QSa ii 11–22)," *Revue de Qumrân* 63: 351–65.

Qimron, E. and J. Strugnell (1994) *Qumran Cave 4. V: Miqsat Ma'ase haTorah* (Discoveries in the Judean Desert 10. Oxford: Clarendon).

Rössler, D. (1960) *Gesetz und Geschichte* (Neukirchen-Vluyn: Neukirchener Verlag).

Rost, L. (1955) "Zum Buch der Kriege der Söhne des Lichtes gegen die Söhne der Finsternis," *Theologische Literaturzeitung* 80: 205–8.

Rowland, C. (1982) *The Open Heaven* (New York: Crossroad).

Sacchi, P. (1990) *L'Apocalittica Giudaica e la sua Storia* (Brescia: Paideia).

Schäfer, P. (1986) *Gershom Scholem Reconsidered. The Aim and Purpose of Early Jewish Mysticism.* (Oxford: Centre for Postgraduate Hebrew Studies).

——— (1992) *The Hidden and Manifest God.* (Albany: State University of New York).

Schiffman, L. H. (1982) "Merkavah Speculation at Qumran: The 4Q Serekh Shirot 'Olat ha-Shabbat," in J. Reinharz and D. Swetschinski, (eds) *Mystics, Philosophers, and Politicians. Essays in Jewish Intellectual History in Honor of Alexander Altmann* (Durham, NC : Duke University Press) 15–47.

—— (1989) *The Eschatological Community of the Dead Sea Scrolls* (Atlanta: Scholars Press).

—— (1994) *Reclaiming the Dead Sea Scrolls* (Philadelphia: Jewish Publication Society).

Scholem, G. (1961) *Major Trends in Jewish Mysticism* (New York: Schocken).

—— (1965) *Jewish Gnosticism, Merkabah Mysticism, and Talmudic Tradition* (2nd edn. New York: The Jewish Theological Seminary).

Schuller, E. (1993) "A Hymn from a Cave Four Hodayot Manuscript: 4Q427 7 i+ii," *Journal of Biblical Literature* 112: 605–28.

—— (1994) "The Cave 4 Hodayot Manuscripts: A Preliminary Description," *Jewish Quarterly Review* 85: 137–50.

Schüpphaus, J. (1977) *Die Psalmen Salomos* (Leiden: Brill).

Smith, M. (1990) "Ascent to the Heavens and Deification in 4QMa," in L. H. Schiffman (ed.) *Archaeology and History in the Dead Sea Scrolls* (Sheffield: Journal for the Study of the Old Testament) 181–8.

Spronk, K. (1986) *Beatific Afterlife in Ancient Israel and in the Ancient Near East* (Kevelaer: Butzon & Bercker).

Starcky, J (1963) "Les quatres étapes du messianisme à Qumrân," *Revue Biblique* 70: 481–505.

Stegemann, H. (1971) *Die Entstehung der Qumrangemeinde* (Bonn: published privately).

—— (1983) "Die Bedeutung der Qumranfunde für die Erforschung der Apokalyptik," in D. Hellholm (ed.) *Apocalypticism in the Mediterranean World and the Near East* (Tübingen: Mohr) 495–530.

—— (1993) *Die Essener, Qumran, Johannes der Täufer und Jesus* (Freiburg: Herder).

Stendahl, K. (ed.) (1957, 1992) *The Scrolls and the New Testament* (New York: Harper; reprinted with a new introduction by J. H. Charlesworth, New York: Crossroad, 1992).

Steudel, A. (1993) "אחרית הימים in the Texts from Qumran," *Revue de Qumrân* 16: 225–46.

—— (1994) *Der Midrasch zur Eschatologie aus der Qumran-Gemeinde (4QMidr-Eschat$^{a.b}$)* (Leiden: Brill).

Stone, M. E. (1978) "The Book of Enoch and Judaism in the Third Century BCE," *Catholic Biblical Quarterly* 40: 479–92 (reprinted in M. E. Stone and D. Satran, (eds) *Emerging Judaism* Minneapolis: Fortress, 1989, 61–75).

—— (1990) *Fourth Ezra* (Hermeneia, Minneapolis: Fortress).

Strugnell, J. (1960) "The Angelic Liturgy at Qumrân, 4Q Serek Šîrôt 'Olat Haššabāt," *Supplements to Vetus Testamentum 7. Congress Volume, Oxford 1959* (Leiden: Brill) 318–45.

Strugnell, J. and D. Dimant (1988) "4QSecond Ezekiel," *Revue de Qumrân* 13: 45–58.

Suter, D. W. (1979) "Fallen Angel, Fallen Priest. The Problem of Family Purity in 1 Enoch 6–16," *Hebrew Union College Annual* 50: 115–35.

Tabor, J. D. and M. O. Wise, (1992) "4Q521 'On Resurrection' and the Synoptic Gospel Tradition. A Preliminary Study," *Journal for the Study of the Pseudepigrapha* 10: 149–62.

Talmon, S. (1989) "Waiting for the Messiah at Qumran," in *The World of Qumran from Within* (Leiden: Brill) 273–300.

Tiller, P. A. (1993) *A Commentary on the Animal Apocalypse of 1 Enoch* (Atlanta: Scholars Press).

Tobin, T. H. (1983) *The Creation of Man: Philo and the History of Interpretation* (Washington, DC: Catholic Biblical Association).

Tov, E. and S. J. Pfann (1993) *The Dead Sea Scrolls on Microfiche Companion Volume* (Leiden: Brill).

Ulrich, E. (1995) "An Index of the Passages in the Biblical Manuscripts from the Judean Desert (Part 2: Isaiah-Chronicles)," *Dead Sea Discoveries* 2: 86–107.

Urbach, E. E. (1975) *The Sages, Their Concepts and Beliefs* (Jerusalem: Magnes).

VanderKam, J. C. (1978) "Enoch Traditions in Jubilees and Other Second Century Sources," in P. J. Achtemeier (ed.) *Society of Biblical Literature Seminar Papers* (Missoula, MT: Scholars Press).

—— (1984) *Enoch and the Growth of an Apocalyptic Tradition* (Washington, DC: Catholic Biblical Association).

—— (1988) "Jubilees and the Priestly Messiah of Qumran," *Revue de Qumrân* 13: 353–65.

—— (1992) "The Jubilees Fragments from Qumran Cave 4," in J. Trebolle Barrera and L. Vegas Montaner, (eds) *The Madrid Qumran Congress*, Leiden: Brill, 635–48.

—— (1994) "Messianism in the Scrolls," in E. Ulrich and J. VanderKam, (eds) *The Community of the Renewed Covenant* (Notre Dame, IN: University of Notre Dame Press) 211–34.

—— (1995a) *The Dead Sea Scrolls Today* (Grand Rapids: Eerdmans).

—— (1995b) *Enoch, A Man for all Generations* (Columbia, SC: University of South Carolina).

VanderKam, J. and J. T. Milik, (1994) "Jubilees," in H. Attridge, *et al.* (eds) *Qumran Cave 4. VIII. Parabiblical Texts, Part 1* (Discoveries in the Judean Desert XIII) (Oxford: Clarendon) 1–185.

Vermes, G. (1979) "The Qumran Messiahs and Messianism," in E. Schuerer, *A History of the Jewish People in the Age of Jesus Christ* (revised edn. Edinburgh: Clark) 2: 550–4.

—— (1981) *The Dead Sea Scrolls. Qumran in Perspective* (Philadelphia: Fortress).

—— (1992a) "Genesis 1–3 in Post-Biblical Hebrew and Aramaic Literature before the Mishnah," *Journal of Jewish Studies* 43: 221–5.

—— (1992b) "The Oxford Forum for Qumran Research Seminar on the Rule of War from Cave 4 (4Q285)," *Journal of Jewish Studies* 43: 85–90.

—— (1995) *The Dead Sea Scrolls in English* (4th edn. London: Penguin).

Vermes, G. and M. Goodman (1989) *The Essenes According to the Classical Sources* (Sheffield: Journal for the Study of the Old Testament).

van der Ploeg, J. (1959) *Le Rouleau de la Guerre* (Leiden: Brill).

von der Osten-Sacken, P. (1969) *Gott und Belial* (Göttingen: Vandenhoeck & Ruprecht).

von Rad, G. (1965) *Theologie des Alten Testaments Vol. 2* (4th edn. Munich: Kaiser).

Wacholder, B. Z. (1983) *The Dawn of Qumran* (Cincinnati: Hebrew Union College).

Wacholder, B. Z and M. Abegg (1991) *A Preliminary Edition of the Unpublished Dead Sea Scrolls. The Hebrew and Aramaic Texts from Cave Four. Fascicle One* (Washington, DC: Biblical Archeology Society).

Wacker, M. T. (1982) *Weltordnung und Gericht. Studien zu 1 Henoch 22* (Würzburg: Echter Verlag).

Wernberg-Møller, P. (1961) "A Reconsideration of the Two Spirits in the Rule of the Community (1QSerek III, 13–IV, 26)," *Revue de Qumrân* 3: 413–41.

White, S. A. (1987) "A Comparison of the 'A' and 'B' Manuscripts of the Damascus Document," *Revue de Qumrân* 12: 537–53.

Widengren, G. (1995) "Les quatre Âges du monde," in G. Widengren, M. Philonenko and A. Hultgård, *Apocalyptique Iranienne et Dualisme Qoumrânien* (Paris: Maisonneuve) 23–62.

Wilson, E. (1955) *The Scrolls from the Dead Sea* (New York: Oxford).

Wise, M. O. (1990a) "The Eschatological Vision of the Temple Scroll," *Journal of Near Eastern Studies* 49: 155–72.

—— (1990b) *A Critical Study of the Temple Scroll from Qumran Cave 11* (Chicago: Oriental Institute).

—— (1991) "4QFlorilegium and the Temple of Adam," *Revue de Qumrân* 15: 103–32.

Wise, M. and J. D. Tabor (1992) "The Messiah at Qumran," *Biblical Archeology Review* November/December: 60–5.

Wolfson, E. R. (1993) "Yeridah la-Merkavah: Typology of Ecstasy and Enthronement in Ancient Jewish Mysticism," in R. A. Herrera (ed.) *Mystics of the Book: Themes, Topics and Typologies* (New York: Peter Lang) 13–44.

—— (1994) "Mysticism and the Poetic-Liturgical Compositions from Qumran," *Jewish Quarterly Review* 85: 185–202.

Yadin, Y. (1962) *The Scroll of the War of the Sons of Light against the Sons of Darkness* (Oxford: Oxford University Press).

Yarbro Collins, A. (1976) *The Combat Myth in the Book of Revelation* (Missoula, MT: Scholars Press).

—— (1979) "Early Christian Apocalypses," *Semeia* 14: 61–121.

—— (1984) "Numerical Symbolism in Apocalyptic Literature," in H. Temporini and W. Haase, (eds) *Aufstieg und Niedergang der Römischen Welt* (Berlin: de Gruyter) II.21.2: 1222–87.

—— (1995) "The Seven Heavens in Jewish and Christian Apocalypses," in J. J. Collins and M. Fishbane, (eds), *Death, Ecstasy and Otherworldly Journeys* (Albany: State University of New York Press) 57–93.

—— (forthcoming) "Revelation, Book of," in *Encyclopedia of the Dead Sea Scrolls* (New York: Oxford).

Zaehner, R. C. (1961) *The Dawn and Twilight of Zoroastrianism* (London: Weidenfeld & Nicolson).

INDEX OF MODERN AUTHORS

INDEX OF PASSAGES